D0308465

FIELD GUIDE
— TO THE —
BIRDS

OF · BRITAIN · AND · IRELAND

LAROUSSE
FIELD GUIDE
TO THE
BIRDS
OF·BRITAIN·AND·IRELAND

JOHN GOODERS
ILLUSTRATED BY ALAN HARRIS

LAROUSSE

Larousse plc,
New Penderel House,
283-288 High Holborn,
London WC1V 7HZ

This edition published by Larousse plc, 1995

10 9 8 7 6 5 4 3 2

A CIP catalogue record for this book is available from the
British Library.

ISBN 0-7523-0023-7

Senior Editor: Michèle Byam
Design: Smiljka Surla

Phototypeset by Tradespools Ltd. Frome, Somerset
Colour separations by Newsele Litho. Milan
Printed in Italy by Vallardi Industrie Grafiche, Milan

CONTENTS

FOREWORD

If you walk into a bookshop and ask for the bird books, you will be directed to a bewildering array of volumes varying from the erudite to the ridiculous. Narrow the choice down to those that aim solely to help you identify birds and the choice will still leave you confused and bemused. How do you make up your mind?

Having been present during the development of several bird encyclopedias and a score or so of bird books, I can tell you that publishers, artists and authors have the same problem. Should the guide cover only the birds of Britain and Ireland or be expanded to include those found in Europe as well? Should every bird that has ever put in an appearance be included or should the contents be restricted to 'regular' birds? Should it be illustrated with paintings or photographs? Should the illustrations and text for each bird be together or should the illustrations be in a separate section? Should the book fit into a pocket to be taken out into the field or should it sit on a bookshelf to be used as a reference work?

To settle these and other fundamental questions compromises are reached and everyone gets on with their part of the production.

It has been my good fortune to be involved in the production of several field guides – with this one I was lucky enough to have publishers who were prepared to listen. As a result, the team responsible had a good idea of the sort of guide I was aiming for and could concentrate on achieving that aim. The first decision we made was to restrict the birds to those that one could reasonably expect to see in Britain and Ireland. Secondly, the book had to be portable, but at the same time have enough space to say what was needed to identify each bird clearly. Cramped, limited space has ruined more field guides than any other single factor and we were determined to avoid making that mistake. Other field guides are ponderously verbose because the author is determined to get in every word no matter what the editors and designers say. We overcame this problem by using a comprehensive checklist of features instead of descriptions of the bird's appearance, voice, behaviour and other characteristics.

So we have the compromise that is in the nature of all information books. Few books even mention this compromise. We hope that by facing up to it we have managed to produce a useful, comprehensive, portable guide to the birds regularly seen in Britain and Ireland.

As you will already have gathered, producing a book of this type is not a simple matter. All sorts of different people are involved at a variety of different levels – my thanks are due to them all. Primarily I must thank Alan Harris for producing one of the finest series of field guide plates I have ever seen. Alan is no studio artist, he is a birder who knows his

Foreword

birds in the field. Are there any other competent artists who are active ringers? Alan's intimate knowledge of birds in the hand and out there in the field shows in his work.

I was also lucky enough to enlist the aid of three top rate birdmen to help with researching and writing the text. My thanks are due to Jim Flegg, Tim Parmenter and the late Peter Grant for their invaluable assistance.

Complex books, such as field guides, are invariably the result of team work and this one is no exception. Deep in the Sussex countryside I enlisted the aid of Caron Hobden and my wife Robbie to turn scribble into readable typescript. At Larousse I was fortunate enough to find Dan Grisewood and Jane Olliver two of the most enthusiastic and sympathetic publishers that I have ever had the pleasure to work with. Jim Miles took overall control of the venture with equal enthusiasm and skill to ensure that everyone produced their very best work almost to schedule. The book was ably edited by Barbara Taylor and Ann Kay and brought to fruition by Michèle Byam, who has a genius for picking up all the bits and pieces that authors and artists invariably forget. To them all I offer heartfelt thanks.

JOHN GOODERS
SUSSEX

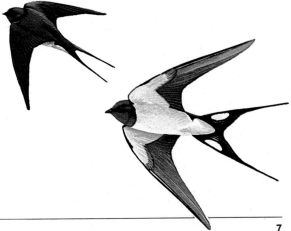

INTRODUCTION

Field guides were invented by the great Roger Peterson in America in the 1930s. They spread to Europe in the 1950s and have proliferated ever since. Today we are offered a huge choice of guides to birds, flowers, mammals, hedgerows, butterflies, reptiles and so on. Because birds are so widespread and attractive, there are more bird guides than there are guides to all the other subjects put together.

Field guides have the sole aim of enabling the observer (you) to put a name to the subject (the bird) without having to blast it away with a shotgun or catch it in a net. It is perhaps not surprising that the first edition of Peterson's European field guide was published in the same year as the random collecting of birds was banned by the Bird Protection Act of 1954.

There is inevitably a sameness about field guides and of necessity they have certain features in common. Paintings or photographs show the bird, a text picks out its characteristic features and describes its behaviour and a map shows where and when it occurs. A blend of all three elements makes the guide work. Ideally they should all be by the same hand. It is unusual, however, for any one person to possess the necessary combination of skills to accomplish this task.

Field guides are then the correct mix of art, words and maps – and no single one of these elements should dominate the others. I have seen guides that depict birds from so many different angles that the beginner is totally daunted. Conversely, I have seen guides that show only the adult male of a species in resplendent summer finery and ignore the fact that male and female birds often look different or that birds may change their appearance according to their age or the time of year.

In this book, we have added three further elements to the normal three field guide ingredients. We have included a detailed checklist, which stands on its own as a simple source of reference and as an indicator key. A monthly calendar not only tells you when a bird is present but also has a numbered scale reflecting the likelihood of sighting the bird in each month of the year. Finally we have added notes around the illustrations to pick out the bird's most important features – just as birders do in their own field notebooks. Together these elements add up to a comprehensive portrait of every regular British bird.

There is no easy, foolproof method of identifying birds. Every year, a large number of birdwatchers, travel with me to foreign parts. Almost without exception they want to learn how to identify the birds they see. Books are an essential part of this process but ultimately there is no substitute for learning the art in the company of a skilled birder.

Introduction

BIRD NAMES

All birds have both an English and a Latin name. The latter is called the scientific name and consists of two parts – a generic and a specific name. The generic name is the first word and it is customary to begin it with a capital letter. All closely related birds have the same generic name. Many of the gulls, for example, belong to the genus *Larus*. The second word is the specific name and this begins with a small letter. The specific name picks out one member of a genus from another. The scientific name of the Herring Gull is *Larus argentatus* while that of its close relative the Black-headed Gull is *Larus ridibundus*.

Many of these scientific names actually mean something – for example, *tridactyla* means 'three-toed'. Other names, such as *Cettia cetti* (Cetti's Warbler), commemorate the person who discovered the bird. Others still are the whims of nineteenth-century bird collectors and some, one can only assume, are very much tongue-in-cheek. Fortunately, most bizarre scientific names apply to birds never encountered in Britain and Ireland.

Scientific names should not be disregarded. Not only do they tell you that one bird is a close relative of another, and therefore likely to be similar in structure and appearance, but they are also the only universally acceptable international language. German or Dutch bird-watchers for example, may have a perfect command of English until they get to bird names. The English name of a bird is unlikely to be a direct translation of its German or Dutch equivalent. So, in order to communicate, one has to resort to pointing at pictures or using the scientific names. You may be surprised just how many non-English speaking birders know a goodly number of scientific bird names.

The English names used here follow general usage and particularly those used in the journal *British Birds*. Unfortunately there is not a list of acceptable English names for all the birds of the world. Gradually, however, things are changing. The Heron is now generally called the Grey Heron to save confusion with other rare European herons. This is, however, hardly the place to debate a universal system of bird nomenclature. Suffice it to say that we have stuck with the hardy old favourites while pushing towards a better system – a typically British approach.

Finally, it may be noted that all the words in the English names begin with a capital letter – unless they follow a hyphen. Thus we have used Great Northern Diver but Black-necked Grebe. Actually, this is a good yardstick of a bird book. If the English names begin with small letters, throw away the book immediately.

Introduction

HOW TO USE THIS BOOK

With a single exception every one of the 256 birds in this book is treated to a whole page. Each page has the same ingredients and a similar design. Like making a cake, each ingredient is an important contribution to the whole. If you miss an ingredient, an inaccurate identification or an inedible cake may result.

The first thing to do when you see an unfamiliar bird is to check the list of general types of bird (waders, birds of prey and so on) on page 26. Then turn to the appropriate pages and leaf through the illustrations to see if your bird is there. If you spot it, or one that looks very similar, check the labels around the illustrations to see if your bird showed the same salient features. Then consult the text, map and monthly abundance chart to confirm your identification. It is unlikely, however, that you will have noted each and every aspect of a bird's plumage and behaviour. This is where the checklist of features for each bird comes in. Use it to check details such as the bird's size, the colour of a particular part of the body or a distinctive piece of behaviour you may have noticed.

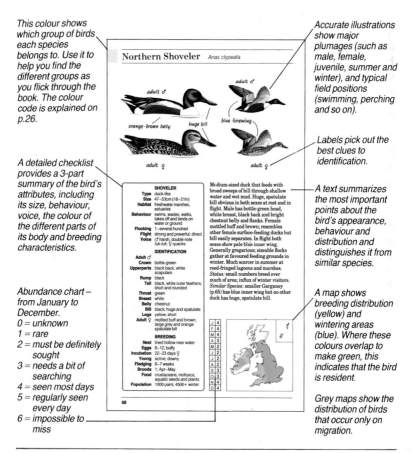

This colour shows which group of birds each species belongs to. Use it to help you find the different groups as you flick through the book. The colour code is explained on p.26.

A detailed checklist provides a 3-part summary of the bird's attributes, including its size, behaviour, voice, the colour of the different parts of its body and breeding characteristics.

Abundance chart – from January to December.
0 = unknown
1 = rare
2 = must be definitely sought
3 = needs a bit of searching
4 = seen most days
5 = regularly seen every day
6 = impossible to miss

Accurate illustrations show major plumages (such as male, female, juvenile, summer and winter), and typical field positions (swimming, perching and so on).

Labels pick out the best clues to identification.

A text summarizes the most important points about the bird's appearance, behaviour and distribution and distinguishes it from similar species.

A map shows breeding distribution (yellow) and wintering areas (blue). Where these colours overlap to make green, this indicates that the bird is resident.

Grey maps show the distribution of birds that occur only on migration.

Northern Shoveler *Anas clypeata*

adult ♂

orange-brown belly

huge bill

blue forewing

adult ♂

adult ♀

adult ♀

SHOVELER
Type duck-like
Size 47–53cm (18–21in)
Habitat freshwater marshes, estuaries
Behaviour swims, wades, walks, takes off and lands on water or ground
Flocking 1–several hundred
Flight strong and powerful; direct
Voice ♂ harsh, double note *tuk-tuk*; ♀ quacks

IDENTIFICATION
Adult ♂
Crown bottle-green
Upperparts black back, white scapulars
Rump black
Tail black, white outer feathers; short and rounded
Throat green
Breast white
Belly chestnut
Bill black; huge and spatulate
Legs yellow; short
Adult ♀ mottled buff and brown; large grey and orange spatulate bill

BREEDING
Nest lined hollow near water
Eggs 8–12; buffy
Incubation 22–23 days ♀
Young active; downy
Fledging 6–7 weeks
Broods 1; Apr–May
Food crustaceans, molluscs, aquatic seeds and plants
Population 1000 pairs; 4500+ winter

Medium-sized duck that feeds with broad sweeps of bill through shallow water and wet mud. Huge, spatulate bill obvious at rest and in flight. Male has bottle-green head, white breast, black back and bright chestnut belly and flanks. Female mottled buff and brown; resembles other female surface-feeding ducks but bill easily separates. In flight both sexes show pale blue inner wing. Generally gregarious; sizeable flocks gather at favoured feeding grounds in winter. Much scarcer in summer at reed-fringed lagoons and marshes. *Status:* small numbers breed over much of area; influx of winter visitors. *Similar Species:* smaller Garganey (p.65) has blue inner wing but no other duck has huge, spatulate bill.

J	4
F	4
M	4
A	3
M	2
J	2
J	2
A	2
S	3
O	3
N	4
D	4

68

Introduction

The illustrations

The first reference points on each page are inevitably the illustrations. Each species is shown in its major plumages and in typical attitudes, as birds are generally seen in the field. Similar species appear on facing pages (wherever possible) and in the same postures to facilitate comparison. Some birds, such as several birds of prey, are treated more diagrammatically than others so that finer points of distinction can be picked out.

The labels

The labels around the illustrations are based on the sort of notes that most competent birders make in the field when they see an unfamiliar bird or a bird they do not recognize. We have used the labels to pick out the most important points to watch for and these may not necessarily be the most obvious. Indeed some are quite subtle. To become more competent at bird identification, it is a good idea to spend some time studying the illustrations and the labels so you know what to look for when you eventually see the bird in the field.

The text

The text is a total compliment to the illustrations and labels. It seeks to put the bird into the field as a living thing by painting a word picture of the appearance of the bird and the way it moves around the landscape it inhabits. Finally, the text describes where the bird usually occurs and in what numbers and points out how to distinguish it from similar species.

The maps

The maps show the usual distribution of almost all of our birds, using different colours to indicate breeding and wintering areas. Where these overlap, the two colours combine to produce a third. Some of these birds also pass through parts of the country where they neither breed nor winter. To keep our maps simple and understandable, we have omitted information about passage from them but mentioned the fact in the text instead. A small number of our regular birds do not breed or winter with us but pass through in spring or autumn, or both. The vast majority of these passage migrants are Arctic breeders, mainly waders. Grey coloured maps show where they regularly occur. The maps show what the birds regularly do. But occasionally, they may depart from their normal behaviour; a summer visitor may stay on through the winter for example. This brings them as much into the realms of rarity as the bird that occurs on our shores only once in a lifetime.

The abundance chart

The seasonal abundance chart uses a scale from 0–6 to indicate the likelihood of seeing the bird in each month of the year. The numbers are not so much a measure of the actual number of birds as a combination of number and visibility. The figures 0–6 have been defined in terms of a full day's birding in the right habitat by a competent birder.

Introduction

IDENTIFYING BIRDS

Let me say at the outset that bird identification is largely a matter of knowledge.
Most birders acquire this from a combination of books and experience. Some
people have a good eye for recognizing
birds and others have a good ear for bird
song but the lack of such attributes will
certainly not prevent you from becoming
a competent birdwatcher.

Reed Warbler

Habitat and appearance

Birds are creatures of habit. Each species has its own place in the world
and exploits it in the same way generation after generation. Knowing
when and where to look for a bird is half the battle in identification.
Reed Warblers, for example, are summer visitors and there is no point
in looking for them in January. They live among reeds and other
aquatic vegetation and you will waste your time looking for them in
oakwoods. They range no further north than Lancashire and Yorkshire
so don't arrange a special trip to Wester Ross to see them.

A knowledge of how birds behave is also a vital clue to their identity.
So too is a knowledge of what to look for when a bird is seen. For
example, you see a flock of black birds on the sea. They look like ducks
and you put them down as Common Scoter without waiting patiently to
see if any of them flap their wings to show a white speculum (patch on
inner wings). Result? You missed a Velvet Scoter. A more obvious but
more advanced example, is the separation of the small, olive-brown
group of warblers. Here the differences are slight and points such as the
length of the eyebrow and bill, slope of the forehead, leg colour and tail
shape are crucial to identification. If you don't know what to look for,
then you won't see it.

*Velvet Scoter can be identified
by a white patch (speculum)
on the inner wing.*

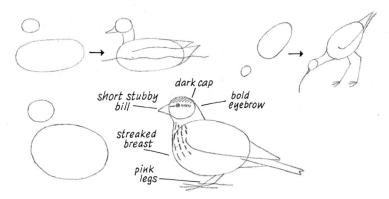

Field descriptions

Perhaps the most important skill to learn when starting to identify birds is to watch, examine and note. Remembering a single feature will probably not be sufficient for an accurate identification. What is required is the patience to watch and note every part of a bird's body as well as when and where it was seen, how it moved, how it fed, how it flew, which other birds it associated with and so on. Such notes are called field descriptions.

Far and away the best form of note taking is to draw an outline of the bird and mark on it any particularly obvious features. I cannot draw birds but I have found that a couple of ovals works quite satisfactorily if I add on legs, bill and tail. This should preferably be done while the bird is still in view. If the bird flies, try to note the pattern on both the upperwing and underwing – if that is impossible, don't worry. An incomplete description is far better than an inaccurate one.

Armed with your field notes and little drawings, check through the guide to find the bird you have seen. If you have difficulty finding it, do not immediately jump to the conclusion that you have found either a bird new to Britain or even a major rarity. The chances are you haven't! Go back over the pages again and keep searching until you find it.

Introduction

MAKING FIELD NOTES

On the next six pages are some of the points to consider when you are making your drawings of birds and compiling your field notes. The most important thing to remember is to note down as much information as you can – even seemingly trivial points may be significant when you come to identify the bird later.

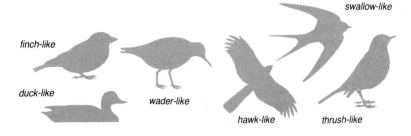

swallow-like

finch-like

duck-like *wader-like*

hawk-like *thrush-like*

What type of bird is it?
The division of birds into groups is not artificial; birds are different and these differences can be seen easily. Consult the list on page 26 to familiarize yourself with the major bird groups. If your bird does not fit into any of the categories you know, then say so.

What is the overall shape of the bird?
Is it, for instance, thin like a wagtail or plump like a Robin?

What shape are the wings?

Are they broad
like a Buzzard?

Are they straight
like a Fulmar?

Are they rounded
like a Partridge?

Or pointed
like a Kestrel?

Or sharply angled
like a Swallow?

Or long and thin
like a Swift?

What shape and size is the bill?

Is it tiny like a Swallow?

Is it thin and pointed like a Robin?

Is it conical like a Greenfinch?

Is it hooked like a Kestrel?

Is it long and thin like a Redshank?

Is it decurved like a Curlew?

It is also useful to note how long the bill is compared to the length of the head. This is particularly important for waders.

What shape is the tail?

There is a whole spectrum of shapes that takes in almost every British and Irish bird. Typical shapes are illustrated below, together with some examples of tail patterns.

| *pointed* | *wedge-shaped* | *rounded* | *square* | *notched* | *forked* |

| *white outer tail feathers* | *inverted 'T' shape* | *black tip* | *white outer tips* |

Introduction

How does it move?

Does it swim, walk, wade, dive, hop, run, climb or flit among vegetation? Different modes of locomotion offer valuable clues to a bird's identity. Treecreepers, Nuthatches and woodpeckers are most often seen climbing the trunks or major branches of trees. Flycatchers perch openly and dart out to catch flying insects. Warblers flit among vegetation but will also behave like flycatchers. Some ducks, such as Pochard, dive for their food while others, such as Wigeon, do not. Swifts fly almost continuously, while other birds, such as Moorhens, seem to take to the air only under duress.

Movement during feeding varies enormously too. Some birds wade and probe into the mud; others pick food from the surface. Some walk, others hop or shuffle. Some are ever-active; others stand still and occasionally pounce.

How does it fly?

Does it fly in a straight line like a Turtle Dove?

Or undulate like a Mistle Thrush?

Does it glide like a shearwater?

Or hang in the air like a gull?

Does it hover like a Kestrel?

Or dive like a Gannet?

Does it soar like a Buzzard?

Or flap and glide like a harrier?

Introduction

When did you see the bird?

Note the date of every observation in your field notebook. Dates can be an important clue to identity.

Where did you see the bird?

Record the place in your notes; some birds simply do not occur in certain parts of the British Isles.

What sort of habitat was the bird using?

Note the type of countryside where the bird was seen. Was it, for instance, at sea, along the shoreline, on a coastal freshwater marsh, a pond or a lake? Was it among reeds or scrub, on heathland or in a wood? Was the wood coniferous, deciduous or mixed? It is impossible to go into too much detail and even identifying the trees and flowers growing in the area can be helpful.

3 June 1995
Lower Twidlemarsh
Worcs.

Wind SW (5-6)
fresh → moderate
50%, sunny later

Teal 10
Redshank 2
Yellowhammer 10
Marsh Warbler
(1 singing)
Goldfinch
Greenfinch
Tree Sparrow
(several
  nesting)

pale eyebrow
steep forehead
uniform underparts
pinkish legs

Marsh Warbler

Note association with
meadowsweet & osiers

osier bed

meadowsweet

Introduction

What call or song did it make?

Most birders know the voices of the majority of our breeding birds and the most obvious calls of our visitors. The ability to recognize a bird from a brief twitter coming from the middle of a dense thicket saves a great deal of time and effort. If an unknown bird calls, try to write down a phonetic rendering or perhaps put it into words. It is not ideal, because each person tends to interpret a bird call in a different way, but it is better than nothing.

Alternatively, carry a tape recorder with you in the field and record calls and songs you don't know. Then, with the aid of a good set of bird recordings and much patience, try to find the owner. This is, incidentally, an excellent way of learning bird calls.

What size is it?

Size is notoriously misleading and everyone is prone to considerable error. For this reason, I do not consider it of great importance nor do I think that too much reliance should be placed on it. The best measure of size is to compare the unknown bird with a known species alongside it. Otherwise, stick to broad scales of size and compare the bird to a familiar species, such as a Sparrow or a Blackbird.

What is its structure?

I have intentionally put structure at the end of the list because it is the most difficult feature to describe and appreciate – even though it is arguably the most important. Picking out a species by its structure must be based on experience although even the beginner should bear it in mind at all times.

Birds differ in structure even within quite closely related groups. The most common waders, for instance, are divided into two groups (the *Calidris* and the *Tringa* sandpipers) based on their structure. The generic names (the first scientific names) of the birds reflect these structural differences and are used to name the groups. Though there are differences within each group, their overall structure is similar.

A Calidris sandpiper – dumpy structure.

A Tringa sandpiper – elegant structure.

Little Stint

Wood Sandpiper

Introduction

What are its field marks?

Field marks are nothing more than bold patches of plumage that stand out when the bird is seen. Head patterns, wingbars and tail and rump patterns are the most obvious and should be fully noted (and drawn) for every unknown bird. In the main, these marks are confined to a particular group of feathers and a sound knowledge of which feathers are which is an invaluable aid to identification. The main diagram below shows the names of each group of feathers and indicates in particular the complex structure of the feathers on a bird's folded wing. Separate diagrams show details of the field markings on the head and open wing. A full, working knowledge of a bird's anatomy is essential to producing an accurate field description.

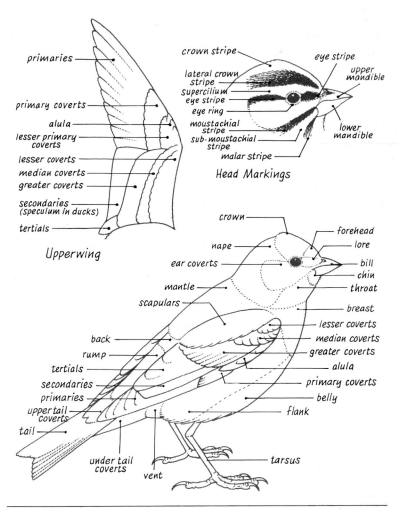

Introduction

BIRDING EQUIPMENT

Birding is a relatively cheap sport compared with say, golf or sailing. It can, however, develop into a passion that devours money at an alarming rate. The only basic equipment you really need is a pair of binoculars and a field guide. Starting with field guides – you have this one so look no further! There are others covering larger areas and including many rarities or vagrants. Buy them as you need them, or wait for Christmas.

Binoculars

Binoculars really are essential and basically you get what you pay for. They vary enormously from dainty little opera glasses to enormous, powerful cross-Channel jobs that need Superman to hold them steady. The specification of a pair of binoculars is shown on the instrument as one number times another – 8 × 30 for instance. The first number is the magnification; the second number is the diameter of the object lens (the large lens at the front) in millimetres.

A magnification that is too low will not bring the bird close enough for the critical examination you require; one that is too high will be impossible to hold steady and give such a narrow field of view that a bird is difficult to locate. A compromise is required. For birding, a magnification of 8, 9, or 10 is perfect. The wider the object lens, the more light is let in and the wider the field of view. Unfortunately larger lenses mean larger, and heavier, binoculars. So compromise again! Carrying binoculars around your neck all day can be a strain, so choose a pair with an object lens of reasonable size. For birdwatching, a diameter of 30 to 50 millimetres is about right.

In practical terms, these factors, together with the range of specifications offered by the manufacturers, limit the choice to the following: 8 × 30, 8 × 40, 10 × 40, and 10 × 50. (Binoculars are seldom made by reputable manufacturers with nine times magnification.) With these specifications in mind, buy what you can afford. Better still, talk to birders you meet about their binoculars or get the back copy of *British Birds* journal that has an article reporting the results of their binocular and telescope survey.

Make sure you buy binoculars with an adjustable eyepiece and a centre wheel for focusing properly at all distances. A plastic rainguard that slips up and down the neck strap is also essential for keeping binoculars free from rain – the birder's nightmare. (If the manufacturer of your binoculars does not make a rainguard, you will have to resort to mail order – consult the RSPB's magazine *Birds*.) Although the rainguard is designed to slip up and down both sides of the strap, many birders thread it through only one side so that it can be pushed aside when they use their binoculars and does not keep falling onto their face. The neck strap itself should be adjusted so that the glasses sit nicely on your chest rather than swinging about on your belly. You may well have to make fresh holes in the strap to get it short enough. So much for binoculars.

Telescopes

Over the past ten years, telescopes have become progressively more widespread. Despite their weight, most birders carry them at all times – many use them with a tripod. A telescope and tripod are cumbersome and heavy to carry around yet the compensations obviously outweigh the disadvantages.

Telescopes are an essential item in a wide variety of birding situations. Their value may be obvious when examining birds at sea or at considerable distances across wide estuaries, but they are also useful at close range when searching through large flocks of gulls or waders. A tripod permits a more leisurely approach, enabling you to examine the flock bird by bird and, at the same time, take the occasional break without losing your position. It also enables individual birds to be passed on to other people by leaving the telescope focused on the bird concerned.

Once upon a time, telescopes were large brass instruments of great inconvenience. Today they are much lighter and more compact. Many are prismatic, less than a foot long, and even 'draw' telescopes are not much more than a couple of feet long. They either have interchangeable eyepieces allowing different magnifications or a zoom eyepiece that enables magnification to be varied *in situ*. In general, these zoom eyepieces reduce the field of view by up to a third and the image is less clear than with a fixed magnification. As with binoculars, the greater the magnification the lower the amount of light entering the eye and the narrower the field of view. About 20 to 30 times is about right for birding. The object lens should be large enough to enable such magnification to be used under most light conditions. Lenses of 60 to 70 millimetres are ideal; larger lenses are not so much heavy, as expensive. Once again, read *British Birds* magazine for their recommendations.

Once you've got a field guide, binoculars, telescope and tripod there is not much more you can use, though you may be surprised how much boots, rainwear, cameras, telephoto lenses, motor drives, encyclopedias, Where-to-Watch guides, memberships, travelling expenses and so on can add up to.

Introduction

WHERE TO WATCH BIRDS

You can watch birds almost anywhere but some places are undoubtedly better than others. A small selection of the best birdwatching sites in the British Isles are marked on the map below and described on the next page. More detailed information can be found in my book *The New Where to Watch Birds*, which has been revised and updated. There are also county guides, which go into greater detail on a local basis.

Having said that, I must also add that there are hosts of good birding places not mentioned in any guide. A local reservoir, an unfrequented headland, a tiny coastal copse, or even the local city park, can all produce interesting and unusual birds. Looking at a map while on a Shetland holiday, it seemed likely that a tiny valley on the north-eastern tip of the Isle of Unst should produce migrants. I went there only once and saw a spring Woodchat Shrike – a good rarity, if not an outrageous one. At the other extreme, a Wood Warbler in my local London park was equally as exciting and unexpected.

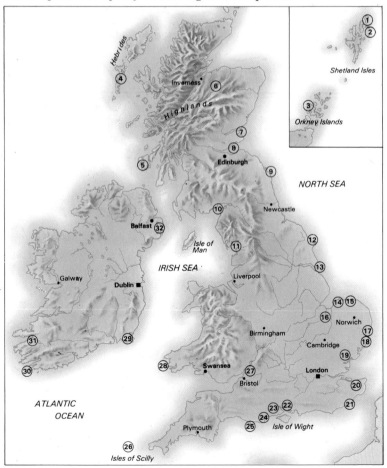

1 *Unst, Shetland*: magnificent cliffs at Hermaness with Gannetry and thousands of breeding seabirds. May–June.

2 *Fetlar, Shetland*: beautiful island with scarce Red-necked Phalarope, Whimbrel and formerly Snowy Owl. May–June.

3 *Marwick Head, Orkney*: a mile of cliffs absolutely alive with breeding seabirds. May–June.

4 *Uists and Benbecula*: three joined islands. Super reserves at Loch Druidibeg and Balranald for Greylag Goose and Red-necked Phalarope. May–June.

5 *Islay*: huge numbers of Barnacle Geese. Nov–Mar.

6 *Speyside*: one of the classic birding areas with scarce mountain species (Snow Bunting, Dotterel, Golden Eagle) and old pine forest birds (Crested Tit, Capercaillie, Scottish Crossbill). May–June.

7 *Tay Estuary*: rich variety of bird areas at mouth include Tentsmuir; particularly impressive range of migrants. Aug–Oct.

8 *Firth of Forth*: seaducks in winter, migrant waders, breeding terns, and Gannet on Bass Rock. All year.

9 *Farne Islands*: splendid seabird colonies, terns, auks, Eider. May–June.

10 *Solway Firth*: winter wildfowl and waders; Barnacle Geese and most other British geese. Nov–Feb.

11 *Morecambe Bay and Leighton Moss*: RSPB reserves with largest wader concentrations and breeding Bittern. All year.

12 *Bempton Cliffs*: only mainland Gannetry plus huge numbers of other seabirds. May–June.

13 *Spurn Point*: bird observatory for seabirds and small migrants with Humber Estuary for waders. All year.

14 *Titchwell*: super RSPB reserve with Bearded Tit and Bittern breeding and wide range of migrants. All year.

15 *Cley*: outstanding marshland with most East Anglian specialities and extraordinary variety of migrants. All year.

16 *Ouse Washes*: wildfowl, including Bewick's Swans; in winter breeding Black-tailed Godwits and Ruff. All year.

17 *Walberswick*: wide variety of habitats with good birds of all types at all seasons. All year.

18 *Minsmere*: RSPB's most famous reserve. Avocet, terns, Marsh Harrier all breed; migrant rarities and good winter birds. All year.

19 *Abberton Reservoir*: Britain's top bird reservoir; excellent winter wildfowl and migrants. All year.

20 *Stodmarsh*: classic breeding area for colonizing marsh birds and scarce migrants. All year.

21 *Dungeness*: bird observatory plus RSPB reserve; good migration spot with some scarce breeders. All year.

22 *Langstone Harbour*: Brent Geese and waders in season with lovely Farlington Marshes nearby. All year.

23 *New Forest*: wonderful heath and woodland with Hobby, Goshawk, Honey Buzzard and much more. May–June.

24 *Studland and Poole Harbour*: excellent estuary birds and best Dartford Warblers at RSPB Arne Reserve. All year.

25 *Portland*: bird observatory for sea-watching and small migrants. Apr–Oct.

26 *Isles of Scilly*: best place for rarities in Britain. Oct.

27 *Slimbridge*: Wildfowl Trust headquarters with good flocks of White-fronted Geese and Bewick's Swans. Jan–Feb.

28 *Skomer*: most accessible of Welsh seabird islands with thousands of auks, gulls etc. May–June.

29 *Wexford Slobs*: estuary with waders and wildfowl at all seasons and good breeding terns. All year.

30 *Cape Clear*: former bird observatory and arguably best place in region for seawatching. Sept–Oct.

31 *Akeagh Lough*: regularly produces American waders and ducks. Aug–Oct.

32 *Strangford Lough*: estuary with waders and wildfowl. All year.

Introduction

HABITAT GUIDE

Birds have, over the centuries, adapted to particular lifestyles and particular niches. Some are confined to one particular niche, while others can exploit a wide range of habitats. Identification is greatly facilitated by a knowledge of what birds are found where.

Open sea: many birds spend their non-breeding lives roaming the oceans well away from land. Fulmar, Manx Shearwater, Storm Petrel, Leach's Petrel, Gannet, Kittiwake, Guillemot, Razorbill, Little Auk, Puffin.

Sea-cliffs: Britain's outstanding bird habitat; our cliff colonies of seabirds are the envy of Europe. Fulmar, Shag, Cormorant, Gannet, Kittiwake, Guillemot, Razorbill, Puffin, Black Guillemot.

Estuary and shoreline: highly variable, from rocky shores to dunes and muddy flats; mostly a wintering zone for waders and wildfowl. Dunlin, Knot, Bar-tailed Godwit, Grey Plover, Ringed Plover, Redshank, Turnstone, Oystercatcher, Wigeon, Pintail, Mallard, Brent Goose, Arctic Tern, Little Tern.

Inland freshwater: includes ponds, lakes, rivers, floods and marshes; great habitat for breeding and migrant birds. Great Crested Grebe, Red-throated Diver, Mallard, Tufted Duck, Greylag Goose, Coot, Moorhen, Common Tern, Black Tern, Grey Wagtail, Dipper, Kingfisher.

Reeds: a scarce but decidedly rich habitat with a few rare breeding birds. Bittern, Marsh Harrier, Water Rail, Bearded Tit, Reed Warbler, Savi's Warbler, Cetti's Warbler, Sedge Warbler.

Fields and hedgerows: agriculture covers the vast majority of our countryside and birds that find a home there tend to be abundant. Kestrel, Lapwing, Golden Plover, Grey Partridge, Little Owl, Barn Owl, Magpie, Jackdaw, Rook, Chaffinch, Yellowhammer.

Towns and gardens: surprisingly good selection of birds despite the presence of people. Black Redstart, Robin, Swift, House Martin, Starling, Blackbird, Blue Tit, Great Tit, Greenfinch, Chaffinch, Bullfinch, Jackdaw.

Conifer woods: native pines are very scarce but modern plantations are beginning to mature. Long-eared Owl, Capercaillie, Black Grouse, Crested Tit, Goldcrest, Firecrest, Redpoll, Crossbill.

Deciduous woods: home to wide variety of birds at all times of the year. Sparrowhawk, Tawny Owl, Great Spotted Woodpecker, Nuthatch, Treecreeper, Willow Warbler, Chiffchaff, Garden Warbler, Spotted Flycatcher, Pied Flycatcher.

Moors and heaths: similar to look at but holding quite different birds according to altitude. Merlin, Hobby, Red Grouse, Stone-curlew, Ptarmigan, Meadow Pipit, Stonechat, Whinchat, Dartford Warbler, Lesser Whitethroat, Yellowhammer.

BIRDS

OF·BRITAIN·AND·IRELAND

Birds of Britain and Ireland

WHICH BIRDS?

Over 500 different species have been seen in Britain and Ireland at one time or another and new species are added to the list every year. Fortunately half the total are vagrants that occur once in a while from distant parts of Europe, Asia and America. They are in no sense 'British Birds'. Most tend to be young, lost birds in rather nondescript juvenile or first winter plumage. They are often difficult to identify and need a somewhat different approach from the normal field guide.

In this book, we cover the 256 birds that are regular and most likely to be seen. These birds either breed regularly, winter regularly or regularly pass through on passage to and from their breeding areas. Of course things are never static; today's regular breeder may disappear and become a rarity. Conversely, today's vagrant may become tomorrow's breeding species. Meanwhile there are 256 species that one could reasonably expect to see and which most keen watchers would be pleased to see in a year.

Order of birds

The birds in this book are arranged in systematic order. This scientifically accepted system arranges birds in their approximate order of evolution. To the beginner, this order may seem chaotic compared with arranging the birds in say order of size, or by habitat, or particularly alphabetically. The systematic order does, however, have one great advantage – it generally groups similar birds together and facilitates comparison. Where this does not happen, we have departed from the strict order to allow similar species to be grouped together.

Use the coloured square at the corner of the pages to help you find the different groups as you flick through the book.

	Divers and grebes		Owls
	Shearwaters, cormorants and gannets		Woodpeckers and allies
	Herons		Larks, swallows and pipits
	Wildfowl		Wrens and allies
	Birds of prey		Chats and thrushes
	Gamebirds, crakes and rails		Warblers and flycatchers
	Waders		Tits, nuthatches and treecreepers
	Gulls, terns and auks		Shrikes and crows
	Pigeons and cuckoos		Sparrows, finches and buntings

grey crown

thin, uptilted bill

red throat

plain back

drooping neck of all divers

white extends above eye

pale speckled back

Summer

Winter

Smallest of the divers and generally the most widespread and numerous throughout year. Breeds on small lakes, usually within flighting distance of sea. Winters in coastal waters, often in loose flocks. Thin, uptilted bill. Pale grey crown and rust-red throat in summer. In winter pale grey or brown back, spotted white. Like other divers, flies fast on long, pointed wings with head and neck drooping.

Status: scarce but widespread breeder in northern and western Scotland and north-western Ireland. Winters along all shores.

Similar Species: Black-throated Diver (p.28) and Great Northern Diver (p.29). All divers similar in winter, though Red-throated paler; smaller size distinguishes throughout year.

RED-THROATED DIVER

Type	duck-like
Size	53–59cm (22in)
Habitat	freshwater, sea
Behaviour	swims, dives from surface, takes off and lands on water
Flocking	summer solitary; small flocks winter
Flight	strong and powerful; direct
Voice	harsh *kuk-kuk-kuk* in flight; wails and cackles in breeding season.

IDENTIFICATION

Ad.summer	
Crown	pale grey
Upperparts	brown
Rump	brown
Tail	brown; short and pointed
Throat	rust-red
Breast	white
Belly	white
Bill	black; short, thin, uptilted
Legs	black; short
Ad.winter	white head and throat; grey cap; pale grey back spotted white; grey bill
Juvenile	as Ad.winter, darker back

BREEDING

Nest	scrape at water's edge
Eggs	2; olive-buff, blotched black
Incubation	24–29 days, mainly ♀
Young	active; downy
Fledging	6 weeks
Broods	1; May–Sept
Food	fish, amphibians
Population	750+ pairs; 12,000+ winter

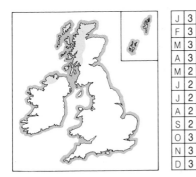

J	3
F	3
M	3
A	3
M	2
J	2
J	2
A	2
S	2
O	3
N	3
D	3

Black-throated Diver *Gavia arctica*

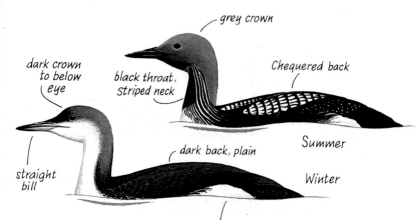

grey crown

Chequered back

dark crown to below eye

black throat, striped neck

Summer

dark back, plain

Winter

straight bill

white flank patch

BLACK-THROATED DIVER

Type	duck-like
Size	56–69cm (25in)
Habitat	freshwater, sea
Behaviour	swims, dives from surface, takes off and lands on water
Flocking	summer solitary; small flocks winter
Flight	strong and powerful; direct
Voice	grunts, croaks and loud wailing in breeding season

IDENTIFICATION

Ad.summer

Crown	grey
Upperparts	black and white, with two chequered ovals
Rump	black
Tail	black; short and pointed
Throat	black
Breast	white
Belly	white
Bill	black; straight and pointed
Legs	black; short
Ad.winter	dark above, white below; white patch on rear flanks
Juvenile	as Ad.winter, speckly above

BREEDING

Nest	scrape at water's edge
Eggs	2; olive-brown, blotched black
Incubation	28–29 days ♂ ♀
Young	active; downy
Fledging	9 weeks
Broods	1; May–Sept
Food	fish, amphibians
Population	150 pairs; 1300 winter

Intermediate in size between Red-throated and Great Northern Divers. Breeds on larger lakes and winters offshore. In summer, largely black and white with two chequered ovals on back. Neck striped black and white with white foreneck. In winter, upperparts plain slate-brown in adult; slightly mottled in juvenile. White patch on rear flanks often obvious. Dark of crown extends below eye giving masked effect.
Status: scarce breeder in north and west Scotland. Winters along all shores, mostly in west.
Similar Species: Red-throated Diver (p.27) always paler and more slightly built. Great Northern Diver (p.29) has more massive head and bill and black, not grey, head in summer.

J	3
F	3
M	3
A	3
M	2
J	2
J	2
A	2
S	2
O	3
N	3
D	3

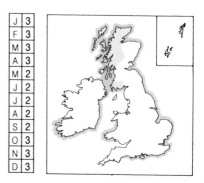

black crown

striped neck patch

chequered back

Summer

dark crown, white above eye

speckled back

heavy bill

Winter

Largest and generally least numerous of the three divers. Size often confusing at sea, but large, angular head and heavy bill distinguish at all seasons. In summer, black head and neck, broken only by narrow oval of stripes on neck. Chequered back pattern more clear-cut than Black-throated. In winter, darker above than Red-throated, but scaly back pattern produces paler effect than Black-throated. Dark crown does not enclose eye. In flight, wing beats slower than the smaller divers.

Status: has bred and regularly summers in northern Scotland. Winter visitor to most coasts; more regular in north and west.

Similar Species: angular crown and mottled upperparts distinguish from winter Black-throated Diver (p.28).

	GREAT NORTHERN DIVER
Type	duck-like, goose-like
Size	69–81cm (30in)
Habitat	freshwater, sea
Behaviour	swims, dives from surface, takes off and lands on water
Flocking	summer solitary; small flocks winter
Flight	strong and powerful; direct
Voice	summer – loud wails, cackling laugh; winter – occasional croaks, moans

IDENTIFICATION

Ad.summer	
Crown	black
Upperparts	black and white, two chequered ovals
Rump	black
Tail	black; short and pointed
Throat	black
Breast	white
Belly	white
Bill	black; straight and pointed
Legs	black; short
Ad.winter	brown above, white below
Juvenile	as Ad.winter, speckly back

BREEDING

Nest	scrape at water's edge
Eggs	2; olive-brown, blackish spots
Incubation	29–30 days ♂ ♀
Young	active; downy
Fledging	12 weeks
Broods	1; May–Sept
Food	fish, amphibians
Population	3500+ winter

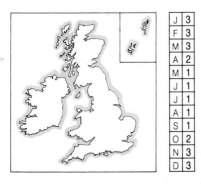

J	3
F	3
M	3
A	2
M	1
J	1
J	1
A	1
S	1
O	2
N	3
D	3

Great Crested Grebe *Podiceps cristatus*

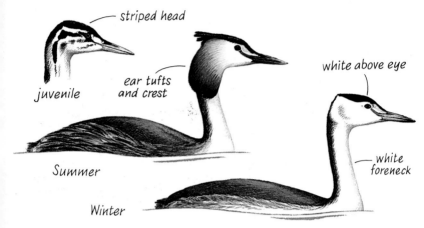

striped head

juvenile

ear tufts and crest

Summer

white above eye

white foreneck

Winter

GREAT CRESTED GREBE	
Type	duck-like
Size	45–51cm (19in)
Habitat	freshwater, sea
Behaviour	swims, dives from surface, takes off and lands on water
Flocking	summer solitary; small flocks winter
Flight	laboured; direct
Voice	harsh barking *ra-ra* and variety croaking sounds

IDENTIFICATION

Ad.summer	
Crown	black; crest
Upperparts	brown
Rump	brown
Tail	brown; short and rounded
Throat	white
Breast	white
Belly	white
Bill	red; straight and sharply pointed
Legs	green; short
Ad.winter	dark cap, white above eye, white neck
Juvenile	as Ad.winter, streaked head

BREEDING

Nest	floating mound in water
Eggs	4; white
Incubation	25–29 days ♂ ♀
Young	active; downy
Fledging	25–29 days
Broods	1 or 2; May–July
Food	fish
Population	3000 pairs; 7000+ winter

Largest grebe; widespread resident and winter visitor to lakes, reservoirs and coastlines. In summer, black cap and prominent russet and black head plumes (erected in display) preclude confusion. In winter, black cap extends *above* eye forming prominent white eyebrow; foreneck white. Juveniles heavily streaked on head. Dives expertly; flies laboriously after lengthy pattering over water's surface.
Status: widespread and quite numerous except in Scottish Highlands and Islands. In winter congregates at larger waters and sheltered coastlines. Some immigration from the Continent.
Similar Species: large size, long neck and sharply pointed bill separate from all grebes except winter Red-necked (p.31), which has no eyebrow and dusky, not white, foreneck.

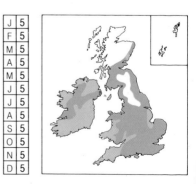

J	5
F	5
M	5
A	5
M	5
J	5
J	5
A	5
S	5
O	5
N	5
D	5

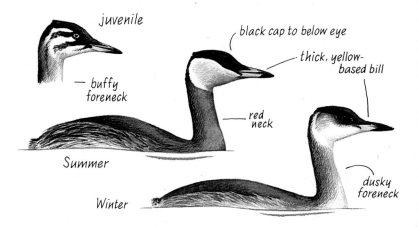

juvenile

buffy foreneck

black cap to below eye

thick, yellow-based bill

red neck

Summer

Winter

dusky foreneck

Mainly winter visitor and passage migrant to coastal waters. In summer, black cap extends to below eye; white cheeks and rust-red neck preclude confusion. In winter, overall pattern remains same but neck becomes dusky grey and cheeks less white. Yellow bill with dark tip. Often found in small groups in winter.

Status: scarce double passage migrant and winter visitor to east coast, extending westward along south coast to Dorset. Absent Ireland.

Similar Species: winter Great Crested Grebe (p.30). Red-necked slightly smaller with grey foreneck; shorter, thicker bill is yellow, not pink.

RED-NECKED GREBE

Type	duck-like
Size	40–46cm (17in)
Habitat	freshwater, sea
Behaviour	swims, dives from surface, takes off and lands on water
Flocking	1–10
Flight	laboured; direct
Voice	silent away from breeding grounds

IDENTIFICATION

Ad.summer	
Crown	black
Upperparts	brown
Rump	brown
Tail	brown; short and rounded
Throat	rust-red
Breast	rust-red
Belly	white
Bill	yellow, dark tip; straight and pointed
Legs	black; short
Ad.winter	smudgy cap, grey foreneck
Juvenile	as Ad.winter; streaked head

BREEDING

Nest	floating mound in water
Eggs	4–5; white
Incubation	22–25 days ♂ ♀
Young	active; downy
Fledging	?
Broods	1; May–June
Food	small fish, crustaceans, molluscs, insects
Population	1 pair; 120+ winter

J	2
F	2
M	2
A	1
M	1
J	1
J	1
A	1
S	2
O	2
N	2
D	2

Slavonian Grebe *Podiceps auritus*

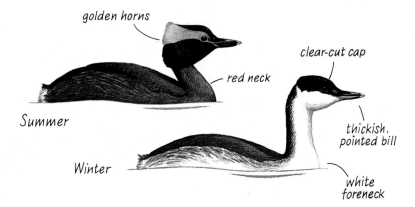

golden horns

red neck

clear-cut cap

thickish, pointed bill

Summer

Winter

white foreneck

SLAVONIAN GREBE

Type	duck-like
Size	31–36cm (13in)
Habitat	freshwater, sea
Behaviour	swims, dives from surface, takes off and lands on water
Flocking	colonial; small flocks (up to 15) winter
Flight	laboured; direct
Voice	trills when breeding

IDENTIFICATION

Ad.summer	
Crown	black, golden 'horns'
Upperparts	almost black
Rump	black
Tail	black; short and rounded
Throat	rust-red
Breast	rust-red
Belly	rust-red
Bill	black; short and pointed
Legs	black; short
Ad.winter	black cap, white throat
Juvenile	browner version of Ad.winter

BREEDING

Nest	floating mound in water
Eggs	4–5; white
Incubation	22–25 days ♂ ♀
Young	active; downy
Fledging	?
Broods	1; May–July
Food	small fish, crustaceans, molluscs, insects
Population	70+ pairs; 430 winter

Small grebe, only slightly larger than Little Grebe. In summer, black head marked by bold golden 'horns' extending through eye; neck and flanks rust-red. In winter, clear-cut black cap contrasts with white foreneck and flanks; back almost black. Generally gregarious at all seasons.
Status: rare breeder in northern Britain; scarce winter visitor, mainly to sheltered coasts and estuaries.
Similar Species: Black-necked (p.33) is separated by black, not red, neck in summer and grey foreneck and less clear-cut cap in winter. At all times, Slavonian has thicker, more symmetrical, bill.

J	2
F	2
M	1
A	2
M	2
J	2
J	2
A	1
S	1
O	1
N	2
D	2

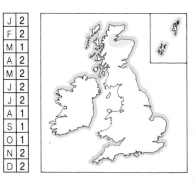

golden fan

black neck

Summer

dusky cap
not clear-cut,
pale hind
crown

thin
uptilted
bill

Winter

dusky
foreneck

Small grebe, similar in size to Slavonian but head rounder and bill thinner and uptilted. Decidedly less maritime than Slavonian in winter, frequenting large reservoirs and gravel pits, usually within easy reach of coast. Winter plumage is dark cap with pale area extending to hind crown; neck smudgy grey. In summer, head, neck and breast black broken only by golden fan of plumes extending from eye. Back black; flanks rust-red.
Status: breeds central Scotland, western Ireland and occasionally elsewhere. Winter visitor to southern Scottish and English waters.
Similar Species: Slavonian Grebe (p.32), especially in winter when Slavonian has more clear-cut cap, white (not grey) neck, and appears more black and white.

BLACK-NECKED GREBE

Type	duck-like
Size	28–33cm (12in)
Habitat	freshwater
Behaviour	swims, dives from surface, takes off and lands on water
Flocking	colonial; small flocks winter
Flight	laboured; direct
Voice	quiet *poo-eep*; variety harsh notes

IDENTIFICATION

Ad.summer	
Crown	black, golden 'fan'
Upperparts	black
Rump	black
Tail	black; short and rounded
Throat	black
Breast	black
Belly	rust-red
Bill	black; short and uptilted
Legs	black; short
Ad.winter	black above, greyish white below, smudgy cap, smudgy grey throat
Juvenile	as Ad.winter but browner

BREEDING

Nest	floating mound in water
Eggs	3–4; white
Incubation	20–21 days ♂ ♀
Young	active; downy
Fledging	?
Broods	2; Apr–June
Food	insects, crustaceans, molluscs
Population	20+ pairs; 120 winter

J	2
F	2
M	2
A	1
M	2
J	2
J	1
A	1
S	2
O	2
N	2
D	2

Little Grebe *Tachybaptus ruficollis*

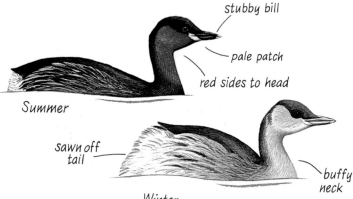

stubby bill

pale patch

red sides to head

Summer

sawn off tail

buffy neck

Winter

	LITTLE GREBE
Type	duck-like
Size	25–29cm (10–11in)
Habitat	freshwater, estuaries
Behaviour	swims, dives from surface, takes off and lands on water
Flocking	colonial; small flocks winter
Flight	laborious; direct
Voice	brief *whit-whit*; loud, far-carrying whinnying song

IDENTIFICATION

	Ad.summer
Crown	black
Upperparts	black
Rump	brown
Tail	buff; short and rounded
Throat	rust-red
Breast	black
Belly	brown
Bill	black with yellow spot at base; short and stubby
Legs	green; short
Ad.winter and juvenile	brown above, buff below, dark cap

BREEDING

Nest	floating mound in water
Eggs	4–6; white
Incubation	19–25 days ♂ ♀
Young	active; downy
Fledging	44–48 days
Broods	2; Apr–July
Food	fish, insects, crustaceans, molluscs
Population	9000–18,000 pairs; 11,000+ winter

Smallest, most widespread and numerous of the grebes, found on variety of inland waters, mostly with plentiful vegetation emerging above water. In summer, rust-red cheeks, throat and neck with bold yellow spot at base of bill. In winter, dark cap and upperparts; buffy throat, neck and flanks.

Status: widespread breeding resident; often quite numerous (semi-colonial) at favoured waters both summer and winter.

Similar Species: can be confused with Slavonian Grebe (p.32) and Black-necked Grebe (p.33) in winter but short, square-cut tail distinguishes.

J	5
F	5
M	5
A	5
M	5
J	5
J	5
A	5
S	5
O	5
N	5
D	5

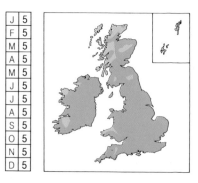

short, stubby bill

stiff wings

thick neck

Stocky, heavily-built seabird; glides and skims water with typical stiff-winged shearwater flight. Flaps wings more frequently than shearwaters. Head, neck and body white; wings, back and tail grey. Lacks any distinctive black and white pattern on wingtips. Short yellow bill; tube-nose visible at close quarters. Thick 'bull-neck' quite unlike any similar species; particularly noticeable in flight. Often gathers in large numbers round trawlers; decidedly gregarious at cliff breeding colonies.

Status: breeds along almost all coasts where suitable cliffs occur. In winter, widespread throughout Atlantic and North Sea.

Similar Species: easily confused with gulls, especially when perched on cliffs. Only grey, stiff-winged species at sea.

FULMAR

Type	gull-like
Size	44–50cm (17–20in)
Habitat	sea and sea-cliffs
Behaviour	swims, perches on rocks, takes off and lands on water or cliffs
Flocking	colonial; sometimes huge flocks
Flight	strong and powerful; gliding
Voice	harsh crackle at breeding colonies

IDENTIFICATION

Adult	
Crown	white
Upperparts	grey
Rump	grey
Tail	grey; short and square
Throat	white
Breast	white
Belly	white
Bill	yellow; short, tube-nosed
Legs	yellow; short

BREEDING

Nest	bare ledge
Eggs	1; white
Incubation	55–57 days ♂ ♀
Young	helpless; downy
Fledging	46–51 days
Broods	1; May–Sept
Food	crustaceans, fish
Population	600,000 pairs

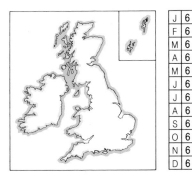

J	6
F	6
M	6
A	6
M	6
J	6
J	6
A	6
S	6
O	6
N	6
D	6

Great Shearwater *Puffinus gravis*

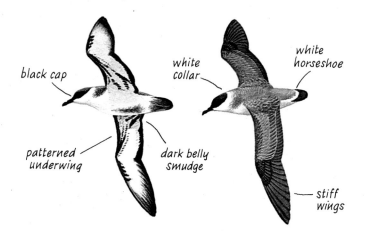

black cap

white collar

white horseshoe

patterned underwing

dark belly smudge

stiff wings

GREAT SHEARWATER

Type	gull-like
Size	42–49cm (16½–19in)
Habitat	sea
Behaviour	swims, takes off and lands on water
Flocking	1–15
Flight	strong and powerful; gliding
Voice	usually silent at sea; some raucous calls from feeding flocks

IDENTIFICATION

Adult	
Crown	black
Upperparts	brown
Rump	white
Tail	black, white horseshoe at base; short and rounded
Throat	white
Breast	white
Belly	white, dark smudge
Bill	black; short and thin
Legs	pink; short

BREEDING

Nest	crevice, burrow
Eggs	1; white
Incubation	?
Young	helpless; downy
Fledging	?
Broods	1
Food	fish, crustaceans, squid
Population	scarce migrant

Large shearwater; flies with long, stiff-winged glides broken by short bouts of wing-flapping. Dark above and pale below. Dark cap, separated from mantle by narrow white collar, contrasts with white cheeks. Wings and rump brown with prominent white horseshoe at base of dark tail. Underparts white with dark ventral smudge. Dark tips to white axillaries (arm pits) and dark wing margins form distinctive underwing pattern.
Status: scarce annual visitor from South Atlantic late summer and autumn; mainly to south and west Ireland, Cornwall, and Durham and Yorkshire coasts. Occasionally gale-blown in large numbers.
Similar Species: similar to Cory's Shearwater (p.37), though flight more like Manx Shearwater (p.39).

J	0
F	0
M	0
A	1
M	1
J	1
J	1
A	2
S	2
O	1
N	1
D	0

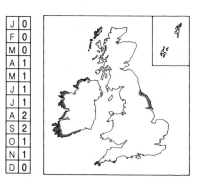

Calonectris diomedea **Cory's Shearwater**

plain
underwing

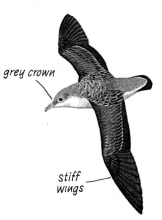

grey crown

stiff
wings

Large shearwater and uncommon visitor to Britain; seen mostly in autumn at sea. Typical long shearwater wings, held straight and stiff in flight, though slightly bowed when gliding. Flaps and soars more than Great Shearwater; flight more like Fulmar than Manx Shearwater. Dark above and pale below, with pale grey-brown head, brown wings and dark brown tail with narrow, pale rump.

Status: uncommon visitor in late summer and autumn, mainly to southern and western Ireland, Cornwall, and Durham and Yorkshire coasts. Breeds in Mediterranean.

Similar Species: Great Shearwater (p.36) has dark cap, prominent white rump and dusky ventral patch.

CORY'S SHEARWATER

Type	gull-like
Size	43–48cm (17–19in)
Habitat	sea
Behaviour	swims, takes off and lands on water
Flocking	1–15
Flight	strong and powerful; gliding
Voice	silent away from breeding grounds

IDENTIFICATION

Adult	
Crown	grey-brown
Upperparts	brown
Rump	brown
Tail	dark brown; short and rounded
Throat	white
Breast	white
Belly	white
Bill	yellow; short and thin
Legs	grey; short

BREEDING

Nest	crevice, burrow
Eggs	1; white
Incubation	60 days? ♂ ♀
Young	helpless; downy
Fledging	?
Broods	1; May–Sept
Food	fish, crustaceans, squid
Population	scarce migrant

J	0
F	0
M	0
A	1
M	1
J	1
J	1
A	2
S	2
O	1
N	0
D	0

Sooty Shearwater _Puffinus griseus_

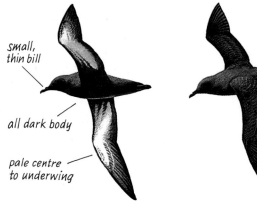

small, thin bill

all dark body

pale centre to underwing

wings set back on body

narrow stiff wings

SOOTY SHEARWATER

Type	gull-like
Size	39–44cm (15–17in)
Habitat	sea
Behaviour	swims, takes off and lands on water
Flocking	1–15
Flight	strong and powerful; gliding; direct
Voice	silent away from breeding grounds

IDENTIFICATION

Adult	
Crown	black
Upperparts	black
Rump	black
Tail	black; short and rounded
Throat	black
Breast	black
Belly	black
Bill	black; short and thin
Legs	black; short

BREEDING

Nest	crevice, burrow
Eggs	1; white .
Incubation	?
Young	helpless; downy
Fledging	?
Broods	1
Food	squid, crustaceans, fish
Population	scarce migrant

Large, narrow-winged shearwater; scarce visitor from South Atlantic. Dark sooty coloration above and below; small head, thin bill; wings set well back on body. Pale underwing may be obvious at considerable range. Flies fast and direct on narrow swept-back wings, flapping frequently – more so than other shearwaters.
Status: regular, but scarce, visitor in summer and autumn to most coasts; more numerous in north and west and decidedly scarce on English coasts of Irish Sea.
Similar Species: with good views, coloration and purposeful flight preclude confusion with other shearwaters.

J	0
F	0
M	0
A	0
M	0
J	0
J	2
A	3
S	3
O	3
N	0
D	0

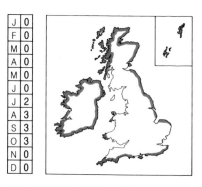

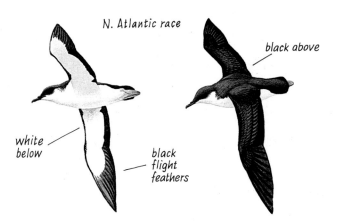

N. Atlantic race

black above

white below

black flight feathers

Most common and widespread of British shearwaters; usually seen in fast careering flight low over sea, or resting on sea awaiting cover of darkness to return to breeding colonies. Black above and white below, with broad black margins to underwing. In typical shearwater flight, flashes alternately black and white as turns low over waves on straight, stiff wings.
Status: breeds on islands in west and north; elsewhere passage migrant.
Similar Species: in some lights may resemble Mediterranean Shearwater.

MANX SHEARWATER

Type	gull-like
Size	30–38cm (11½–15in)
Habitat	sea and small islands
Behaviour	swims, takes off and lands on water and ground
Flocking	1–many thousands
Flight	strong and powerful; gliding; undulating
Voice	loud wails and screams at breeding colonies

IDENTIFICATION

Ad.N.Atlan.

Crown	black
Upperparts	black
Rump	black
Tail	black; short and rounded
Throat	white
Breast	white
Belly	white
Bill	black; short and thin
Legs	grey; short

BREEDING

Nest	burrow, crevice
Eggs	1; white
Incubation	52–54 days ♂ ♀
Young	helpless; downy
Fledging	59–62 days
Broods	1; May–Sept
Food	fish, squid, crustaceans
Population	300,000 pairs+

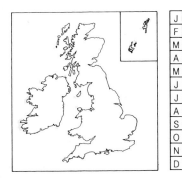

J	0
F	1
M	2
A	2
M	3
J	4
J	3
A	3
S	2
O	2
N	1
D	1

European Storm-petrel *Hydrobates pelagicus*

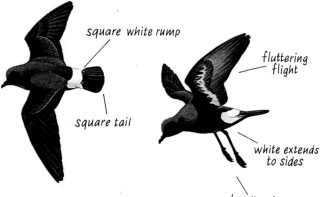

square white rump

square tail

fluttering flight

white extends to sides

dangling legs

EUROPEAN STORM-PETREL

Type	swallow-like
Size	14–16cm (5–6in)
Habitat	sea and small offshore islets
Behaviour	swims, takes off and lands on water or ground
Flocking	1–several hundred
Flight	flitting, gliding; undulating
Voice	on nest, purr ending in hiccough; also high-pitched, repeated squeaks; silent at sea

IDENTIFICATION

Adult	
Crown	black
Upperparts	black
Rump	white
Tail	black; medium length and square
Throat	black
Breast	black
Belly	black
Bill	black; short and thin
Legs	black; medium length

BREEDING

Nest	burrow, crevice
Eggs	1; white
Incubation	38–40 days ♂ ♀
Young	helpless; downy
Fledging	56–64 days
Broods	1; May–July
Food	small fish, plankton
Population	50,000 pairs+

Tiny, black, bat-like seabird with prominent white rump. Usually seen at sea flying with non-stop wing action, dipping to surface with feet dangling to pick up food. Wings straight, broad and rounded; white underwing bar. Tail square-cut, with broad white rump extending to sides of underparts. Feet do not project beyond tail. Often follows ships, picking up food from wake.
Status: highly localized breeder on small islands off coasts of Scotland, Wales and Ireland. Elsewhere on passage or storm-driven.
Similar Species: Leach's Storm-petrel (p.41).

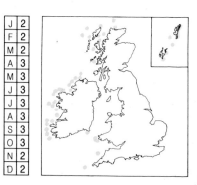

J	2
F	2
M	2
A	3
M	3
J	3
J	3
A	3
S	3
O	3
N	2
D	2

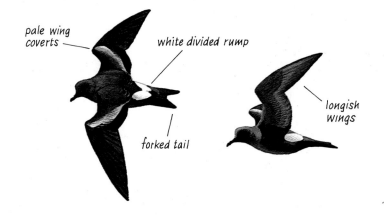

pale wing coverts

white divided rump

longish wings

forked tail

Usually black-brown bird with long, pointed, angled wings; pale edges to coverts form pale inner wing. Tail distinctly forked; white rump has dark central stripe. Feet do not extend beyond tail. Flight is shearwater-like; short glides between bouts of leisurely wing-flapping. Seldom follows ships. *Status:* confined to handful of remote islands off coast of Scotland and possibly Ireland. Otherwise scarce passage migrant and storm-driven waif.

Similar Species: smaller and more numerous European Storm-petrel (p.40) is blacker, has less angled wings and lacks forked tail and pale inner wing. European Storm-petrel's flight more bat-like, with non-stop flitting action and no graceful glides.

LEACH'S STORM-PETREL

Type	swallow-like
Size	19–22cm (7½–9in)
Habitat	sea and small offshore islets
Behaviour	swims, takes off and lands on water or ground
Flocking	1–20
Flight	hovers, glides; undulating
Voice	croons on nest; variety of screeches and repeated notes at colonies

IDENTIFICATION

Adult	
Crown	dark brown
Upperparts	dark brown
Rump	white, dark central stripe
Tail	dark brown; medium length and forked
Throat	dark brown
Breast	dark brown
Belly	dark brown
Bill	black; short and thin
Legs	black; medium length

BREEDING

Nest	burrow, crevice
Eggs	1; white
Incubation	41–42 days ♂ ♀
Young	helpless; downy
Fledging	63–70 days
Broods	1; May–June
Food	fish, plankton
Population	several thousand pairs

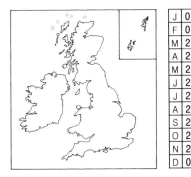

J	0
F	0
M	2
A	2
M	2
J	2
J	2
A	2
S	2
O	2
N	2
D	0

Great Cormorant *Phalacrocorax carbo*

adult summer

white face

white patch

pale belly
first winter

adult winter

thick bill

thick neck

white face

GREAT CORMORANT

Type	goose-like
Size	84–89cm (33–38in)
Habitat	sea, estuaries, freshwater, islands, trees
Behaviour	swims, dives, perches on rocks and buoys, takes off and lands on water and ground
Flocking	colonial; small flocks
Flight	laboured; glides; direct
Voice	croaks and grunts on breeding grounds

IDENTIFICATION

Adult	
Crown	black
Upperparts	black
Rump	black
Tail	black; medium length and rounded
Throat	white
Breast	black
Belly	black
Bill	yellow; straight and thick
Legs	black; short
Juvenile	brown above, buff below

BREEDING

Nest	mound of seaweed on cliff or tree
Eggs	3–4; pale blue
Incubation	28–29 days ♂ ♀
Young	helpless; naked
Fledging	50–60 days
Broods	1; Apr–June
Food	fish
Population	8000 pairs; 20,000+ winter

Common, goose-like waterbird, occurring on coasts and less frequently on inland waters; often seen perched with wings outstretched. Adult glossy green-black with white face and round white flank patch in summer. Immature browner, with pale breast and belly. Swims low in water with uptilted head and heavy, yellow bill. Dives easily; often flies in 'V' formation like geese.

Status: found on all coasts, breeding mainly in north and west; also inland in lowland England and north and central Ireland.

Similar Species: Shag (p.43) is considerably smaller.

J	5
F	5
M	5
A	5
M	5
J	5
J	5
A	5
S	5
O	5
N	5
D	5

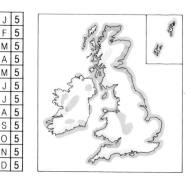

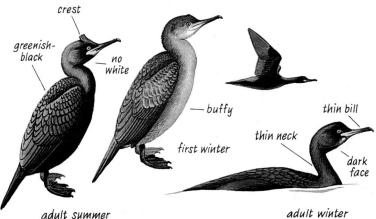

crest

greenish-
black

no
white

— buffy

first winter

thin bill

thin neck

dark
face

adult summer

adult winter

Smaller version of Great Cormorant,
though essentially marine along
predominantly rocky coasts. Swims,
dives and hangs out wings like Great
Cormorant but seldom flies very high.
Adult glossy green-black, with short
tufted crest in summer. Bill black
with yellow gape. Immatures
brownish with black scaling to
feathers; underparts buffy, chin paler.
Status: widespread in north and west,
scarce where does not breed.
Similar Species: separated from
Great Cormorant (p.42) at all times
by smaller size, steeper forehead,
smaller, thinner bill and thinner
neck.

	SHAG
Type	goose-like
Size	72–80cm (28–31in)
Habitat	sea, sea-cliffs
Behaviour	swims, dives, perches on rocks and buoys, takes off and lands on water and ground
Flocking	colonial; 1–several thousand
Flight	laboured; glides; direct
Voice	grunts and hisses at breeding grounds

IDENTIFICATION

Ad.summer	
Crown	green-black; crest
Upperparts	green-black
Rump	green-black
Tail	green-black; medium length and rounded
Throat	green-black
Breast	green-black
Belly	green-black
Bill	black with yellow gape; straight and thinnish
Legs	grey; short
Ad.winter	no crest, dark face
Juvenile	brown above, buff below

BREEDING

Nest	mound of seaweed on cliff
Eggs	3; pale blue
Incubation	30 days ♂ ♀
Young	helpless; naked
Fledging	55 days
Broods	1; Mar–Apr
Food	fish
Population	32,000 pairs; 100,000+ winter

J	3
F	3
M	3
A	4
M	4
J	4
J	4
A	4
S	3
O	3
N	3
D	3

Northern Gannet *Morus bassanus*

dark, speckled

juvenile

white head and fore-wing

some black tips to wing feathers

white, black wingtips

thick neck and bill

first summer

second summer

third summer

adult

NORTHERN GANNET

Type	goose-like
Size	86–96cm (34–37in)
Habitat	sea, sea-cliffs
Behaviour	swims, dives from air, takes off and lands on water and ground
Flocking	colonial; 1–several thousand
Flight	strong and powerful; glides, dives; direct
Voice	variety grunts and cackles at breeding colonies

IDENTIFICATION

Adult	
Crown	yellow
Upperparts	white, black wingtips
Rump	white
Tail	white; medium length and pointed
Throat	white
Breast	white
Belly	white
Bill	grey; straight and thickish
Legs	black; short
Juvenile	speckled dark brown, white rump
Second Year	dark brown, head and forewing becoming whiter

BREEDING

Nest	mound of seaweed
Eggs	1; white
Incubation	43–45 days ♂ ♀
Young	helpless; downy
Fledging	14 weeks
Broods	1; Apr–June
Food	fish
Population	150,000 pairs

Large black and white seabird that nests at a few colonies, mainly on remote islets. At sea, appears white and cigar-shaped with pointed head and tail. Wings long, straight and pointed with large black tips. Flies low over water on stiff, shearwater-like wings, before rising in series of flaps and starting another glide. Makes dramatic dives for fish, often from great height. Adult has yellow wash over head. Immatures share same basic shape, but are dark brown; gradually become whiter over period of four years. *Status:* seen passing offshore, especially in north and west where main breeding colonies located; can be seen off all coasts during passage. *Similar Species:* all-dark juveniles separated from Great Cormorant (p.42) by different flight and behaviour

J	4
F	4
M	6
A	6
M	6
J	6
J	6
A	6
S	6
O	6
N	4
D	4

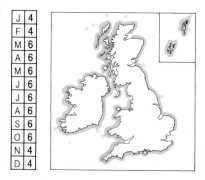

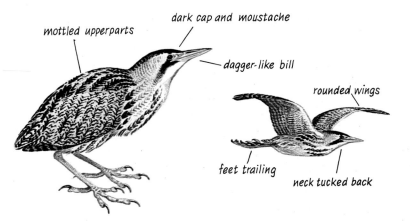

mottled upperparts

dark cap and moustache

dagger-like bill

rounded wings

feet trailing

neck tucked back

Large, secretive heron of dense reedbeds; more often heard than seen. Characteristic booming sounds more like distant foghorn than bird. Heavily camouflaged in shades of brown and buff; spends most of life hidden among reeds. Seen by chance during excursions across open areas, or in occasional flights with head tucked back and legs trailing behind. Close views reveal delicate plumage details as well as black crown and moustachial streak. Legs greenish yellow.
Status: decidedly scarce, breeding regularly only in East Anglia and Lancashire. Some winter wandering and immigration from the Continent.
Similar Species: rare Purple Heron (p.47) also appears brownish in flight.

BITTERN

Type	heron-like
Size	70–80cm (27–31in)
Habitat	freshwater marshes
Behaviour	wades, takes off and lands on ground
Flocking	solitary
Flight	laboured
Voice	deep, far-carrying *urrwoomp*, repeated

IDENTIFICATION

Adult	
Crown	black
Upperparts	brown and black, streaked
Rump	buff and brown, streaked
Tail	buff and brown, streaked; short and rounded
Throat	white
Breast	buff and brown, streaked
Belly	buff and brown, streaked
Bill	yellow; straight and thin
Legs	greenish yellow; medium length

BREEDING

Nest	platform of twigs, reeds on ground
Eggs	3–4; pale greenish blue
Incubation	21 days ♂ ♀
Young	helpless; downy
Fledging	6 weeks
Broods	1, sometimes 2; Apr–May
Food	fish, amphibians
Population	less than 20 pairs

J	1
F	1
M	1
A	1
M	1
J	1
J	1
A	1
S	1
O	1
N	1
D	1

Grey Heron *Ardea cinerea*

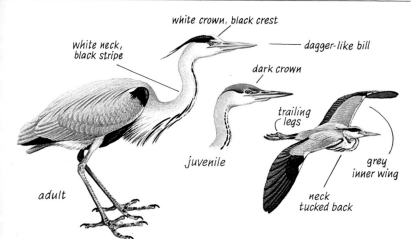

white crown, black crest

white neck, black stripe

dagger-like bill

dark crown

trailing legs

grey inner wing

neck tucked back

juvenile

adult

GREY HERON

Type	heron-like
Size	90–100cm (35–39in)
Habitat	freshwater margins and marshes
Behaviour	wades, walks, takes off and lands on ground
Flocking	1–50
Flight	laboured; glides; direct
Voice	harsh *snark*

IDENTIFICATION

Adult	
Crown	black; crest
Upperparts	grey
Rump	grey
Tail	grey; short and square
Throat	white
Breast	white, streaked black
Belly	white, streaked black
Bill	yellow; straight and thin
Legs	orange-yellow; very long
Juvenile	greyer, lacks crest

BREEDING

Nest	platform of twigs high in trees
Eggs	3–5; pale greenish blue
Incubation	23–28 days ♂ ♀
Young	helpless; downy
Fledging	50–55 days
Broods	1; Feb–Apr
Food	fish, amphibians
Population	10,000 pairs

Large, grey and white heron with long neck and dagger-like yellow bill. Flies with orange-yellow legs trailing behind and neck tucked into shoulders. Grey back; wings deeply bowed in flight. White head, neck and underparts; black crest and black streaking on neck. Frequents all wetlands. Nests colonially in heronries among tall trees; many have been used for more than a century.
Status: widespread resident throughout Britain and Ireland; population reduced by hard winters.
Similar Species: rare Purple Heron (p.47) could possibly be confused.

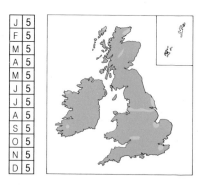

J	5
F	5
M	5
A	5
M	5
J	5
J	5
A	5
S	5
O	5
N	5
D	5

Ardea purpurea **Purple Heron**

brown neck

black and brown head and neck

adult

mottled brown inner wing

juvenile

Slightly smaller than Grey Heron and considerably darker, both at rest and in flight. Head and neck warm brown with black crest and black streaking on neck. Back and wings grey with buffy tips to scapulars. Generally rather skulking.

Status: decidedly scarce, though annual, summer visitor to marshes and reedbeds; mostly southern and eastern England.

Similar Species: could be confused with Bittern (p.45) in flight, especially brown, mottled juvenile.

PURPLE HERON

Type	heron-like
Size	75–85cm (29–33in)
Habitat	freshwater margins and marshes
Behaviour	wades, walks, takes off and lands on ground
Flocking	solitary
Flight	laboured; glides; direct
Voice	similar to Grey Heron but higher pitched

IDENTIFICATION

Adult	
Crown	black; crest
Upperparts	grey and buff
Rump	grey
Tail	grey; short and square
Throat	brown and black, streaked
Breast	brown and black, streaked
Belly	black
Bill	yellow; straight and thin
Legs	yellow; very long
Juvenile	brown above, buff below mottled, lacks crest

BREEDING

Nest	platform of reeds in reedbed
Eggs	4–5; greenish blue
Incubation	24–28 days ♂ ♀
Young	helpless; downy
Fledging	42 days
Broods	1; Apr–May
Food	fish, insects, amphibians
Population	scarce migrant

J	0
F	0
M	0
A	1
M	1
J	1
J	1
A	1
S	1
O	1
N	0
D	0

Spoonbill *Platalea leucorodia*

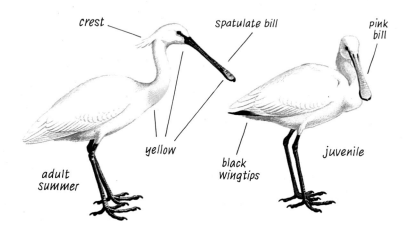

crest — spatulate bill

pink bill

yellow

black wingtips

juvenile

adult summer

SPOONBILL

Type	heron-like
Size	78–80cm (27–31in)
Habitat	freshwater marshes, estuaries
Behaviour	wades, walks, takes off and lands on water or ground
Flocking	1 or 2
Flight	glides, soars; strong, powerful and direct
Voice	silent

IDENTIFICATION

Ad.summer

Crown	white; crest
Upperparts	white
Rump	white
Tail	white; short and square
Throat	yellow
Breast	yellow
Belly	white
Bill	black, tipped yellow; large and spatulate
Legs	black; very long
Ad.winter	no crest or neck wash
Juvenile	as winter but black wingtips and pink bill

BREEDING

Nest	platform of reeds and twigs in tree or bush
Eggs	4; spotted reddish
Incubation	21 days ♂ ♀
Young	helpless; downy
Fledging	7 weeks
Broods	1; Apr–May
Food	insects, crustaceans, molluscs, fish
Population	scarce passage migrant

Large, white, heron-like bird with large spatulate bill. Plumage all white with droopy crest and yellow wash at base of neck in breeding plumage; crest and neck wash lost in winter. Bill black with yellow tip; bare yellow patch on throat; long legs black. Flies with neck extended rather than tucked back like heron. Feeds with side-to-side scything action of bill in shallow water. Juveniles show black wingtips.
Status: scarce visitor, mostly spring and autumn, to south and east coasts. Breeds Holland.
Similar Species: rare Little and Great White Egrets are only other all-white, heron-like birds. Spoonbill can be picked-out at considerable distance by slightly creamy white (not pure white) plumage.

J	0
F	0
M	0
A	1
M	1
J	1
J	1
A	1
S	1
O	0
N	0
D	0

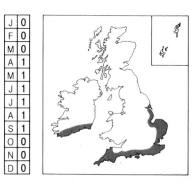

noisy wing beats

black knob

grey-blue bill

juvenile

orange bill

'S' shaped neck

adult ♂

Huge, familiar, white waterbird found on all types of freshwater; also occurs on estuaries and occasionally the sea. Adult completely white; legs black; bill orange with large black knob at base. Juvenile grey-buff with grey bill. Swims easily and walks with rolling gait. At all times holds neck in gentle 'S' shape. Flies with noisy wing beats after laborious pattering take-off over water.

Status: widespread and numerous resident throughout lowland Britain; gathers in substantial flocks outside breeding season. Sometimes nests in colonies.

Similar Species: Bewick's Swan (p.50) and Whooper Swan (p.51) are winter visitors that often join Mute Swan flocks. Both have black and yellow bills and noisy calls in flight.

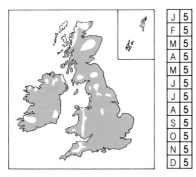

MUTE SWAN	
Type	goose-like
Size	145–160cm (57–63in)
Habitat	freshwater, estuaries, fields
Behaviour	swims, up-ends, walks, takes off and lands on water
Flocking	1–30, exceptionally several hundred
Flight	laboured; direct
Voice	various hisses and grunts of aggression during breeding season; silent in flight

IDENTIFICATION	
Adult	
Crown	white
Upperparts	white
Rump	white
Tail	white; short and square
Throat	white
Breast	white
Belly	white
Bill	orange with black knob at base; duck-like
Legs	black; short
Juvenile	grey-buff with grey-blue bill

BREEDING	
Nest	huge mound of vegetation, freshwater margins
Eggs	5–7; white, blue-grey wash
Incubation	34–38 days, mainly ♀
Young	active; downy
Fledging	4 months
Broods	1; Apr–May
Food	aquatic vegetation
Population	5000–6000 pairs

J	5
F	5
M	5
A	5
M	5
J	5
J	5
A	5
S	5
O	5
N	5
D	5

Bewick's Swan *Cygnus columbianus*

concave profile

concave profile

truncated yellow area

pinkish bill

noisy calls in flight

juvenile

adult

BEWICK'S SWAN

Type	goose-like
Size	116–128cm (45–50in)
Habitat	freshwater, estuaries, fields
Behaviour	swims, up-ends, walks, takes off and lands on water or ground
Flocking	gregarious, 1–several hundred
Flight	laboured; direct
Voice	goose-like honking flight call

IDENTIFICATION

Adult

Crown	white
Upperparts	white
Rump	white
Tail	white; short and square
Throat	white
Breast	white
Belly	white
Bill	black with yellow base; duck-like
Legs	black; short
Juvenile	brownish grey, pinkish bill

BREEDING

Nest	huge mound of vegetation
Eggs	4; creamy white
Incubation	29–30 days
Young	active; downy
Fledging	40–45 days
Broods	1; June–July
Food	grass, grain, roots
Population	16,000+ winter

Smallest of the three swans; size most apparent in flight when faster wing beats and noisy calls resemble goose. Black bill has truncated yellow area at base. Rounded crown with concave forehead and bill profile. Neck often held straight. Usually gregarious, forming large flocks at suitable feeding grounds; grazes in goose-like fashion. *Status:* localized winter visitor from Siberia to traditional feeding grounds, such as Ouse Washes and Slimbridge; most numerous in southern England. Late winter influxes due to hard weather in Germany and Holland. *Similar Species:* Whooper Swan (p.51) is much larger, has pointed yellow area on bill and flat crown and bill profile.

J	2
F	2
M	2
A	2
M	0
J	0
J	0
A	0
S	0
O	1
N	2
D	2

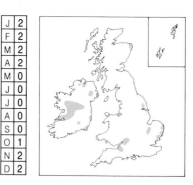

straight profile

straight profile

straight profile

straight neck

pointed yellow area

juvenile

adult

Winter visitor forming medium-sized flocks, often in association with other swans. Neck usually held straight. Yellow base to black bill, which extends forward to form clear point, accentuating flat crown-bill profile. Generally noisy, especially in flight, when wing beats produce whistling noise.

Status: regular winter visitor mainly from Iceland; largest numbers in Scotland and Ireland.

Similar Species: Mute Swan (p.49) is same size but has orange bill and holds neck in 'S'. Smaller Bewick's Swan (p.50) has concave (not flat) crown-bill profile.

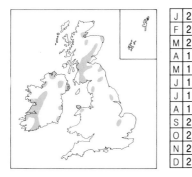

J	2
F	2
M	2
A	1
M	1
J	1
J	1
A	1
S	2
O	2
N	2
D	2

WHOOPER SWAN

Type	goose-like
Size	145–160cm (57–63in)
Habitat	freshwater, estuaries, fields
Behaviour	swims, up-ends, walks, takes off and lands on water or ground
Flocking	1–100
Flight	laboured; direct
Voice	loud, trumpeting *whoop*

IDENTIFICATION

Adult	
Crown	white
Upperparts	white
Rump	white
Tail	white; short and square
Throat	white
Breast	white
Belly	white
Bill	black with yellow base; duck-like
Legs	black; short
Juvenile	brownish grey, pinkish bill

BREEDING

Nest	mound of vegetation at water's edge, usually island
Eggs	5–6; creamy white
Incubation	35–42 days ♀
Young	active; downy
Fledging	?
Broods	1; May–June
Food	grass, grain, roots
Population	1 or 2 pairs; 5000+ winter

Bean Goose *Anser fabalis*

dark head and neck

orange bill

uniform brown wing

large head and bill

orange legs

	BEAN GOOSE
Type	goose-like
Size	71–89cm (28–35in)
Habitat	freshwater marshes, grassland
Behaviour	swims, walks, takes off and lands on water and ground
Flocking	1–100
Flight	strong and powerful; direct
Voice	low *ung-unk*, generally less vocal than other geese

IDENTIFICATION

	Adult
Crown	brown
Upperparts	brown, barred buff
Rump	white
Tail	white with grey terminal band; short and square
Throat	brown
Breast	buff
Belly	buff, barred brown
Bill	orange, black base; duck-like
Legs	orange; medium length

BREEDING

Nest	lined scrape near water
Eggs	4–6; white
Incubation	27–29 days ♀
Young	active; downy
Fledging	8 weeks
Broods	1; June–July
Food	grass, grain
Population	200–300 winter

Large, 'grey' goose with dark neck and dark head. Favours damp grassland habitat. Upperparts brown, closely barred buff. Underparts buffy, narrowly barred brown on flanks. Orange legs; bill orange with variable black base. Gregarious.
Status: scarce winter visitor with only two small regular flocks in Solway and East Anglia. Elsewhere rare winter visitor after hard weather.
Similar Species: closely-related Pink-footed Goose (p.53) is smaller and prefers estuaries to damp grassland. Pink-footed and Greylag Goose both show obvious pale forewing in flight, commonly lacking in Bean Goose.

J	1
F	1
M	1
A	1
M	0
J	0
J	0
A	0
S	0
O	1
N	1
D	1

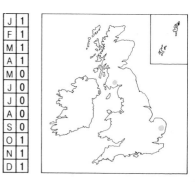

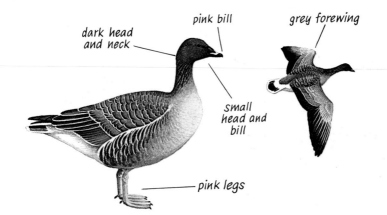

Anser brachyrhynchus **Pink-footed Goose**

dark head and neck

pink bill

grey forewing

small head and bill

pink legs

Small 'grey' goose; highly localized winter visitor to Scotland and northern Britain. Small dark head and small pink bill with variable dark base; legs pink. Upperparts greyish brown, closely barred buffy white. Shows bold grey forewing in flight.

Status: numerous winter visitor from Iceland and Greenland forming enormous roosting flocks at traditional sites, mainly Scotland and Lancashire. Elsewhere rather scarce visitor after hard weather.

Similar Species: dark head and neck separate from all other 'grey' geese except Bean Goose (p.52), which lacks grey forewing and has larger head and thicker neck.

PINK-FOOTED GOOSE

Type	goose-like
Size	61–76cm (24–30in)
Habitat	freshwater, estuaries, grassland
Behaviour	swims, walks, takes off and lands on water and ground
Flocking	1–many thousands
Flight	strong and powerful; direct
Voice	highly vocal; high-pitched *unk-unk* and *wink-wink-wink*

IDENTIFICATION

Adult	
Crown	brown
Upperparts	grey-brown, barred buff
Rump	white
Tail	white with dark terminal band; short and square
Throat	brown
Breast	buff
Belly	buff, barred brown
Bill	pink, dark based; small and duck-like
Legs	pink; medium length

BREEDING

Nest	lined scrape, cliff-ledge
Eggs	4–5; white
Incubation	25–28 days ♀
Young	active; downy
Fledging	8 weeks
Broods	1; June–July
Food	grass, grain, potatoes
Population	100,000 winter

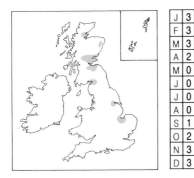

J	3
F	3
M	3
A	2
M	0
J	0
J	0
A	0
S	1
O	2
N	3
D	3

53

White-fronted Goose *Anser albifrons*

white forehead

uniform brown wing

orange legs

barred belly

barred belly

WHITE-FRONTED GOOSE

Type	goose-like
Size	65–76cm (26–30in)
Habitat	freshwater marshes, grassland
Behaviour	swims, walks, takes off and lands on water and ground
Flocking	1–6000
Flight	strong and powerful; direct
Voice	high-pitched *kow-yow* and *ryo-ryok*; more musical than other geese

IDENTIFICATION

Ad.Russian

Crown	brown
Upperparts	brown; barred
Rump	white
Tail	white with grey terminal band; short and square
Throat	brown
Breast	buff
Belly	brown, barred black
Bill	pink; duck-like
Legs	orange; medium length
Ad.Greenland	bill orange

BREEDING

Nest	lined scrape in bog or thicket
Eggs	5–6; white
Incubation	27–28 days ♀
Young	active; downy
Fledging	?
Broods	1; June–July
Food	grass, cereals, potatoes
Population	5000 Russian; 16,000+ Greenland winter

Most widespread of the 'grey' geese; found in variety of habitats throughout Britain and Ireland. Small size, broad white base to bill and bold smudgy bars on belly separate from similar geese. Pink or orange bill (see below); legs orange. In flight, lack of grey forewing distinguishes from other 'grey' geese, except Bean Goose (p.52).
Status: widespread winter visitor. Pink-billed (from Russia) visit England and Wales; orange-billed (from Greenland) visit Ireland, west Scotland and west Wales.
Similar Species: other 'grey' geese (pp.52, 53, 55) and as above. Juvenile lacks white face and black bars on belly.

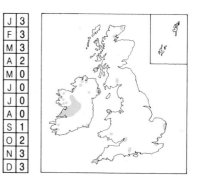

J	3
F	3
M	3
A	2
M	0
J	0
J	0
A	0
S	1
O	2
N	3
D	3

large head
and bill

orange bill

grey forewing

pink
legs

Largest and most frequently seen 'grey' goose; ancestor of most domestic geese. Upperparts dark brown, closely barred buff. Underparts, head and neck buff; some faint barring on flanks. Pink legs; orange bill (pink in eastern sub-species). In flight shows prominent pale grey forewing.

Status: native birds breed only in Outer Hebrides and nearby Scottish mainland, but many successful re-introductions in various parts of the country. Widespread visitor, mainly from Iceland.

Similar Species: overall size, large pale head and neck with large bill separate from all other 'grey' geese. Eastern sub-species has orange legs.

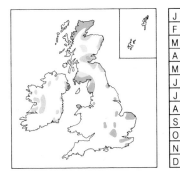

GREYLAG GOOSE	
Type	goose-like
Size	76–89cm (30–35in)
Habitat	freshwater, estuaries, grassland
Behaviour	swims, walks, takes off and lands on water or ground
Flocking	1–several hundred
Flight	strong and powerful; direct
Voice	deep *aahng-ung-ung*; highly vocal

IDENTIFICATION	
Adult	
Crown	brown
Upperparts	brown, barred buff
Rump	white
Tail	white with grey terminal band; short and square
Throat	brown
Breast	buff
Belly	buff
Bill	orange; large and duck-like
Legs	pink; medium length

BREEDING	
Nest	scrape near water
Eggs	4–6; white
Incubation	27–28 days ♀
Young	active; downy
Fledging	8 weeks
Broods	1; Apr–May
Food	grass, grain, roots
Population	700–800 pairs; 100,000 winter

J	3
F	3
M	3
A	3
M	2
J	2
J	2
A	2
S	2
O	3
N	3
D	3

Canada Goose _Branta canadensis_

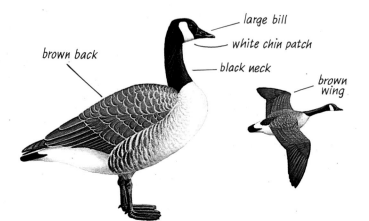

- large bill
- white chin patch
- black neck
- brown back
- brown wing

CANADA GOOSE

Type	goose-like
Size	90–100cm (36–40in)
Habitat	freshwater, marshes and margins, grassland
Behaviour	swims, walks, takes off and lands on water or ground
Flocking	1–1000
Flight	strong and powerful; direct
Voice	loud _wagh-onk_ repeated

IDENTIFICATION

Adult	
Crown	black
Upperparts	brown, barred buff
Rump	white
Tail	white with black terminal band; short and square
Throat	black and white
Breast	buff
Belly	brown
Bill	black; large and duck-like
Legs	black; medium length

BREEDING

Nest	lined hollow beside water, often on island
Eggs	5–6; white
Incubation	28–30 days ♀
Young	active; downy
Fledging	9 weeks
Broods	1; Apr–May
Food	grass, aquatic vegetation, cereals, grain
Population	34,000 individuals

Largest of the 'black' geese; about same size as bulkier Greylag. Familiar inhabitant of ponds, lakes, reservoirs and other freshwater habitats; generally tame and often aggressive. Buffy brown above and buff below; long black head and neck broken only by white chin patch. Forms large flocks at end of breeding season (for moulting), otherwise in pairs and family parties. _Status:_ prospering after introduction from native North America, where is long distance migrant. Fresh birds continually flying free from wildfowl collections. Widespread in Britain but highly local in Ireland. Most birds resident, but some long distance migrations (for moulting) developing. _Similar Species:_ Barnacle Goose (p.57) has white face, grey (not brown) back and is much smaller.

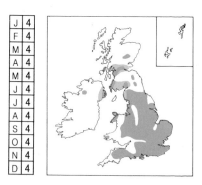

J	4
F	4
M	4
A	4
M	4
J	4
J	4
A	4
S	4
O	4
N	4
D	4

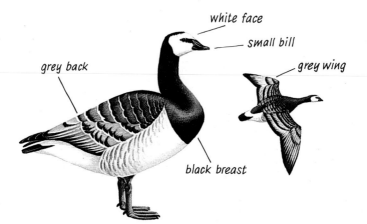

white face

small bill

grey back

grey wing

black breast

Strikingly attractive 'black' goose; highly localized winter visitor, forming large flocks in favoured areas. Back grey, heavily barred black and white. Neck and breast black. White face and black crown. Underparts white. In flight shows grey wings with black trailing edge. Small, black bill and black feet.

Status: largest numbers in western Scotland and western Ireland, but has prospered under careful conservation and now occurs irregularly in small numbers at other, mainly coastal, sites.

Similar Species: Canada Goose (p.56) and Brent Goose (p.58).

BARNACLE GOOSE

Type	goose-like
Size	58–69cm (23–27in)
Habitat	grassland, estuaries
Behaviour	swims, walks, takes off and lands on water and ground
Flocking	1–several thousand
Flight	strong and powerful; direct
Voice	barking, puppy-like yaps with deeper growls

IDENTIFICATION

Adult	
Crown	black
Upperparts	grey, barred black and white
Rump	white
Tail	white with black terminal band; short and square
Throat	black and white
Breast	black
Belly	white
Bill	black; small and duck-like
Legs	black; medium length

BREEDING

Nest	lined depression, ledges of cliffs
Eggs	3–5; white
Incubation	24–25 days ♀
Young	active; downy
Fledging	7 weeks
Broods	1; June–July
Food	grass
Population	33,000 winter

J	3
F	3
M	3
A	2
M	1
J	0
J	0
A	0
S	1
O	3
N	3
D	3

Brent Goose *Branta bernicla*

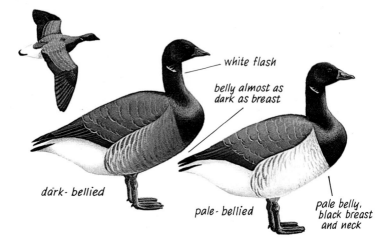

white flash

belly almost as
dark as breast

dark-bellied

pale-bellied

pale belly,
black breast
and neck

BRENT GOOSE

Type	goose-like
Size	56–61cm (22–24in)
Habitat	estuaries, grassland
Behaviour	swims, walks, takes off and lands on water or ground
Flocking	1–several thousand
Flight	strong and powerful; direct
Voice	grumbling *krook*, garrulous in flocks

IDENTIFICATION

Ad.dark

Crown	black
Upperparts	brown
Rump	white
Tail	white with black terminal band; short and square
Throat	black
Breast	black
Belly	brown
Bill	black; duck-like
Legs	black; medium length
Ad.pale	as above but belly buff
Juveniles	white wingbars; no neck flash

BREEDING

Nest	lined scrape near water, mostly near sea
Eggs	3–5; white-yellow
Incubation	24–26 days ♀
Young	active; downy
Fledging	?
Broods	1; June–July
Food	eelgrass, salting plants, growing cereals, grass
Population	Dark-bellied 92,000+ winter; Pale-bellied 13,000+ winter

Smallest, darkest 'black' goose; predominantly estuarine species regularly found feeding among coastal fields. Two sub-species occur: Pale-bellied *B.b. hrota* brown above and pale below; black head and neck ends in clear-cut breast band. Adults have small white neck flash. Dark-bellied *B.b. bernicla* similar, but lacks contrast between breast and belly. Juveniles of both sub-species have white bars across folded wing and lack neck flash. *Status:* has prospered with protection, now increasing and spreading winter visitor along most coastlines; large flocks confined to favoured estuaries. Dark-bellied mostly southern and eastern England; Pale-bellied in Ireland and north-east England. *Similar Species:* Barnacle Goose (p.57) and Canada Goose (p.56).

J	3
F	3
M	3
A	2
M	0
J	0
J	0
A	0
S	1
O	2
N	2
D	3

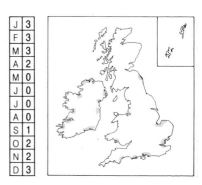

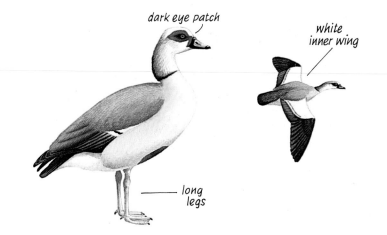

Alopochen aegyptiacus **Egyptian Goose**

dark eye patch

white inner wing

long legs

More like Shelduck than goose. Pinkish buff plumage, darker above and paler below. Shows black wingtips and tail and broad green speculum. Small pink bill with dark base and tip; dark patch around eye. Legs long and pink. Flies fast on broad wings; black on wings contrasts with white inner forewing, forming bold pattern. Spends much time on land and even perches in trees.
Status: scarce. Introduced from Africa in eighteenth century, now confined to parks and marshes in northern East Anglia.
Similar Species: none.

EGYPTIAN GOOSE	
Type	goose-like
Size	66–72cm (26–28in)
Habitat	freshwater, parks, fields
Behaviour	swims, wades, walks, takes off and lands on water or ground
Flocking	1–15
Flight	strong and powerful; direct
Voice	usually silent; some hissing and cackling

IDENTIFICATION

Adult	
Crown	pinkish buff
Upperparts	rust or grey-brown
Rump	rust-brown or grey-brown
Tail	black and brown; short and square
Throat	pinkish buff
Breast	pinkish buff
Belly	pinkish buff
Bill	pink; small and duck-like
Legs	pink; long
Juvenile	as adult but lacks eye ring; bill and legs yellowish grey

BREEDING

Nest	hole in tree or among rocks
Eggs	5–8; creamy-white
Incubation	28–30 days ♂ ♀
Young	active; downy
Fledging	?
Broods	1; Apr–May
Food	grass, other vegetation
Population	small feral, 500?

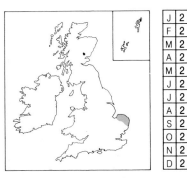

J	2
F	2
M	2
A	2
M	2
J	2
J	2
A	2
S	2
O	2
N	2
D	2

Common Shelduck *Tadorna tadorna*

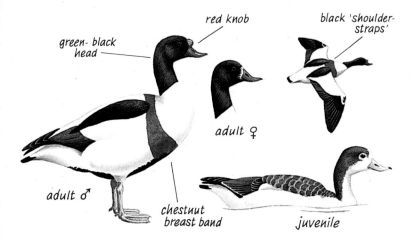

green-black head

red knob

black 'shoulder-straps'

adult ♀

adult ♂

chestnut breast band

juvenile

COMMON SHELDUCK	
Type	duck-like, goose-like
Size	58–64cm (22–25in)
Habitat	shorelines, estuaries, freshwater marshes
Behaviour	swims, wades, walks, takes off and lands on water or ground
Flocking	1–several hundred
Flight	strong and powerful; direct
Voice	whistling and growling

IDENTIFICATION

Adult ♂	
Crown	bottle-green
Upperparts	white and black
Rump	white
Tail	white with black terminal band; short and square
Throat	bottle-green
Breast	chestnut
Belly	white
Bill	red with knob; duck-like
Legs	pink; medium length
Adult ♀	as ♂ but less clear-cut markings and pink-red, knobless bill
Juvenile	as ♀ but lacks breast band; grey-brown crown

BREEDING

Nest	down-lined cup in burrow, hollow tree
Eggs	8–15; cream
Incubation	28–30 days ♀
Young	active; downy
Fledging	8 weeks
Broods	1; May–June
Food	crustaceans, molluscs
Population	12,000 pairs; 66,000+ winter

Large, goose-like duck showing bold black and white pattern. Head and neck dark bottle-green; rest of plumage white with broad, chestnut breast band and black stripe along folded wing. Bill bright red in adult male with bulbous knob at base. Females and immatures have pinkish red bills (without knob) and less clear-cut breast and wing markings. In flight, main wing feathers are black and contrast with white forewing. Generally gregarious, forming large flocks in winter and for moulting. Mainly coastal; favours estuaries and muddy shores, though often breeds inland.

Status: resident along most coasts; most migrate late summer to N. Germany to moult; return in autumn.
Similar Species: none.

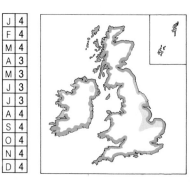

J	4
F	4
M	4
A	3
M	3
J	3
J	3
A	4
S	4
O	4
N	4
D	4

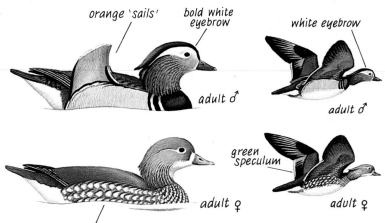

Aix galericulata **Mandarin Duck**

orange 'sails'

bold white eyebrow

adult ♂

white eyebrow

adult ♂

green speculum

adult ♀

adult ♀

spotted flanks

One of the smaller ducks, most often found on small lakes among wooded countryside. Male has elaborate, multi-coloured plumage with dark drooping crest, white slash over eye, green nape, chestnut 'whiskers' and orange flanks. Two orange 'sails' stand up on back; in flight, they lie flat on lower back. Best field marks are white slash over eye and green speculum. Female much duller, with grey head marked by narrow white eyebrow. Back brown; underparts buff, heavily spotted cream. A limp crest hangs from hind crown. *Status:* introduced, highly localized resident, mostly in south-east England. *Similar Species:* female may be confused with escaped female American Wood Duck.

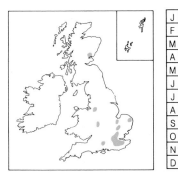

J	2
F	2
M	2
A	2
M	2
J	2
J	2
A	2
S	2
O	2
N	2
D	2

MANDARIN DUCK

Type	duck-like
Size	41–47cm (16–18½in)
Habitat	freshwater, woodland
Behaviour	swims, walks, takes off and lands on water, vegetation or ground
Flocking	1–15
Flight	strong and powerful; direct
Voice	♂ whistle; ♀ kek

IDENTIFICATION

Adult ♂	
Crown	brown; crest
Upperparts	brown and black; orange 'sails'
Rump	black
Tail	black; short and rounded
Throat	brown and black
Breast	black and white
Belly	white
Bill	red; duck-like
Legs	yellow; short
Ad. ♀ and juv.	head grey, upperparts brown, underparts spotted

BREEDING

Nest	tree-hole
Eggs	9–12; buffy
Incubation	28–30 days ♀
Young	active; downy
Fledging	?
Broods	1; Apr–May
Food	nuts, seeds, insects
Population	300–400 pairs

Eurasian Wigeon *Anas penelope*

chestnut head

golden crown

white wing patch

adult ♂

adult ♂

cinnamon above and below

adult ♀

adult ♀

EURASIAN WIGEON

Type	duck-like
Size	43–48cm (16–19in)
Habitat	estuaries, shores, marshes, grassland
Behaviour	swims, wades, walks, takes off and lands on water or ground
Flocking	1–several thousand
Flight	strong and powerful; direct
Voice	♂ high pitched whistle; ♀ growls

IDENTIFICATION

Adult ♂	
Crown	yellow and chestnut
Upperparts	grey
Rump	grey
Tail	black and white; short and pointed
Throat	chestnut
Breast	buff
Belly	white
Bill	silver-grey; small and duck-like
Legs	grey; short
Adult ♀	rufous; barred above and below

BREEDING

Nest	lined hollow near water
Eggs	7–8; creamy
Incubation	22–25 days ♀
Young	active; downy
Fledging	6 weeks
Broods	1; May–June
Food	grass, eelgrass, aquatic vegetation
Population	300–500 pairs; up to 300,000 winter

Abundant winter visitor; often forming large flocks in favoured areas. Male has golden blase extending from forehead over crown. Rest of head and neck chestnut; body grey with white flash along flanks. Rear flanks white with black end to body. In flight, shows white patch on inner wing; lacking in female and first winter male. Small silver-grey bill. Female cinnamon-brown with delicate rounded head. Largest flocks feed on coastal grassland and most roost on estuaries. Often found alongside geese; also occurs at inland reservoirs and flooded ground. *Status:* widespread and numerous winter visitor; small numbers breed, mainly in north of Britain. *Similar Species:* male none; female more cinnamon than other surface-feeding ducks.

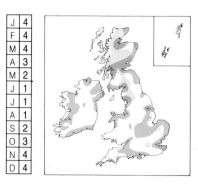

J	4
F	4
M	4
A	3
M	2
J	1
J	1
A	1
S	2
O	3
N	4
D	4

Anas acuta **Northern Pintail**

long tail

chocolate head

pale forewing

adult ♂

adult ♂

heavily spotted

adult ♀

base of neck low
in water

pointed tail

adult ♀

Slim, elegant duck; characteristic
swimming attitude with foreparts
lower in water than hindparts. Male
has chocolate-brown head with vertical
white stripe up back of long neck.
Upperparts grey; long drooping black
and white scapulars. Grey underparts;
white rear flank patch and black rear
end. Long tail has pointed central tail
feathers. Bill silver-blue. Female grey-
buff, boldly blotched brown above and
below – the palest surface-feeding
duck. In flight, male shows pale inner
forewing; female virtually featureless.
Pointed rear end more obvious in male
than female.
Status: scarce, very localized breeder.
Winter visitor everywhere, but only
common at favoured areas.
Similar Species: Eurasian Wigeon
(p.62) also has pointed tail in flight.

J	3
F	3
M	3
A	3
M	1
J	1
J	1
A	1
S	2
O	3
N	3
D	3

NORTHERN PINTAIL

Type	duck-like
Size	♂ 63–70cm (25–27in); ♀ 53–59cm (21–23in)
Habitat	marshes, estuaries
Behaviour	swims, up-ends, takes off and lands on water or ground
Flocking	1–several thousand
Flight	strong and powerful; direct
Voice	♂ growls and whistles; ♀ quacks

IDENTIFICATION

Adult ♂	
Crown	brown
Upperparts	grey; black and cream scapulars
Rump	grey
Tail	black; long and pointed
Throat	brown
Breast	white
Belly	white
Bill	silver-blue; duck-like
Legs	black; short
Adult ♀	buff and brown with distinctive spotting; pointed tail

BREEDING

Nest	lined hollow in vegetation
Eggs	7–9; yellowish white
Incubation	21–23 days ♀
Young	active; downy
Fledging	7 weeks
Broods	1; Apr–June
Food	aquatic vegetation, invertebrates
Population	less than 50 pairs; c 25,000 winter

Common Teal *Anas crecca*

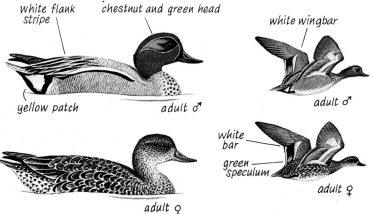

white flank stripe

chestnut and green head

yellow patch

adult ♂

white wingbar

adult ♂

white bar

green speculum

adult ♀

adult ♀

COMMON TEAL

Type	duck-like
Size	34–38cm (13–15in)
Habitat	freshwater, estuaries
Behaviour	swims, wades, walks, takes off and lands on water or ground
Flocking	1–several hundred
Flight	strong and powerful
Voice	♂ whistles; ♀ quacks

IDENTIFICATION

Adult ♂	
Crown	chestnut-brown
Upperparts	grey
Rump	black
Tail	grey; short and rounded
Throat	brown
Breast	buff, spotted brown
Belly	buff
Bill	grey; duck-like
Legs	black; short
Adult ♀	mottled brown and buff

BREEDING

Nest	lined hollow in marsh
Eggs	8–12; creamy buff
Incubation	21–28 days ♀
Young	active; downy
Fledging	44 days
Broods	1; Apr–May
Food	aquatic vegetation, seeds
Population	3500–6000 pairs; 150,000+ winter

Small, fast-flying, highly gregarious duck. Often forms compact flocks that fly in twisting, turning formation, like waders. Male's chestnut head has bottle-green, yellow-edged area round eye. At any distance appears simply dark headed. Breast buff, spotted brown. Grey back and flanks separated by narrow black and white 'lateral line'. Black rear end encloses large yellow patch. In flight, shows inconspicuous bottle-green speculum and clearer white wingbar. Female brown and buff.
Status: uncommon but widespread breeder; huge winter influx.
Similar Species: similar to, but smaller than, all female surface-feeding ducks except Garganey (p.65), from which separated by green speculum and different face pattern.

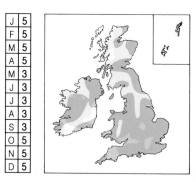

J	5
F	5
M	5
A	5
M	3
J	3
J	3
A	3
S	3
O	5
N	5
D	5

Anas querquedula Garganey

white eyebrow

adult ♂

blue-grey forewing

adult ♂

striped face pattern

adult ♀

blue-grey forewing

adult ♀

Dainty, Teal-sized duck easily overlooked in eclipse and female plumages. Male has maroon-brown head with bold white eyebrow, drooping black and white scapulars and grey underparts. Female has striped face pattern. In flight, shows pale blue inner wing like Shoveler. *Status:* scarce summer visitor, mainly to south and east England; winters in Africa.

Similar Species: female and eclipse male like similar plumages of Common Teal (p.64) and much larger Mallard (p.67). Female similar to other female surface-feeding ducks but separated by pronounced face pattern. Some female and eclipse Common Teal, and many Mallard, show similar pattern but less pronounced.

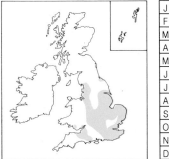

J	0
F	0
M	1
A	2
M	2
J	2
J	2
A	1
S	1
O	0
N	0
D	0

GARGANEY

Type	duck-like
Size	37–41cm (14–16in)
Habitat	freshwater and marshes
Behaviour	swims, up-ends, takes off and lands on water or ground
Flocking	1–10
Flight	strong and powerful; direct
Voice	♂ crackling rattle; ♀ quacks

IDENTIFICATION

Adult ♂	
Crown	maroon-brown
Upperparts	buff and brown
Rump	buff and brown
Tail	buff; short and square
Throat	brown
Breast	buff and brown
Belly	grey
Bill	grey; duck-like
Legs	grey; short
Adult ♀	spotted buff and brown with distinctive striped face pattern

BREEDING

Nest	lined hollow, well-hidden near water
Eggs	8–11; buffy
Incubation	21–23 days ♀
Young	active; downy
Fledging	5–6 weeks
Broods	1; Apr–May
Food	aquatic invertebrates and plants
Population	less than 100 pairs

Gadwall *Anas strepera*

grey back and flanks

black rear end

adult ♂

white in wing

adult ♂

adult ♀

orange-yellow bill edges

adult ♀

GADWALL

Type	duck-like
Size	48–54cm (18–21in)
Habitat	freshwater marshes, estuaries
Behaviour	swims, walks, takes off and lands on water or ground
Flocking	1–15
Flight	strong and powerful; direct
Voice	♂ whistles; ♀ quacks

IDENTIFICATION

Adult ♂	
Crown	brown
Upperparts	grey
Rump	black
Tail	black; short and square
Throat	brown
Breast	grey, spotted
Belly	grey, barred
Bill	black; duck-like
Legs	yellow; short
Adult ♀	mottled buff and brown with white speculum (as ♂) and yellow sides to bill

BREEDING

Nest	lined hollow by water
Eggs	8–12; creamy
Incubation	25–27 days ♀
Young	active; downy
Fledging	7 weeks
Broods	1; May–June
Food	aquatic vegetation
Population	250 pairs; 4000 winter

Rather nondescript grey and brown duck, slightly smaller than Mallard. Resident at marshes and waters with growth of reeds. Male has mottled brown head and upperparts with dark eye stripe, similar to females of other surface-feeding ducks. Flanks finely barred grey. Best field mark is black rear end and white speculum, particularly in flight. Female has white speculum and yellow sides to bill. *Status:* nowhere numerous, mostly introduced and resident. Some Scottish birds migrate to Ireland; some winter visitors from northern Europe. *Similar Species:* only adult male Eurasian Wigeon (p.62) show white in dark wing in flight. Female Northern Pintail, Common Teal (pp.63–64), Mallard and Northern Shoveler (pp.67–68) resemble both sexes adult Gadwall but all lack Gadwall's white in wing.

J	3
F	3
M	3
A	3
M	2
J	2
J	2
A	2
S	2
O	3
N	3
D	3

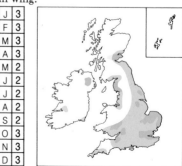

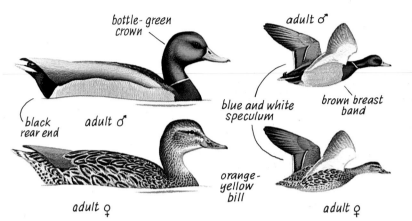

bottle-green crown

adult ♂

black rear end

adult ♂

brown breast band

blue and white speculum

adult ♀

orange-yellow bill

adult ♀

Common and widespread throughout year in wide variety of aquatic habitats, from wild marshes and floods to city-centre ponds. Male's bottle-green head separated from chocolate-brown breast by narrow white neck ring. Back and wings pale grey; underparts paler grey. Black rear end with two upward-curling feathers. In flight.head appears dark; dark blue speculum bordered fore and aft by white bars. Female resembles other female surface-feeding ducks; dark cap, dark eye stripe and orange-yellow bill aid separation. Generally gregarious. *Status:* mainly resident; breeds throughout area. Large winter influx from the Continent.
Similar Species: female and eclipse male often show similar face pattern to much smaller Garganey (p.65).

MALLARD	
Type	duck-like
Size	55–62cm (22–24in)
Habitat	freshwater, marshes, estuaries
Behaviour	swims, up-ends, takes off and lands on water or ground
Flocking	1–several thousand
Flight	strong and powerful; direct
Voice	♂ whistles and grunts; ♀ familiar quack

IDENTIFICATION

Adult ♂	
Crown	bottle-green
Upperparts	pale grey
Rump	black
Tail	white;short and rounded
Throat	bottle-green
Breast	chocolate-brown
Belly	very pale grey
Bill	yellow; duck-like
Legs	orange; short
Adult ♀	mottled buffs and browns, orange-yellow bill, blue and white speculum

BREEDING

Nest	lined hollow on ground
Eggs	10–12; creamy
Incubation	28–29 days ♀
Young	active; downy
Fledging	7–8 weeks
Broods	1; Mar–July
Food	aquatic seeds, plants, invertebrates
Population	70,000–150,000 pairs; 500,000 winter

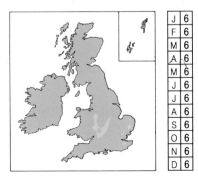

J	6
F	6
M	6
A	6
M	6
J	6
J	6
A	6
S	6
O	6
N	6
D	6

Northern Shoveler *Anas clypeata*

adult ♂

orange-brown belly

huge bill

adult ♂

blue forewing

adult ♀

adult ♀

NORTHERN SHOVELER

Type	duck-like
Size	47–53cm (18–21in)
Habitat	freshwater marshes, estuaries
Behaviour	swims, wades, walks, takes off and lands on water or ground
Flocking	1–several hundred
Flight	strong and powerful; direct
Voice	♂ harsh, double note *tuk-tuk*; ♀ quacks

IDENTIFICATION

Adult ♂	
Crown	bottle-green
Upperparts	black back, white scapulars
Rump	black
Tail	black, white outer feathers; short and rounded
Throat	green
Breast	white
Belly	chestnut
Bill	black; huge and spatulate
Legs	yellow; short
Adult ♀	mottled buff and brown; large grey and orange spatulate bill

BREEDING

Nest	lined hollow near water
Eggs	8–12; buffy
Incubation	22–23 days ♀
Young	active; downy
Fledging	6–7 weeks
Broods	1; Apr–May
Food	crustaceans, molluscs, aquatic seeds and plants
Population	1000 pairs; 17,000+ winter

Medium-sized duck that feeds with broad sweeps of bill through shallow water and wet mud. Huge, spatulate bill obvious in both sexes at rest and in flight. Male has bottle-green head, white breast, black back and bright chestnut belly and flanks. Female mottled buff and brown; resembles other female surface-feeding ducks but bill easily separates. In flight both sexes show pale blue inner wing. Generally gregarious; sizeable flocks gather at favoured feeding grounds in winter. Much scarcer in summer at reed-fringed lagoons and marshes. *Status:* small numbers breed over much of area; influx of winter visitors. *Similar Species:* smaller Garganey (p.65) has blue inner wing but no other duck has huge, spatulate bill.

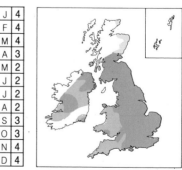

J	4
F	4
M	4
A	3
M	2
J	2
J	2
A	2
S	3
O	3
N	4
D	4

Aythya ferina **Common Pochard**

grey back

rusty head

grey wings

adult ♂

adult ♂

pale eye ring and line

buff-grey wings

adult ♀

adult ♀

Compact diving duck with prominent sloping forehead and large bill. Male has grey body, chestnut head and black breast. At any distance whole of foreparts appear dark; body pale grey with dark rear end. Female greyish-brown, darker on head and neck. In flight shows inconspicuous pale grey wingbar. Highly gregarious, forming huge rafts at suitable waters. Flocks generally spend much time sleeping during the day. Dives mainly for aquatic vegetation.
Status: widespread, but not a common breeder; often abundant winter visitor.
Similar Species: none.

COMMON POCHARD

Type	duck-like
Size	44–48cm (17–19in)
Habitat	freshwater, sea, estuaries
Behaviour	swims, dives from surface, walks, takes off and lands on water
Flocking	1–2000
Flight	strong and powerful; direct
Voice	generally quiet; ♀ growls in flight

IDENTIFICATION

Adult ♂	
Crown	chestnut
Upperparts	grey
Rump	black
Tail	grey; short and rounded
Throat	chestnut
Breast	black
Belly	grey
Bill	grey; large and duck-like
Legs	black; short
Adult ♀	greyish brown with darker head and breast and dark rear end

BREEDING

Nest	mound of vegetation at or near water's edge
Eggs	6–11; greenish
Incubation	24–26 days ♀
Young	active; downy
Fledging	7–8 weeks
Broods	1; Apr–June
Food	aquatic plants, invertebrates
Population	400 pairs; 80,000 winter

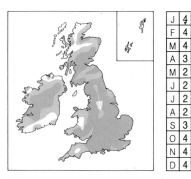

J	4
F	4
M	4
A	3
M	2
J	2
J	2
A	2
S	3
O	4
N	4
D	4

Tufted Duck *Aythya fuligula*

black back
crest
rounded head
adult ♂

white wingbar
adult ♂

hint of crest
adult ♀

adult ♀

TUFTED DUCK	
Type	duck-like
Size	41–45cm (16–17in)
Habitat	freshwater, estuaries
Behaviour	swims, dives from surface, takes off and lands on water or ground
Flocking	1–2000
Flight	strong and powerful; direct
Voice	generally silent; ♀ growls

IDENTIFICATION

Adult ♂	
Crown	black, glossed purple; crest
Upperparts	black
Rump	black
Tail	black; short and rounded
Throat	black
Breast	black
Belly	white
Bill	grey; duck-like
Legs	black; short
Adult ♀	brown above, buffy on flanks; reduced crest

BREEDING

Nest	lined hollow near water; well-hidden
Eggs	5–12; greenish
Incubation	23–25 days ♀
Young	active; downy
Fledging	6 weeks
Broods	1; Apr–June
Food	aquatic invertebrates, plants
Population	9000 pairs; 90,000 winter

Dainty diving duck, with round head, drooping crest and short neck. Male has all-black breast, back and tail; black head has purple sheen; white flanks and underparts. Inconspicuous crest extends from hind crown. Female sooty brown, with paler barred flanks and less obvious crest. Grey bill often has white base in female. In flight both sexes show prominent, broad, white wingbar. Gregarious, often gathering in large winter flocks, frequently in company of Pochard. Dives easily, mainly for invertebrates.
Status: widespread breeding bird in small numbers; abundant winter visitor.
Similar Species: Goldeneye (p.76) is similarly black and white. White-faced females resemble female Greater Scaup (p.71).

J	5
F	5
M	5
A	5
M	4
J	4
J	4
A	4
S	4
O	5
N	5
D	5

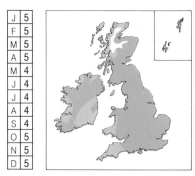

Aythya marila **Greater Scaup**

grey back

sloping hind crown

large bill

white wingbar

adult ♂

adult ♂

clear-cut white at base of bill

adult ♀

adult ♀

Marine equivalent of Tufted Duck and generally similar. Male has black, green-glossed head, black breast and rear end, grey back and white flanks and belly. Female has large, clear-cut white area at base of bill. In all plumages, steep forehead and backward-sloping crown create distinct head shape. Essentially coastal, gathering in large, sometimes huge, flocks at favoured feeding grounds; small numbers storm-driven inland. *Status:* occasional rare breeder in extreme north; common winter visitor but large flocks highly localized, mainly in north.
Similar Species: female usually separated from female Tufted Duck (p.70) by white on face, but beware white-faced female Tufted inland. Male like male Tufted, but grey-backed.

GREATER SCAUP

Type	duck-like
Size	46–51cm (18–20in)
Habitat	freshwater marshes, sea, estuaries
Behaviour	swims, dives from surface, takes off and lands on water or ground
Flocking	1–10,000
Flight	strong and powerful; direct
Voice	generally silent; ♀ growls

IDENTIFICATION

Adult ♂	
Crown	black, green-glossed
Upperparts	grey
Rump	black
Tail	black; short and rounded
Throat	black
Breast	black
Belly	white
Bill	grey; duck-like
Legs	black; short ·
Adult ♀	brown above, buffy on flanks, white face

BREEDING

Nest	lined hollow near water; open sites
Eggs	6–15; greenish
Incubation	24–28 days ♀
Young	active; downy
Fledging	5–6 weeks
Broods	1; May–June
Food	molluscs, aquatic vegetation
Population	c5 pairs; 5000–10,000 winter

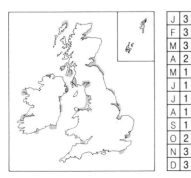

J	3
F	3
M	3
A	2
M	1
J	1
J	1
A	1
S	1
O	2
N	3
D	3

Common Eider *Somateria mollissima*

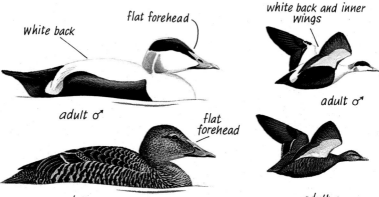

white back

flat forehead

white back and inner wings

adult ♂

adult ♂

flat forehead

adult ♀

adult ♀

COMMON EIDER

Type	duck-like
Size	55–61cm (21–24in)
Habitat	sea, estuaries
Behaviour	swims, dives from surface, takes off and lands on water
Flocking	1–several hundred
Flight	strong and powerful; direct
Voice	♂ dove-like cooing; ♀ repeated *gok-gok-gok*

IDENTIFICATION

Adult ♂	
Crown	white, black sides
Upperparts	white
Rump	black
Tail	black; short and rounded
Throat	white
Breast	white, pink-tinge
Belly	black
Bill	grey; duck-like
Legs	brown; short
Adult ♀	barred buff and brown above and below

BREEDING

Nest	lined hollow on island, coast or nearby river
Eggs	4–6; greenish
Incubation	27–28 days ♀
Young	active; downy
Fledging	60–75 days
Broods	1; May–June
Food	molluscs, crustaceans, other invertebrates
Population	15,000–25,000 pairs; 70,000 winter

Large, stocky seaduck. Male mainly white above and black below with pink tinge to white breast. Bold black mark extends over each side of crown. Pale green nape visible at close range. Female warm buff and brown, finely barred. Long, sloping forehead and longish bill form continuous line, creating wedge-shaped head with feathering reaching half way to bill tip. Immature male like female, but white developing from breast to back over first summer creates patchy effect. Forms small flocks in coastal waters; breeds colonially.
Status: resident along coasts of Scotland, northern Ireland and north-east England. Winter visitor elsewhere.
Similar Species: none.

J	4
F	4
M	4
A	4
M	4
J	4
J	4
A	4
S	4
O	4
N	4
D	4

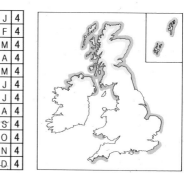

Clangula hyemalis **Long-tailed Duck**

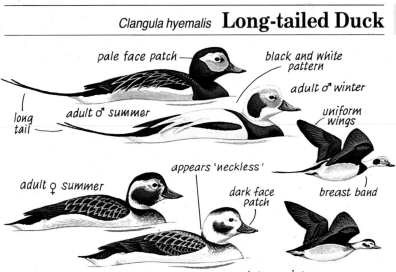

pale face patch

black and white pattern

adult ♂ winter

long tail

adult ♂ summer

uniform wings

adult ♀ summer

appears 'neckless'

dark face patch

breast band

adult ♀ winter

Small, stocky seaduck. Large head, small bill and pointed tail; male has extended central tail feathers. Variable plumage always includes face patch. Summer male has dark brown head and neck; face silvery grey. Winter male has white head with grey patch on side of face. Female always has pale patch around eye; remaining upperparts broadly edged buff in summer, browner in winter. In flight, wings uniform brown in all plumages. Gregarious around coasts.
Status: winter visitor; most numerous on inshore waters in north and east where large flocks amount to at least half of British population.
Similar Species: none.

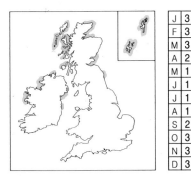

LONG-TAILED DUCK	
Type	duck-like
Size	♂ 54–58cm (21–23in); ♀ 41–45cm (16–17in)
Habitat	sea, estuaries
Behaviour	swims, dives from surface, takes off and lands on water
Flocking	1–1000
Flight	strong and powerful; direct
Voice	♂ yodelling call; ♀ quacks

IDENTIFICATION

Ad.♂summer	
Crown	blackish brown
Upperparts	brown and black, edged buff
Rump	blackish brown
Tail	dark brown, white outer feathers; long and pointed
Throat	blackish brown
Breast	blackish brown
Belly	buff-grey
Bill	pink; small and duck-like
Legs	black; short
Ad.♂winter	paler on head with black and white back
Adult ♀	brown above with distinctive pale face patch

BREEDING

Nest	lined hollow hidden in vegetation
Eggs	5–9; yellow
Incubation	23–25 days ♀
Young	active; downy
Fledging	5 weeks
Broods	1; May–July
Food	molluscs, crustaceans
Population	20,000 winter

J	3
F	3
M	3
A	2
M	1
J	1
J	1
A	1
S	2
O	3
N	3
D	3

Common Scoter *Melanitta nigra*

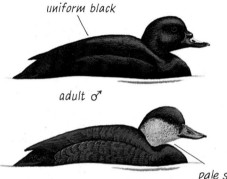

uniform black

adult ♂

adult ♂

adult ♀

pale sides to face

adult ♀

COMMON SCOTER

Type	duck-like
Size	46–51cm (18–20in)
Habitat	sea
Behaviour	swims, dives from surface, takes off and lands on water
Flocking	1–several hundred
Flight	strong and powerful; low; direct
Voice	often silent; occasional harsh whistles

IDENTIFICATION

Adult ♂	
Crown	black
Upperparts	black
Rump	black
Tail	black; short and rounded
Throat	black
Breast	black
Belly	black
Bill	yellow, black knob at base; duck-like
Legs	grey; short
Adult ♀	brown with creamy cheeks; black bill with smaller knob

BREEDING

Nest	lined hollow near water
Eggs	6–9; creamy
Incubation	27–31 days ♀
Young	active; downy
Fledging	6–7 weeks
Broods	1; June–July
Food	cockles, mussels, crustaceans
Population	160–190 pairs; 25,000–30,000 winter

All-black seaduck most often seen as small dark blobs bouncing among waves, or as all-dark birds flying fast and low over sea. Male black with yellow bill and black knob at base. Female brown with pale cheeks that may be picked out at considerable distances. Gregarious, usually forming flocks 10–100 strong.

Status: scarce breeder in extreme north and north-west; winter visitor to most coasts; non-breeders in summer.

Similar Species: Velvet Scoter (p.75).

J	3
F	3
M	3
A	3
M	3
J	2
J	2
A	2
S	3
O	3
N	3
D	3

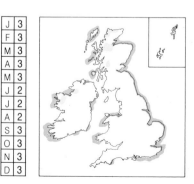

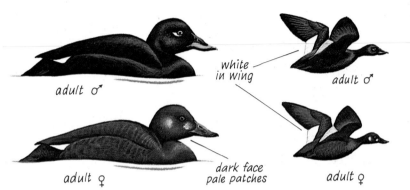

white in wing

adult ♂

adult ♂

adult ♀

dark face pale patches

adult ♀

Similar to Common Scoter, but generally scarcer; often forms mixed flocks. Male black with larger yellow bill. Female brown with two pale face patches. Both sexes show white in wing in flight; may also be visible at rest. When observing all-dark ducks on the sea at a distance, Velvet Scoter may betray their presence by flapping wings to reveal white patches.

Status: less numerous than Common Scoter. Winter visitor to inshore waters, except western Ireland.

Similar Species: Common Scoter (p.74) has no white in wing.

VELVET SCOTER

Type	duck-like
Size	53–59cm (20–23in)
Habitat	sea
Behaviour	swims, dives from surface, takes off and lands on water
Flocking	small flocks
Flight	strong and powerful; low; direct
Voice	mostly silent; some croaking

IDENTIFICATION

Adult ♂	
Crown	black
Upperparts	black
Rump	black
Tail	black; short and rounded
Throat	black
Breast	black
Belly	black
Bill	yellow; large and duck-like
Legs	red; short
Adult ♀	dark brown; pale face patches, grey bill

BREEDING

Nest	lined hollow in open country, near water
Eggs	7–10; creamy
Incubation	27–28 days ♀
Young	active; downy
Fledging	6–7 weeks
Broods	1; June–July
Food	mussels, crabs, shrimps
Population	2500–5000 winter

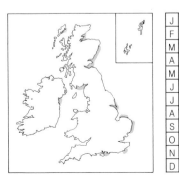

J	2
F	2
M	2
A	1
M	1
J	0
J	0
A	0
S	1
O	2
N	2
D	2

Goldeneye *Bucephala clangula*

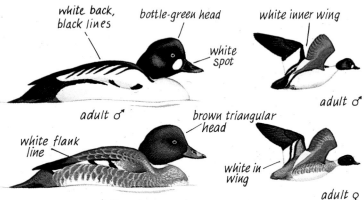

white back, black lines

bottle-green head

white spot

white inner wing

adult ♂

adult ♂

brown triangular head

white flank line

white in wing

adult ♀

adult ♀

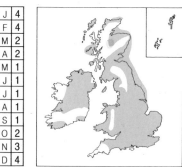

GOLDENEYE

Type	duck-like
Size	40–48cm (16–19in)
Habitat	freshwater, sea, estuaries
Behaviour	swims, dives from surface, takes off and lands on water
Flocking	1–15
Flight	strong and powerful; direct
Voice	silent except in courtship

IDENTIFICATION

Adult ♂	
Crown	black, glossed green
Upperparts	black; white wing, streaked black
Rump	black
Tail	black; short and rounded
Throat	black
Breast	white
Belly	white
Bill	black; duck-like
Legs	yellow; short
Adult ♀	mottled grey with dark brown head and white neck-ring

BREEDING

Nest	unlined tree hole
Eggs	6–11; blue-green
Incubation	27–32 days ♀
Young	active; downy
Fledging	51–60 days
Broods	1; Apr–June
Food	molluscs, crustaceans
Population	27–57 pairs; 10,000–15,000 winter

Medium-sized diving duck found on freshwater as often as on sea. Both sexes marked by steep forehead, peaked crown and sloping hind crown, giving head uniquely characteristic shape. Male has black, green-glossed head with white patch between bill and eye; upperparts black with transverse streaks across folded wing. Flanks and underparts white; rear end black. Female has chocolate-brown head, white neck band and grey body. In flight, both sexes have white inner wing with narrow, dark, central band(s). Generally gregarious, forming small, loose flocks.

Status: small numbers breed in Scotland; widespread winter visitor.
Similar Species: male Tufted Duck (p.70) also black and white, but should present no difficulties.

J	4
F	4
M	2
A	2
M	1
J	1
J	1
A	1
S	1
O	2
N	3
D	4

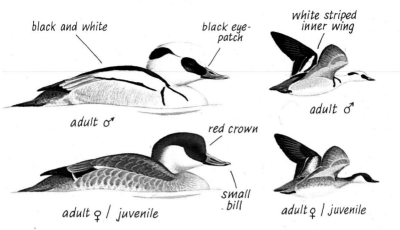

black and white

black eye-patch

white striped inner wing

adult ♂

adult ♂

red crown

small bill

adult ♀ / juvenile

adult ♀ / juvenile

Compact little duck and scarce winter visitor. Male white with narrow black lines on crown, back and flanks. Steep forehead and hint of crest create large-headed appearance; small bill, black facial mask. Female and first winter male – 'redheads' – have chestnut crown extending to below eye, white face, grey back and pale grey underparts. Mostly found in small flocks on inland waters, with 'redheads' predominating.

Status: scarce late winter visitor in variable numbers to south and east England; regular at a few favoured waters. Hard weather may bring larger numbers from the Continent.

Similar Species: male none; at distance, 'redheads' could be confused with Slavonian Grebe (p.32).

SMEW

Type	duck-like
Size	36–43cm (14–17in)
Habitat	freshwater, estuaries
Behaviour	swims, dives from surface, takes off and lands on water
Flocking	1–25
Flight	strong and powerful; direct
Voice	usually silent

IDENTIFICATION

Adult ♂	
Crown	white, black lines; slight crest
Upperparts	white, black lines
Rump	grey
Tail	grey; short and rounded
Throat	white
Breast	white
Belly	white
Bill	grey; small and duck-like
Legs	grey; short
Adult ♀	grey above, paler grey below; white cheeks, chestnut crown

BREEDING

Nest	unlined tree hole
Eggs	6–9; creamy
Incubation	30 days ♀
Young	active; downy
Fledging	10 weeks
Broods	1; May–June
Food	fish
Population	100 winter

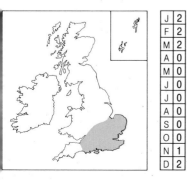

J	2
F	2
M	2
A	0
M	0
J	0
J	0
A	0
S	0
O	0
N	1
D	2

Red-breasted Merganser *Mergus serrator*

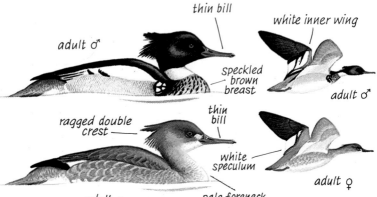

adult ♂

thin bill

white inner wing

speckled brown breast

adult ♂

ragged double crest

thin bill

white speculum

adult ♀

pale foreneck

adult ♀

RED-BREASTED MERGANSER

Type	duck-like
Size	51–61cm (20–24in)
Habitat	freshwater, sea, estuaries
Behaviour	swims, dives from surface, takes off and lands on water
Flocking	1–several hundred
Flight	strong and powerful; direct
Voice	mostly silent; purrs and croaks in display

IDENTIFICATION

Adult ♂	
Crown	green; double crest
Upperparts	black
Rump	grey
Tail	grey; short and rounded
Throat	white
Breast	brown, spotted black
Belly	pale grey
Bill	red; long, straight and thin
Legs	red; short
Adult ♀	grey with reddish head and similar double crest

BREEDING

Nest	lined hollow, well hidden among rocks or tree roots
Eggs	7–12; buffy
Incubation	29–35 days ♀
Young	active; downy
Fledging	59 days
Broods	1; May–June
Food	fish
Population	2000–3000 pairs; 11,000 winter

Long, slim duck with long, thin bill – a typical 'sawbill'. Male has dark bottle-green head with double crest extending from hind crown. Breast rufous brown, spotted black; forms breast band in flight. Head and breast separated by broad white collar. Upperparts black; flanks and underparts pale grey. Female has rusty head with similar double crest; foreneck and chin white. In flight, male shows black and white inner wing; female white speculum. Mergansers dive well to catch fish.
Status: breeds along rivers in north and west; large flocks in north-east in autumn, more widespread along most coasts in winter.
Similar Species: female Goosander (p.79); Red-breasted Merganser has thinner, horizontal-pointing crest and white foreneck.

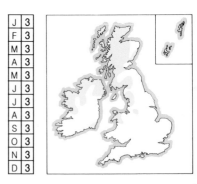

J	3
F	3
M	3
A	3
M	3
J	3
J	3
A	3
S	3
O	3
N	3
D	3

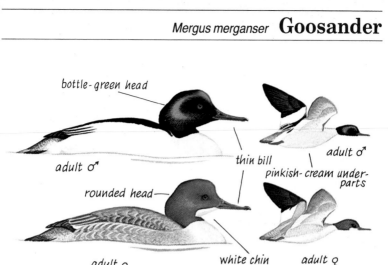

bottle-green head

adult ♂

thin bill

adult ♂

pinkish-cream under-parts

rounded head

adult ♀

white chin
dark neck

adult ♀

Typical 'sawbill' duck, found mainly on freshwater throughout year. Larger and bulkier than Red-breasted Merganser but with similar shape and similar long, thin, serrated bill. Male has green-glossed, black head with rounded crest, giving head unique shape. Back black; flanks and underparts white with warm, pinkish flush. White inner wing shows in flight. Female has white chin, rusty foreneck and hint of crest. Generally found on inland waters, occasionally larger flocks on sheltered estuaries.
Status: breeds on lakes, mostly in forested country in north.
Similar Species: Red-breasted Merganser (p.78); females most similar but Goosander has less ragged crest angled sharply downward towards back.

GOOSANDER

Type	duck-like
Size	57–69cm (22–27in)
Habitat	freshwater
Behaviour	swims, dives from surface, takes off and lands on water
Flocking	1–50
Flight	strong and powerful; direct
Voice	generally silent; various courtship croaks and cackles

IDENTIFICATION

Adult ♂	
Crown	black, green gloss; crest
Upperparts	black, white sides
Rump	grey
Tail	grey; short and rounded
Throat	green
Breast	white
Belly	pinkish white
Bill	red; long, straight and thin
Legs	red; short
Adult ♀	grey with reddish head and rounded crest

BREEDING

Nest	lined tree hole or similar cavity
Eggs	7–14; creamy
Incubation	32–35 days ♀
Young	active; downy
Fledging	5 weeks
Broods	1; Mar–June
Food	fish
Population	900–1250 pairs; 5000 winter

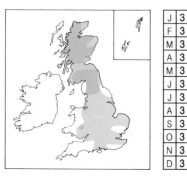

J	3
F	3
M	3
A	3
M	3
J	3
J	3
A	3
S	3
O	3
N	3
D	3

Ruddy Duck *Oxyura jamaicensis*

long tail

blue bill, white face

uniform upper wing

adult ♂

adult ♂

tail often hidden in water

bold face stripe

adult ♀

adult ♀

RUDDY DUCK

Type	duck-like
Size	36–43cm (14–17in)
Habitat	freshwater
Behaviour	swims, dives from surface, takes off and lands on water
Flocking	1–15
Flight	strong and powerful; direct
Voice	generally silent; quiet courtship grunts and hisses

IDENTIFICATION

Adult ♂	
Crown	black
Upperparts	russet
Rump	russet
Tail	brown; long and pointed
Throat	russet
Breast	russet
Belly	russet
Bill	bright blue; duck-like
Legs	blue; short
Adult ♀	buff-brown, barred below; dark cap and pale cheek with distinctive line; greyer bill than ♂

BREEDING

Nest	floating mound
Eggs	6–10; white
Incubation	20–21 days ♀
Young	active; downy
Fledging	?
Broods	1; May–June
Food	larvae, seeds
Population	2000+ individuals

Dumpy little duck of strangely 'weight forward' appearance; stiff tail often held cocked upright but equally often horizontal and invisible. Male russet, with dark cap and hind crown enclosing white face. Brilliant blue bill. Female brown above, barred buff and brown below; dark cap and distinctive dark line across face. Bill greyer blue than male.

Status: introduced from North America to West Midlands where now regular breeder; spreading eastwards. Some birds move as far south as Kent and Sussex in winter.

Similar Species: none.

J	2
F	2
M	2
A	2
M	2
J	2
J	2
A	2
S	2
O	2
N	2
D	2

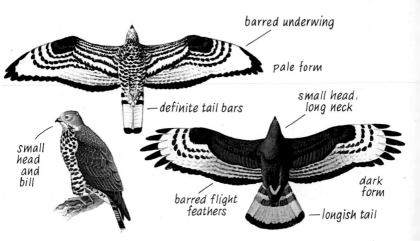

barred underwing

pale form

—definite tail bars

small head, long neck

small head and bill

barred flight feathers

dark form

—longish tail

Rare summer visitor to large areas of woodland in southern England. Slimmer and more angular than similar Buzzard. Small head, thin neck and waisted, 'wasp-like' wings. Tail longer than Buzzard; wings droop when soaring. Plumage highly variable but carpals always dark and underwing has regularly spaced barring. Tail with terminal band and two other similar bands. Unique 'butterfly-like' display flight of male involves holding wings high above back and fluttering before diving. *Status:* very scarce summer visitor and passage migrant.
Similar Species: Common Buzzard (p.90).

HONEY BUZZARD

Type	hawk-like
Size	50–58cm (20–23in)
Habitat	forests and woods
Behaviour	takes off and lands on vegetation and ground
Flocking	usually solitary
Flight	soars, glides; strong and powerful
Voice	high-pitched *kee-a*

IDENTIFICATION

Adult	
Crown	brown
Upperparts	brown
Rump	brown
Tail	buff with brown bands; longish and square
Throat	white
Breast	brown, buff and brown barred or white
Belly	varies (as breast)
Bill	brown; hooked
Legs	yellow; medium length

BREEDING

Nest	sticks high in tree
Eggs	1–3; white, speckled reddish
Incubation	30–35 days, mainly ♀
Young	helpless; downy
Fledging	40–44 days
Broods	1; June
Food	larvae and adult wasps and bees; also amphibians, birds
Population	*c* 20 pairs

J	0
F	0
M	0
A	0
M	2
J	2
J	2
A	2
S	2
O	1
N	0
D	0

Red Kite   *Milvus milvus*

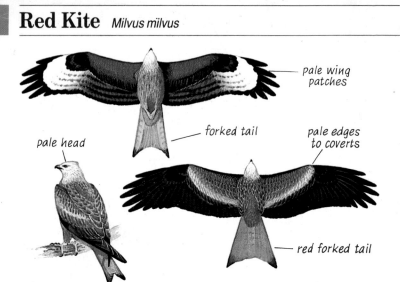

pale wing patches

forked tail

pale head

pale edges to coverts

red forked tail

RED KITE

Type	hawk-like
Size	58–64cm (22–25in)
Habitat	forests and woods
Behaviour	perches openly, takes off from vegetation and ground
Flocking	usually solitary
Flight	soars, glides; strong and powerful
Voice	repeated *he-he-heea*

IDENTIFICATION

Adult	
Crown	white
Upperparts	rufous
Rump	rufous
Tail	rufous; long and forked
Throat	white
Breast	rufous, streaked
Belly	rufous, streaked
Bill	yellow; hooked
Legs	yellow; medium length

BREEDING

Nest	twigs, plus rubbish in tree
Eggs	2–3; white, spotted red
Incubation	28–30 days ♀
Young	helpless; downy
Fledging	45–50 days
Broods	1; Mar–May
Food	mammals, birds, carrion
Population	*c* 100 pairs

Uncommon raptor, similar in size to Buzzard, but much more angular and less bulky with longer wings and tail. Rufous above and below with pale, almost whitish, head. In flight, upperwing brown with rufous coverts; underwing brown with prominent whitish patches on outer wing. Tail rufous and deeply forked, almost translucent against light. Often hangs on rising air; circles and weaves in slow, effortless flight on bowed wings with tail twisting as rudder. Mostly found over hillside woods and pastures. *Status:* resident in central Wales; scarce passage migrant elsewhere, mostly southern England. *Similar Species:* none.

J	2
F	2
M	2
A	2
M	2
J	2
J	2
A	2
S	2
O	2
N	2
D	2

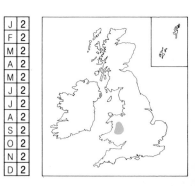

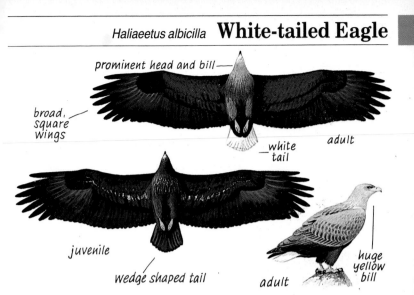

Haliaeetus albicilla **White-tailed Eagle**

prominent head and bill —

broad, square wings

white tail

adult

juvenile

wedge shaped tail

adult

huge yellow bill

Huge, bulky eagle with enormous broad wings and prominent head and bill. Adult mostly dark brown with pure white tail; large pale head with very large yellow bill. In flight, prominent head and bill and short white tail contrast with huge, square-cut dark wings. Juveniles share this shape, but have dark tails or only white centres to tail feathers, depending on age. Found by sea or near freshwater.

Status: exterminated as breeding bird in Scotland in 1916 but re-introduced to Rhum since 1975; first bred in 1985. Otherwise rare winter visitor.

Similar Species: immatures superficially similar to adult Golden Eagle (p.87); adult similar to immature Golden Eagle, which also has white tail but with black terminal band.

WHITE-TAILED EAGLE

Type	hawk-like
Size	69–91cm (27–36in)
Habitat	moors, sea
Behaviour	dives from air, perches openly, takes off from vegetation or ground
Flocking	usually solitary
Flight	soars, glides, aerial dive; strong and powerful
Voice	laughing *kok-kok-kok* while courting

IDENTIFICATION

Adult	
Crown	buff
Upperparts	dark brown
Rump	dark brown
Tail	white; short and rounded
Throat	dark brown
Breast	brown, streaked
Belly	brown
Bill	yellow; large and hooked
Legs	yellow; medium length
Juvenile	all brown but with white centres to tail feathers

BREEDING

Nest	huge mass of twigs on cliff or tree
Eggs	2; white
Incubation	34–45 days ♂ ♀
Young	helpless; downy
Fledging	70 days
Broods	1; Mar–May
Food	fish, carrion
Population	8 pairs reintroduced

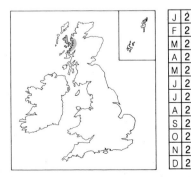

J	2
F	2
M	2
A	2
M	2
J	2
J	2
A	2
S	2
O	2
N	2
D	2

Hen Harrier *Circus cyaneus*

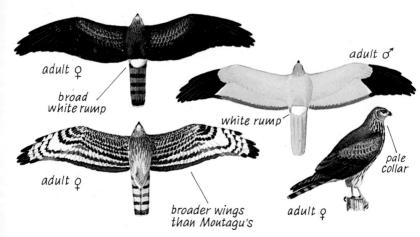

adult ♀

broad
white rump

adult ♀

broader wings
than Montagu's

adult ♂

white rump

adult ♀

pale
collar

HEN HARRIER

Type	hawk-like
Size	43–51cm (17–20in)
Habitat	freshwater and marshes, moors and heaths, estuaries and shores
Behaviour	perches openly, takes off and lands on vegetation or ground
Flocking	1 or 2
Flight	hovers, soars, glides; laboured; undulating
Voice	mostly silent, cackles and squeals in courtship

IDENTIFICATION

Adult ♂	
Crown	grey
Upperparts	grey
Rump	white
Tail	grey; long and square
Throat	grey
Breast	grey
Belly	white
Bill	black; hooked
Legs	yellow; medium length
Ad. ♀ and juv.	all brown with white rump, streaked below

BREEDING

Nest	platform of sticks and twigs hidden in low vegetation
Eggs	4–6; pale blue
Incubation	29–39 days ♀
Young	helpless; downy
Fledging	37 days
Broods	1; Apr–June
Food	small birds and mammals
Population	500–600 pairs; 1000 winter

Medium-sized harrier, between Montagu's and Marsh Harrier in size and bulk. Male pale grey above with white rump and black wingtips; breast grey, remaining underparts white. Female and juvenile brown above with bold white rump; streaked brown or buff below. Hunts low over moors and young conifer plantations in summer. *Status:* scarce but increasing resident; breeds in hilly districts, more common in north than west. Regular passage migrant and winter visitor in small numbers, mainly to coasts (particularly east coast).
Similar Species: Montagu's Harrier (p.85). Females and juveniles especially similar – often jointly called 'ring-tail' harriers – though Hen Harrier bulkier, with larger white rump and paler head than breast.

J	3
F	3
M	3
A	3
M	3
J	3
J	3
A	3
S	3
O	3
N	3
D	3

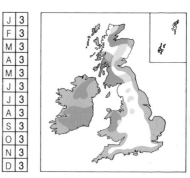

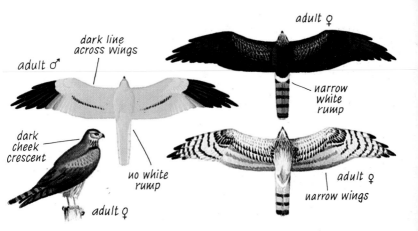

adult ♀

adult ♂

dark line
across wings

narrow
white
rump

dark
cheek
crescent

no white
rump

adult ♀

adult ♀

narrow wings

adult ♀

Smaller and slimmer than Hen Harrier
and much less common. Male pale grey
above with black wingtips and black
line across upperwing. Underwing has
several lines of bars. Tail and rump
grey with no more than hint of white
on rump. Underparts white, streaked
chestnut. Female brown like female
Hen Harrier but more lightly built,
with narrower white rump and head
same tone as breast. Juvenile more
uniformly rufous below.
Status: passage migrant and rare
summer visitor to England, Wales and
southern Ireland.
Similar Species: Hen Harrier (p.84).

MONTAGU'S HARRIER

Type	hawk-like
Size	39–46cm (15–18in)
Habitat	freshwater marshes, heaths, fields and hedges
Behaviour	perches openly, takes off and lands on vegetation or ground
Flocking	1 or 2
Flight	hovers, soars, glides; laboured; undulating
Voice	shrill courtship *kek-kek-kek*

IDENTIFICATION

Adult ♂	
Crown	grey
Upperparts	grey
Rump	grey
Tail	grey; long and square
Throat	grey
Breast	grey
Belly	white, streaked chestnut
Bill	black; hooked
Legs	yellow; medium length
Ad. ♀ and juv.	all brown, buffy and streaked below with white rump

BREEDING

Nest	platform of reeds, twigs, grass on ground
Eggs	4–5; bluish
Incubation	27–40 days ♀
Young	helpless; downy
Fledging	35–40 days
Broods	1; May–June
Food	small birds and mammals
Population	7–14 pairs

J	0
F	0
M	0
A	1
M	1
J	1
J	1
A	1
S	1
O	1
N	0
D	0

85

Marsh Harrier *Circus aeruginosus*

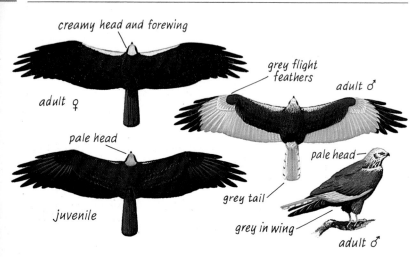

creamy head and forewing

adult ♀

grey flight feathers

adult ♂

pale head

juvenile

grey tail

pale head

grey in wing

adult ♂

<table>
<tr><td colspan="2">MARSH-HARRIER</td></tr>
<tr><td>Type</td><td>hawk-like</td></tr>
<tr><td>Size</td><td>48–56cm (19–22in)</td></tr>
<tr><td>Habitat</td><td>freshwater marshes, moors, heaths, estuaries, shores</td></tr>
<tr><td>Behaviour</td><td>perches openly, takes off from vegetation or ground</td></tr>
<tr><td>Flocking</td><td>1 or 2</td></tr>
<tr><td>Flight</td><td>hovers, soars, glides; laboured; undulating</td></tr>
<tr><td>Voice</td><td>high-pitched kee-a in courtship</td></tr>
</table>

IDENTIFICATION

Adult ♂	
Crown	buff
Upperparts	brown, dark wingtips
Rump	brown
Tail	grey; long and square
Throat	buff
Breast	brown, streaked
Belly	brown
Bill	black; hooked
Legs	yellow; medium length
Adult ♀	all brown with creamy head and forewing
Juvenile	all brown or similar to female

BREEDING

Nest	platform of reeds in large reedbed
Eggs	4–5; blue-white
Incubation	33–38 days ♀
Young	helpless; downy
Fledging	35–40 days
Broods	1; Apr–May
Food	birds, eggs, small mammals, carrion
Population	92–111 pairs

Largest of the harriers with typical slow, flap-and-glide flight creating lumbering appearance. Long wings, long tail and gliding flight near ground with wings held in 'V' identify as a harrier. Male brown with pale buff head and forewing edges. In flight, grey tail and large grey area on inner wing contrasts with dark wingtips and brown wing coverts. Female all brown with creamy head and forewing. Juveniles all brown with creamy head, similar to female. Found mostly over large reedbeds and marshes.
Status: rare breeder, mostly in East Anglia; scarce passage migrant and winter visitor, mostly east coasts.
Similar Species: Hen Harrier (p.84) and Montagu's Harrier (p.85). Marsh Harrier is bulkier and broader-winged than other harriers.

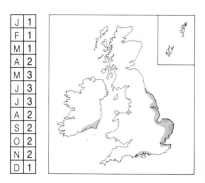

J	1
F	1
M	1
A	2
M	3
J	3
J	3
A	2
S	2
O	2
N	2
D	1

Aquila chrysaetos **Golden Eagle**

tawny across wings

prominent head

white wingbars

adult

tawny crown
and nape

white tail
black band

juvenile

adult

Large eagle of mountains and moorlands; virtually confined to Scotland. Adult dark brown with pale tawny crown and forewing. In flight, appears all dark from below. Juvenile has white tail with broad black terminal band and white base to outer primaries. From below, white tail less noticeable, but bold white line extends along all flight feathers. Flight powerful with deep wing beats; quarters hillsides like huge harrier. Long, broad wings held in shallow 'V' when soaring; dives on folded wings. *Status:* sedentary in Scottish Highlands and Lake District. *Similar Species:* White-tailed Eagle (p.83). Often confused with much smaller buzzards (p.90–91) but proportions of head, wings and tail quite different.

GOLDEN EAGLE	
Type	hawk-like
Size	76–90cm (30–35in)
Habitat	moors and heaths, forests and woods
Behaviour	perches openly, takes off from vegetation or ground
Flocking	solitary
Flight	soars, glides; strong and powerful; laboured
Voice	yelping *kaa*; generally silent

IDENTIFICATION

Adult	
Crown	tawny-buff
Upperparts	brown
Rump	brown
Tail	brown; medium length, square
Throat	brown
Breast	brown
Belly	brown
Bill	yellow; hooked
Legs	yellow; medium length
Juvenile	brown with white wing flashes above and below; white tail with black band

BREEDING

Nest	massive structure of twigs on cliff or tree
Eggs	2; white, blotched brown
Incubation	43–45 days, usually ♀
Young	helpless; downy
Fledging	63–70 days
Broods	1; Feb–May
Food	small mammals, large birds
Population	420+ pairs

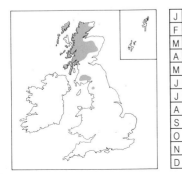

J	3
F	3
M	3
A	3
M	3
J	3
J	3
A	3
S	3
O	3
N	3
D	3

Northern Goshawk *Accipiter gentilis*

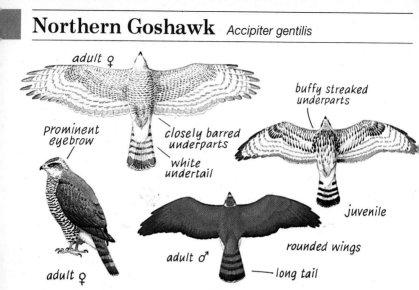

adult ♀

prominent eyebrow

closely barred underparts

white undertail

buffy streaked underparts

juvenile

rounded wings

adult ♂

long tail

adult ♀

NORTHERN GOSHAWK

Type	hawk-like
Size	48–58cm (19–23in)
Habitat	forests and woods, fields and hedgerows
Behaviour	perches openly, takes off from vegetation or ground
Flocking	solitary
Flight	soars, glides, aerial dive; strong and powerful; direct
Voice	chattering *gek-gek-gek*

IDENTIFICATION

Adult	
Crown	grey, dark cap
Upperparts	brownish grey
Rump	grey
Tail	grey; long and square
Throat	white
Breast	white, barred grey
Belly	white, barred grey
Bill	black; hooked
Legs	yellow; medium length
Juvenile	browner; streaked below where adult finely barred

BREEDING

Nest	twigs in tree
Eggs	2–3; pale blue
Incubation	36–41 days ♀
Young	helpless; downy
Fledging	45 days
Broods	1; Apr–June
Food	birds and mammals
Population	150–230 pairs

Like large European Sparrowhawk with rounded wings and long, banded tail. Adult brownish grey with darker cap and bold white eyebrow. Closely barred pale grey below, with particularly prominent white undertail coverts. Female about Common Buzzard-sized; much larger than male, which is only a little larger than female European Sparrowhawk. Juvenile browner; streaked below. Dives and soars in spectacular display, often with white undertail coverts spread. Hunts like European Sparrowhawk.

Status: scarce but increasing resident in parts of England and Scotland following escape from falconry in 1960s. Rare passage migrant.

Similar Species: European Sparrowhawk (p.89); Goshawk is larger, bulkier and has slower wing beats and bulging secondaries.

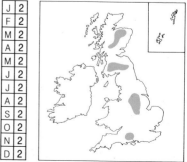

J	2
F	2
M	2
A	2
M	2
J	2
J	2
A	2
S	2
O	2
N	2
D	2

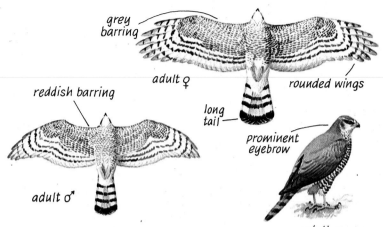

Accipiter nisus # European Sparrowhawk

grey barring

adult ♀

rounded wings

reddish barring

long tail

prominent eyebrow

adult ♂

adult ♀

Fast-flying, agile hawk of woodlands and fields. Grey or grey-brown above, with clear, pale eyebrow in female. Male barred russet below; female barred grey. Both have long tails with at least four distinct bars showing. Dashing flight in pursuit of small birds makes confusion with Common Kestrel impossible. When soaring or travelling, shape is similar but Sparrowhawk flaps rounded wings quickly for a few beats before gliding. *Status:* widespread; increasing after 1960s pesticide disaster.
Similar Species: Common Kestrel (p.92) has longer, more pointed wings and often hovers in flight. Northern Goshawk (p.88) is larger and more bulky, although large female Sparrowhawk may be confused with small male Northern Goshawk.

J	4
F	4
M	4
A	4
M	4
J	4
J	4
A	4
S	4
O	4
N	4
D	4

EUROPEAN SPARROWHAWK

Type	hawk-like
Size	28–38cm (11–15in)
Habitat	forests and woods, fields and hedgerows, heaths
Behaviour	perches openly, takes off and lands on vegetation or ground
Flocking	solitary
Flight	soars, glides, aerial dive; strong and powerful; direct
Voice	loud *kek-kek-kek*

IDENTIFICATION

Adult ♂	
Crown	grey
Upperparts	grey or grey-brown
Rump	grey
Tail	grey and white, banded; long and square
Throat	white
Breast	whitish, reddish barring
Belly	whitish, reddish barring
Bill	black; hooked
Legs	yellow; medium length
Adult ♀	larger than ♂, brown above, pale eyebrow; heavily barred grey below

BREEDING

Nest	twigs in trees
Eggs	4–5; white, blotched dark brown
Incubation	42 days ♀
Young	helpless; downy
Fledging	32 days
Broods	1; Apr–June
Food	small birds
Population	33,000+ pairs

Common Buzzard *Buteo buteo*

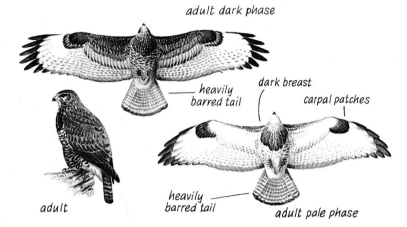

adult dark phase

heavily barred tail

dark breast

carpal patches

adult

heavily barred tail

adult pale phase

COMMON BUZZARD	
Type	hawk-like
Size	50–56cm (20–22in)
Habitat	moors and heaths, forests and woods, fields and hedgerows
Behaviour	perches openly, takes off and lands on vegetation or ground
Flocking	1; small soaring groups
Flight	soars, glides; laboured
Voice	mewing *pee-oo*

IDENTIFICATION

Ad.dark	
Crown	brown
Upperparts	brown
Rump	brown
Tail	brown, barred;short and square
Throat	brown
Breast	buff, dark patches on sides
Belly	brown
Bill	black; hooked
Legs	yellow; medium length
Ad.pale	variable, often almost white below, especially in flight

BREEDING

Nest	bulky sticks and twigs in tree, on cliff, rock outcrop, occasionally ground
Eggs	3–4; white, blotched reddish
Incubation	42 days, mainly ♀
Young	helpless; downy
Fledging	40–45 days
Broods	1; Mar–May
Food	small mammals
Population	8000–10,000 pairs

Most common of the larger raptors; prefers wooded areas with open fields as well as moorland and heath. Highly variable plumage from dark brown with pale wing linings to pure creamy white with dark wing edges. Tail heavily barred or almost pure creamy white. Always shows dark patches at carpal joint and at sides of breast. Soars on broad wings held forward in shallow 'V'; small head and short tail. *Status:* common resident of hilly districts in north of Ireland and west of Britain, also in West Midlands. In the south, occurs as far east as Hampshire. Scarce passage migrant and winter visitor elsewhere.
Similar Species: Rough-legged Buzzard (p.91).

J	4
F	4
M	4
A	4
M	4
J	4
J	4
A	4
S	4
O	4
N	4
D	4

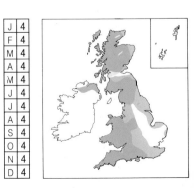

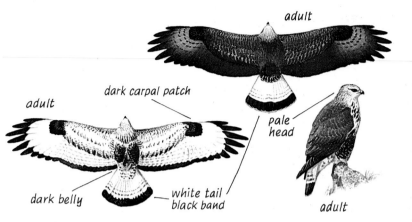

adult

dark carpal patch

adult

pale head

dark belly

white tail black band

adult

Similar to Common Buzzard, but with less variable plumage pattern. Flight feathers always very pale, mostly white with a few indistinct bars. Underwing coverts vary from brown to white; carpal patch always black and prominent. Tail white with broad black sub-terminal band and up to four narrow, less distinct, bars towards tip. Dark belly or flank patches more obvious than Common Buzzard. Always pale headed. Soars on flat wings and frequently hangs on wind or hovers.
Status: scarce winter visitor, mainly to east coasts; numbers vary from year to year.
Similar Species: Common Buzzard (p.90) and see above.

ROUGH-LEGGED BUZZARD

Type	hawk-like
Size	50–61cm (20–24in)
Habitat	freshwater marshes, moors, estuaries
Behaviour	perches openly, takes off and lands on vegetation or ground
Flocking	1–4
Flight	hovers, soars, glides; laboured
Voice	mostly silent

IDENTIFICATION

Adult	
Crown	white
Upperparts	brown
Rump	brown
Tail	white with black band and narrow bars near tip; medium length, square
Throat	buff
Breast	white, streaked brown
Belly	brown, blackish patches on sides
Bill	black; hooked
Legs	yellow; medium length

BREEDING

Nest	twigs on rock outcrop
Eggs	2–3; white, blotched brown
Incubation	28 days, mainly ♀
Young	helpless; downy
Fledging	40–42 days
Broods	1; May–June
Food	small mammals
Population	c20 winter

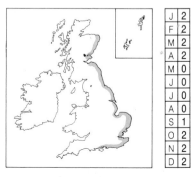

J	2
F	2
M	2
A	2
M	0
J	0
J	0
A	0
S	1
O	2
N	2
D	2

Common Kestrel *Falco tinnunculus*

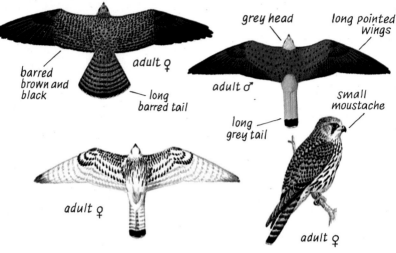

barred brown and black

adult ♀

grey head

long pointed wings

adult ♂

long grey tail

long barred tail

small moustache

adult ♀

adult ♀

COMMON KESTREL	
Type	hawk-like
Size	33–36cm (13–14in)
Habitat	towns, marshes, moors, heaths, cliffs, forests, fields
Behaviour	perches openly, takes off and lands on vegetation or ground
Flocking	solitary
Flight	hovers, soars, aerial dive; strong and powerful; direct
Voice	high-pitched *kee-kee-kee*

IDENTIFICATION

Adult ♂	
Crown	grey
Upperparts	brown, spotted black
Rump	grey
Tail	grey, black terminal band; long and square
Throat	buff
Breast	buff, spotted black
Belly	buff, streaked on flanks
Bill	black; hooked
Legs	yellow; long
Ad. ♀ and juv.	browner, heavily barred back; lacks grey on head and tail

BREEDING

Nest	bare ledge or hole
Eggs	4–5; white, heavily speckled brown
Incubation	27–29 days, mainly ♀
Young	helpless; downy
Fledging	27–39 days
Broods	1; Apr–June
Food	small mammals and birds
Population	30,000–80,000 pairs

Most common raptor frequenting farmland, moors, parks, heaths, coastlines, marshes and city-centres. Often seen hovering, especially over motorway verges. Male has grey head with thin black moustachial streak; · grey tail with broad black sub-terminal band. Upperparts rufous brown spotted black with dark brown flight feathers. Underparts tawny with spotted streaks; underwing pale. Female all brown above with dark streaking on head, heavily barred back, and multiple dark tail bands. In flight, long tail and shallow beats of long, pointed wings distinctive.
Status: common and widespread resident.
Similar Species: European Sparrowhawk (p.89) has rounded wings and distinctive flight.

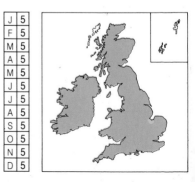

J	5
F	5
M	5
A	5
M	5
J	5
J	5
A	5
S	5
O	5
N	5
D	5

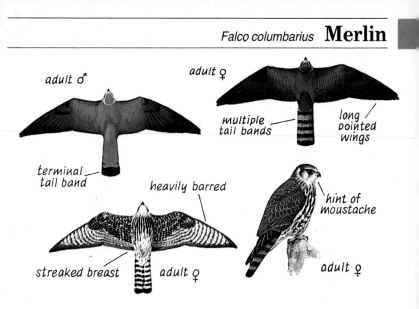

Falco columbarius **Merlin**

adult ♂

adult ♀

multiple tail bands

long pointed wings

terminal tail band

heavily barred

hint of moustache

streaked breast   adult ♀

adult ♀

Small, dark, fast-flying falcon of hills and moors; haunts coastlines and adjacent marshes in winter. Male smaller; blue-grey above with dark terminal band on tail. Female brown with multiple-barred buff and brown tail. Both sexes heavily streaked below and heavily barred across underwing. Flies low and fast in pursuit of smaller birds.

Status: resident in hilly districts of north and west, but nowhere common. Winter visitor elsewhere, mostly to coasts.

Similar Species: Hobby (p.94), a summer visitor, is also dark but with prominent white sides to neck and clear-cut, dark moustache; wings are longer, narrower and more angular.

	MERLIN
Type	hawk-like
Size	27–32cm (10–13in)
Habitat	moors, estuaries, freshwater marshes
Behaviour	perches openly, takes off and lands on vegetation or ground
Flocking	solitary
Flight	soars, glides, aerial dive; strong and powerful; direct
Voice	chattering *kee-kee-kee*

IDENTIFICATION

Adult ♂	
Crown	blue-grey
Upperparts	blue-grey
Rump	blue-grey
Tail	blue, dark terminal band
Throat	buff
Breast	buff, heavy blackish streaks
Belly	buff, heavy blackish streaks
Bill	yellow; hooked
Legs	yellow; short
Ad. ♀ and juv.	brown above, heavily barred and streaked below

BREEDING

Nest	hollow on ground
Eggs	5–6; buff, heavily spotted reddish
Incubation	28–32 days, mainly ♀
Young	helpless; downy
Fledging	25–30 days
Broods	1; Apr–May
Food	small birds
Population	600–800 pairs

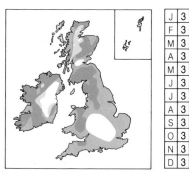

J	3
F	3
M	3
A	3
M	3
J	3
J	3
A	3
S	3
O	3
N	3
D	3

Hobby *Falco subbuteo*

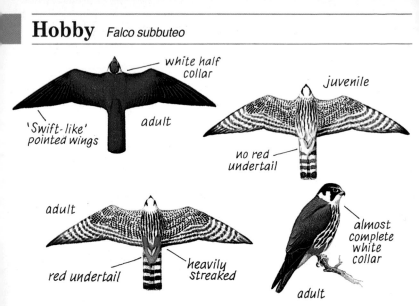

white half collar

'Swift-like' pointed wings

adult

juvenile

no red undertail

adult

red undertail

heavily streaked

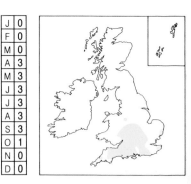

almost complete white collar

adult

HOBBY

Type	hawk-like
Size	30–36cm (12–14in)
Habitat	heaths, fields and hedges
Behaviour	perches openly, takes off and lands on vegetation
Flocking	1 or 2
Flight	soars, glides, aerial dive; strong and powerful; direct
Voice	*kew-kew* repeated; also high-pitched *ki-ki-ki*

IDENTIFICATION

Adult

Crown	black
Upperparts	slate-grey, white 'neck ring' and black moustache
Rump	grey
Tail	grey, undertail coverts rust-red; medium length, square
Throat	white
Breast	buff, heavily streaked
Belly	buff, heavily streaked
Bill	yellow; hooked
Legs	yellow; short
Juvenile	dark brown above; lacks red undertail

BREEDING

Nest	old nest of other species in tree
Eggs	2–3; yellowish, speckled reddish
Incubation	28 days, mainly ♀
Young	helpless; downy
Fledging	28–32 days
Broods	1; May–June
Food	insects, small birds
Population	150–450 pairs

Rare summer visitor to heaths and downland; often hunts over water or marshland for insects and small birds. Resembles Common Kestrel but wings longer and narrower, almost Swift-like; tail slightly shorter. Upperparts slate-grey; prominent black moustache and almost complete white 'neck ring'. Neck ring is most prominent field mark.
Underparts heavily streaked and barred; undertail coverts rust-red. Juvenile dark brown above; lacks rusty undertail coverts.
Status: scarce summer visitor to central and southern England; scarce bird of passage elsewhere.
Similar Species: Merlin (p.93) and Common Kestrel (p.92) both have broader wings and lack white 'neck ring'.

J	0
F	0
M	0
A	3
M	3
J	3
J	3
A	3
S	3
O	1
N	0
D	0

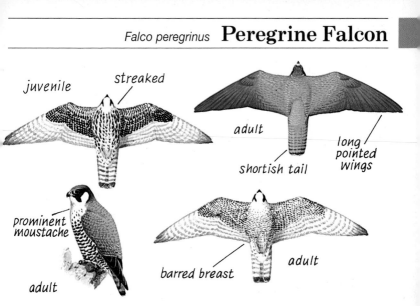

Falco peregrinus **Peregrine Falcon**

juvenile

streaked

adult

shortish tail

long pointed wings

prominent moustache

adult

barred breast

adult

adult

Large, robust falcon with shortish tail and long, angular wings. Flies with deep sweeps of long, pointed wings producing impression of immense speed and power. Upperparts slate-grey with paler rump and delicately barred tail. White face and sides of neck with bold black moustaches. Underparts and underwing finely barred. Juvenile brown above with heavily streaked body. Haunts cliffs, both coastal and inland; in winter also frequents estuaries where rests on ground or small hummock.
Status: scarce resident in hilly and coastal districts of north and west; elsewhere scarce winter visitor.
Similar Species: no other large falcons.

PEREGRINE FALCON

Type	hawk-like
Size	38–48cm (15–19in)
Habitat	moors, sea-cliffs, estuaries and shores
Behaviour	perches openly, takes off and lands on ground
Flocking	solitary
Flight	soars, glides, aerial stoop; strong and powerful; direct
Voice	loud *kek-kek-kek*; repeated *wee-chew*

IDENTIFICATION

Adult	
Crown	slate-grey
Upperparts	slate-grey, white face and sides of neck; prominent black moustache
Rump	grey
Tail	grey; shortish and square
Throat	white
Breast	white, barred black
Belly	white, barred black
Bill	yellow; hooked
Legs	yellow; short
Juvenile	brown above; heavily streaked

BREEDING

Nest	bare scrape on cliff
Eggs	3–4; buff, speckled red
Incubation	28–29 days, mainly ♀
Young	helpless; downy
Fledging	35–42 days
Broods	1; Apr–June
Food	birds
Population	1000+ pairs

J	3
F	3
M	3
A	3
M	3
J	3
J	3
A	3
S	3
O	3
N	3
D	3

Osprey *Pandion haliaetus*

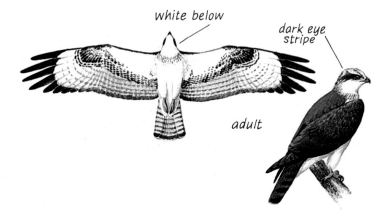

white below

dark eye stripe

adult

OSPREY

Type	hawk-like
Size	51–59cm (20–23in)
Habitat	freshwater, sea, estuaries, forests and woods
Behaviour	perches openly; dives from air; takes off and lands on vegetation, ground, or water
Flocking	solitary
Flight	hovers, soars, glides, aerial dive; strong and powerful; direct
Voice	whistling *chew-chew*

IDENTIFICATION

Adult	
Crown	white
Upperparts	brown and grey
Rump	brown
Tail	brown; medium length, square
Throat	white
Breast	white, faint brown band
Belly	white
Bill	black; hooked
Legs	grey; medium length

BREEDING

Nest	mass of sticks in tree
Eggs	3; creamy, blotched reddish
Incubation	35–38 days ♂ ♀
Young	helpless, downy
Fledging	51–59 days
Broods	1; Mar–June
Food	fish
Population	70+ pairs

Large, pale raptor, sometimes mistaken for large gull. Upperparts dark brown and grey; underparts white with black carpal patches, wingtips and wingbar. Flies gull-like on bowed wings. Head and nape white with prominent black eye stripe. Small head and long neck apparent at all times. Catches fish in spectacular feet-first dive; often after hovering high overhead. Found in lakes in forested areas in summer; reservoirs and other large waters at other times. Hunts in sea abroad.

Status: recolonised in 1955 after lengthy absence. Scarce (but spreading) summer visitor to Highlands of Scotland; elsewhere increasing passage migrant.

Similar Species: none.

J	0
F	0
M	0
A	3
M	3
J	3
J	3
A	3
S	3
O	3
N	0
D	0

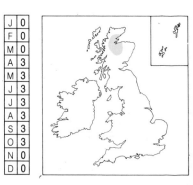

prominent head pattern

long angled wings

cigar-shaped body

adult ♂

adult ♀

Small, fast-flying, migratory gamebird; more often heard than seen. Ventriloquial call makes bird's location difficult to assess. Good views of bird on ground exceptional. Usually seen when flushed (deliberately or accidentally); flies when almost trodden on. Combination of stocky body and long, pointed wings is unique. Upperparts brown, streaked and barred; underparts warm buffy orange. Pattern of bold creamy eyebrow and dark facial streaks more pronounced in male than female.
Status: scarce and declining summer visitor.
Similar Species: none.

COMMON QUAIL

Type	partridge-like
Size	17–18.5cm (6–7in)
Habitat	moors, heaths, fields, hedges
Behaviour	walks, runs, takes off and lands on ground
Flocking	solitary
Flight	glides; strong and powerful; direct
Voice	distinctive *whic-we-wic*, repeated; often rendered 'wet-me-lips'

IDENTIFICATION

Adult	
Crown	black and white
Upperparts	brown and black, pale streaks
Rump	brown
Tail	brown; short and rounded
Throat	white; ♂ black central stripe
Breast	buffy orange
Belly	white
Bill	black; short and stubby
Legs	grey; short

BREEDING

Nest	hollow on ground
Eggs	7–12; creamy, spotted brown
Incubation	16–21 days ♀
Young	active; downy
Fledging	19 days
Broods	1 sometimes 2; May.–June
Food	seeds, insects
Population	less than 100 pairs

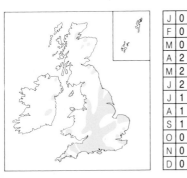

J	0
F	0
M	0
A	2
M	2
J	2
J	1
A	1
S	1
O	0
N	0
D	0

Red Grouse *Lagopus lagopus*

red comb

rich, dark chestnut

rufous brown

adult ♂

adult ♀

RED GROUSE	
Type	partridge-like
Size	33–39cm (13–19in)
Habitat	moors
Behaviour	walks, takes off and lands on ground
Flocking	1–15
Flight	glides; strong and powerful; direct
Voice	characteristic *go-back, go-back, go-back, back-back-back*

IDENTIFICATION

Adult ♂	
Crown	red-brown, barred black
Upperparts	red-brown, barred black
Rump	red-brown, barred black
Tail	red-brown, barred black
Throat	red-brown, barred black
Breast	red-brown, barred black
Belly	red-brown, barred black
Bill	grey; short and stubby
Legs	white; short
Adult ♀	paler, reduced red comb

BREEDING

Nest	hollow on ground
Eggs	6–11; yellowish, blotched dark brown
Incubation	20–26 days
Young	active; downy
Fledging	12–13 days
Broods	1; May–June
Food	heather
Population	less than 500,000 pairs

The grouse of grouse-moor fame; widespread resident of hilly, heather-clad regions. Sub-species of Willow Grouse, which is widespread in northern hemisphere. Most numerous in northern Britain where moorland is managed to suit its needs. Both sexes dark reddish brown, heavily spotted and barred black. Male considerably darker than female, with bolder red comb above eye. Generally seen when flushed from heather; flies away strongly before gliding back to cover on bowed wings. In early morning, often seen along moorland roads collecting grit. Colour and dumpy, rotund shape identify.

Status: largely confined to moorland of north and west Britain and Ireland.
Similar Species: Ptarmigan (p.99) is much scarcer and less widespread.

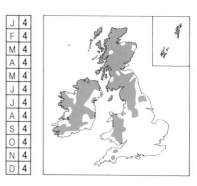

J	4
F	4
M	4
A	4
M	4
J	4
J	4
A	4
S	4
O	4
N	4
D	4

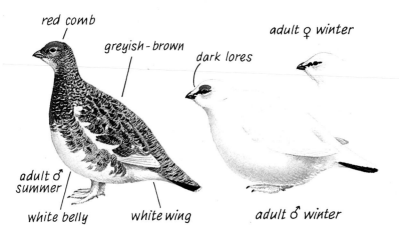

red comb

greyish-brown

adult ♀ winter

dark lores

adult ♂ summer

white belly

white wing

adult ♂ winter

Close relative of Red Grouse that lives at higher altitudes but is similarly resident and unknown away from breeding grounds. Mottled greys and browns camouflage against scant vegetation and broken rocks of high mountain tops. In winter, whole plumage white; in summer, only wingtips white. Even intermediate white and grey patchy birds difficult to see. Male has prominent red comb in summer; black mark between bill and eye in winter.
Status: scarce resident of mountain tops of Scottish Highlands.
Similar Species: in summer, Red Grouse (p.98) but Ptarmigan paler, in shades of grey-brown rather than russet. Slightly smaller than Red Grouse.

J	2
F	2
M	2
A	2
M	2
J	2
J	2
A	2
S	2
O	2
N	2
D	2

PTARMIGAN

Type	partridge-like
Size	33–36cm (13–14in)
Habitat	moors
Behaviour	walks, perches openly, takes off and lands on ground
Flocking	1–15
Flight	glides; strong and powerful; direct
Voice	cackling *aar-aar-ka-ka-ka*

IDENTIFICATION

Ad.♂summer	
Crown	grey-brown
Upperparts	grey-brown, barred black; white wingtips
Rump	grey-brown
Tail	black; short and rounded
Throat	grey-brown
Breast	grey-brown, barred black
Belly	white
Bill	black; short and stubby
Legs	white; short
Ad.♀summer	mottled brown and buff; underparts less white than ♂
Ad.winter	all white; ♂ dark area between bill and eye

BREEDING

Nest	bare hollow on ground
Eggs	5–10; white, blotched dark brown
Incubation	24–26 days ♀
Young	active; downy
Fledging	10 days
Broods	1; May–June
Food	shoots, berries
Population	less than 10,000 pairs

Black Grouse *Tetrao tetrix*

red comb

dark, barred breast

white in wing

adult ♀

adult ♂

white undertail

lyre-shaped tail

notched tail

BLACK GROUSE

Type	partridge-like
Size	♂ 51–56cm (20–22in); ♀ 40–44cm (15–17in)
Habitat	moors, fields and hedgerows, forests
Behaviour	walks, takes off and lands on ground
Flocking	1–15
Flight	glides; strong and powerful; direct
Voice	*roo-koo* repeated at lek; a sneezed *chew-oosh*

IDENTIFICATION

Adult ♂	
Crown	black
Upperparts	black, white wingbar
Rump	black
Tail	black, undertail white; long and forked
Throat	black
Breast	black
Belly	black and white
Bill	black; short and stubby
Legs	black; short
Adult ♀	mottled brown and black above, black and buff below; notched tail
Juvenile	like small, dull ♀

BREEDING

Nest	hollow on ground
Eggs	6–10; buffy, spotted brown
Incubation	23–26 days ♀
Young	active; downy
Fledging	4 weeks
Broods	1; May–June
Food	shoots, berries
Population	10,000–50,000 pairs

Large grouse of woodland margins and birch scrub, best seen at communal lekking grounds in early morning or evening. Generally gregarious, forming small flocks and family groups. Sexes quite distinct. Male (Blackcock) predominantly black, with longish lyre-shaped tail, erected in display to show bold white undertail. Large red comb above eye, bold white wingbar in flight. Female (Greyhen) heavily barred brown and black above, black and buff below. Longish tail shows distinct notch in flight.
Status: resident of moorlands in northern and western Britain; absent Ireland.
Similar Species: Capercaillie (p.101) is larger, has white bill and tail is a different shape.

J	3
F	3
M	3
A	3
M	3
J	3
J	3
A	3
S	3
O	3
N	3
D	3

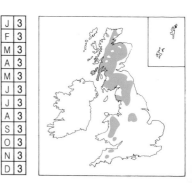

Tetrao urogallus **Capercaillie**

Largest of the grouse; huge male reminiscent of Turkey. Native birds shot out of existence in eighteenth century but successfully re-introduced in nineteenth. Male black with brown back and wings; long tail spread and raised to form fan in display. Large head with ragged 'beard'; red wattle above eye; fearsome white bill. Highly aggressive, will even attack human intruders. Female smaller and camouflaged in barred shades of brown with distinctive orange breast. Confined to conifer forests.
Status: resident in Scottish Highland forests; unknown elsewhere.
Similar Species: smaller Black Grouse (p.100) has lyre-shaped tail in male; female lacks orange breast.

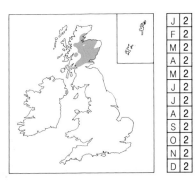

J	2
F	2
M	2
A	2
M	2
J	2
J	2
A	2
S	2
O	2
N	2
D	2

CAPERCAILLIE

Type	partridge-like
Size	♂ 82–90cm (32–35in); ♀ 58–64cm (22–25in)
Habitat	forests and woods
Behaviour	walks, perches openly, takes off and lands on vegetation and ground
Flocking	1–10
Flight	glides; strong and powerful; direct
Voice	crowing *ko-ko-kok*; series of clicks ending in pop

IDENTIFICATION

Adult ♂	
Crown	black
Upperparts	brown
Rump	black
Tail	black; long and rounded
Throat	black
Breast	black
Belly	black; spotted white
Bill	white; short and stubby
Legs	grey; medium length
Adult ♀	smaller; buff and brown with orange breast

BREEDING

Nest	lined depression on ground
Eggs	5–8; buff, blotched reddish
Incubation	26–29 days ♀
Young	active; downy
Fledging	2–3 weeks
Broods	1; Apr–June
Food	shoots, berries, conifer needles
Population	1000–10,000 pairs

Red-legged Partridge *Alectoris rufa*

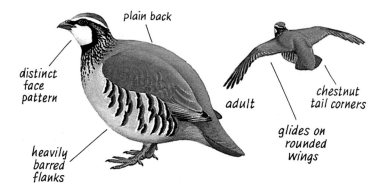

plain back

distinct face pattern

heavily barred flanks

adult

chestnut tail corners

glides on rounded wings

RED-LEGGED PARTRIDGE

Type	partridge-like
Size	33–36cm (13–14in)
Habitat	heaths, fields
Behaviour	walks, runs, perches openly, takes off and lands on ground
Flocking	1–15
Flight	glides; strong and powerful; direct
Voice	loud *chuk-chuk-chukar-chukar*

IDENTIFICATION

Adult	
Crown	buff
Upperparts	buff
Rump	buff
Tail	buff; short and rounded
Throat	black and white
Breast	grey
Belly	orange
Bill	red; short and stubby
Legs	red; medium length

BREEDING

Nest	hollow on ground
Eggs	10–16; yellowish, spotted reddish
Incubation	23–25 days; often 2 nests, one incubated ♂, one incubated ♀
Young	active; downy
Fledging	10 + days
Broods	1 or 2; Apr–May
Food	seeds, leaves, insects
Population	100,000–200,000 pairs

Rotund, stocky bird successfully introduced from the Continent. Distinctive facial pattern consists of black eye stripe extending across ear coverts and neck to join broad, speckled breast band and enclose creamy chin and throat. Blue flanks barred black and chestnut. Gregarious, found in small flocks in open fields; also in overgrown areas with scattered vegetation. Flies low over ground and glides on bowed wings. In recent years, closely related Chukar introduced; hybrids may be found in some areas. *Status:* resident mainly in south and east Britain; absent Ireland. *Similar Species:* Grey Partridge (p.103) is similar shape but Red-legged is more boldly marked. Chukar has 'clean-cut' (not spotted) black breast band and fewer, broader bars on flanks.

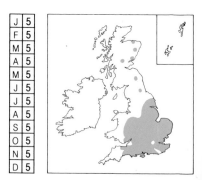

J	5
F	5
M	5
A	5
M	5
J	5
J	5
A	5
S	5
O	5
N	5
D	5

streaked back

chestnut
tail corners

grey
breast

chestnut
horseshoe

♂

Stocky gamebird of open fields that prefers to run when threatened. When pressed, flies low over ground on bowed wings. Generally gregarious, occurring in small flocks (coveys). Pale, washed-out coloration makes it appear buffy at any distance. A closer approach reveals pale orange face, grey breast, brown bars on flanks and bold chestnut horseshoe on belly – reduced to chestnut smudge in female.
Status: declining resident of agricultural land throughout Britain and Ireland.
Similar Species: Red-legged Partridge (p.102).

GREY PARTRIDGE

Type	partridge-like
Size	29–32cm (11–13in)
Habitat	heaths, fields
Behaviour	walks, runs, takes off and lands on ground
Flocking	1–15
Flight	glides; strong and powerful; direct
Voice	decelerating *krikrikri-kri-krikri*; also rusty hinge sound, *kirr-ik*

IDENTIFICATION

Adult	
Crown	buff
Upperparts	brown and black, streaked
Rump	buff
Tail	buff; short and rounded
Throat	orange
Breast	grey
Belly	buff; ♂ chestnut horseshoe, ♀ chestnut smudge
Bill	grey; short and stubby
Legs	grey; medium length

BREEDING

Nest	hollow on ground
Eggs	9–20; buff
Incubation	23–25 days ♀
Young	active; downy
Fledging	16 days
Broods	1; Apr–May
Food	seeds, leaves, insects
Population	less than 500,000 pairs

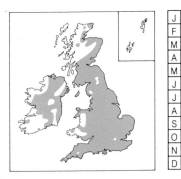

J	5
F	5
M	5
A	5
M	5
J	5
J	5
A	5
S	5
O	5
N	5
D	5

Golden Pheasant *Chrysolophus pictus*

yellow crown

♀

brown legs

red underparts

♂

GOLDEN PHEASANT

Type	partridge-like
Size	♂ 89–109cm (35–43in); ♀ 61–71cm (24–28in)
Habitat	forests and woods
Behaviour	walks, runs, takes off and lands vegetation or ground
Flocking	1–15
Flight	laboured
Voice	harsh *chak*

IDENTIFICATION

Adult ♂	
Crown	yellow
Upperparts	yellow
Rump	red
Tail	brown and black; long and pointed
Throat	yellow
Breast	red
Belly	red
Bill	yellow; short and stubby
Legs	yellow; medium length
Adult ♀	rusty and black above; heavily barred buff below; long pointed tail

BREEDING

Nest	hollow on ground
Eggs	5–12; buffy
Incubation	22 days
Young	active; downy
Fledging	12–14 days
Broods	1; Apr–May
Food	shoots, berries, seeds
Population	1000–2000 individuals

Exotic pheasant introduced from South East Asia since end of nineteenth century; present breeding population from birds escaped from captivity. Male highly colourful and unmistakable with bright red underparts, golden crown and rump and long tail. Female much more subdued; mainly shades of rust and buff, heavily barred. Secretive and difficult to locate among dense stands of rhododendrons and conifers. Hybridizes with Lady Amherst's.
Status: still scarce; headquarters in Breckland and Galloway.
Similar Species: female similar to female Common Pheasant (p.106) but more rufous above. Female also easily confused with female Lady Amherst's Pheasant (p.105) but has brownish, rather than blue, legs.

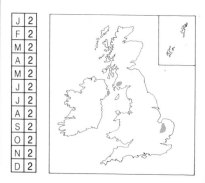

J	2
F	2
M	2
A	2
M	2
J	2
J	2
A	2
S	2
O	2
N	2
D	2

Lady Amherst's Pheasant

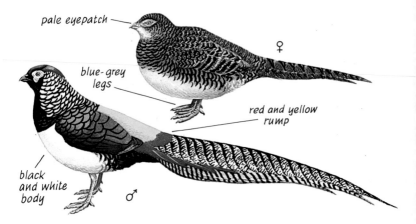

pale eyepatch

♀

blue-grey legs

red and yellow rump

black and white body

♂

Introduced in twentieth century from South East Asia. Male magnificent in black and white with orange rump, red uppertail coverts and extremely long black and white marbled tail. Female barred black and chestnut. Secretive; confined to conifer woods with dense undergrowth and rhododendron scrub. *Status:* confined to area around Woburn where introduced. *Similar Species:* female very similar to female Golden Pheasant (p.104) but has bluish legs and darker, more chestnut, breast.

LADY AMHERST'S PHEASANT

Type	partridge-like
Size	♂ 115–150cm (45–59in); ♀ 58–68cm (23–27in)
Habitat	forests and woods
Behaviour	walks, runs, takes off and lands on vegetation or ground
Flocking	1–15
Flight	laboured
Voice	*su-ik-ik-ik*

IDENTIFICATION

Adult ♂	
Crown	black, with black and white nape
Upperparts	green
Rump	red and yellow
Tail	black and white; very long and pointed
Throat	black
Breast	black
Belly	white
Bill	grey; short and stubby
Legs	bluish, medium length
Adult ♀	rusty and black above, heavily barred buff below; long pointed tail

BREEDING

Nest	hollow on ground
Eggs	6–12; buffy
Incubation	23 days ♀
Young	active; downy
Fledging	12–14 days
Broods	1; Apr–May
Food	shoots, berries, seeds
Population	200–500 individuals

J	2
F	2
M	2
A	2
M	2
J	2
J	2
A	2
S	2
O	2
N	2
D	2

Common Pheasant *Phasianus colchicus*

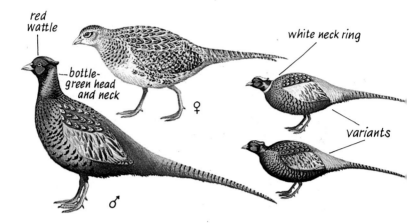

red wattle

bottle-green head and neck

white neck ring

variants

♀

♂

COMMON PHEASANT	
Type	partridge-like
Size	♂ 75–90cm (30–35in); ♀ 52–64cm (20–25in)
Habitat	heaths, forests and woods, fields and hedges
Behaviour	walks, runs, takes off and lands on vegetation or ground
Flocking	1–15
Flight	glides; strong and powerful; direct
Voice	far carrying *kok . . . kok-kok*

IDENTIFICATION

Adult ♂	
Crown	green
Upperparts	brown, spotted black; lower back grey
Rump	russet
Tail	brown, barred black; long and pointed
Throat	green
Breast	brown, spotted black
Belly	brown, spotted black
Bill	buff; short and stubby
Legs	grey; medium length
Adult ♀	mottled buff and brown, speckled black; long, pointed, buff and black tail

BREEDING

Nest	hollow on ground
Eggs	7–15; plain olive-brown
Incubation	23–27 days ♀
Young	active; downy
Fledging	12–14 days
Broods	1; Apr–June
Food	shoots, seeds, berries
Population	8,000,000 individuals

Widespread, ground-dwelling gamebird of woods, hedgerows and fields. Plumage of male highly variable due to introduction of sub-species from different parts of natural range. Female buffy; heavily speckled black above and on flanks. Generally found in small groups. When disturbed, often runs or flies to cover; takes off powerfully and then glides on bowed wings, often quite low. Seldom makes prolonged flights. Among vegetation, often crouches and is difficult to find. *Status:* widespread resident (except north-western Scotland); locally abundant when reared. *Similar Species:* Golden Pheasant (p.104) and Lady Amherst's Pheasant (p.105). Males of these species are quite distinct; females smaller and more russet.

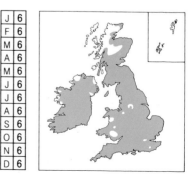

J	6
F	6
M	6
A	6
M	6
J	6
J	6
A	6
S	6
O	6
N	6
D	6

long red
bill

plain
grey

white
undertail

pinkish legs

trailing legs

barred flanks

Highly secretive, marsh-dwelling bird, similar to Moorhen but with long, red bill. More frequently heard than seen; calls sound more like a squealing pig than a bird. Laterally compressed for easy passage through dense vegetation, especially reeds. In winter, may emerge on open ground, though seldom far from water and cover. Upperparts dark brown, heavily streaked black; sides of head, throat and breast metallic grey. Flanks and belly barred black and white. Long legs and toes and short, rounded wings. Short, cocked tail frequently flicked showing white undertail coverts. *Status:* widespread resident but not common; Continental birds are winter visitors.
Similar Species: only rail with long bill.

WATER RAIL

Type	rail-like
Size	27–29cm (10–11in)
Habitat	freshwater marshes
Behaviour	wades, takes off and lands on water or ground
Flocking	1–2
Flight	laboured; legs trailing
Voice	repeated *kip-kip-kip*; variety of shrill squeals and harsh grunts

IDENTIFICATION

Adult	
Crown	brown and black
Upperparts	brown, streaked black
Rump	brown and black
Tail	brown and black, undertail white; short and pointed
Throat	grey
Breast	grey
Belly	black and white, barred
Bill	red; very long and thin
Legs	pinkish or greenish; long

BREEDING

Nest	cup of reeds hidden above water
Eggs	6–10; creamy, spotted reddish
Incubation	19–20 days, mainly ♀
Young	active; downy
Fledging	7–8 weeks
Broods	2; Apr–June
Food	amphibians, vegetation, invertebrates
Population	2000–4000 pairs

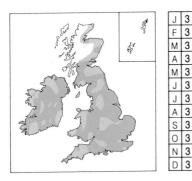

J	3
F	3
M	3
A	3
M	3
J	3
J	3
A	3
S	3
O	3
N	3
D	3

Spotted Crake *Porzana porzana*

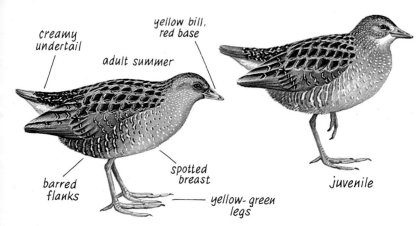

creamy undertail

yellow bill, red base

adult summer

barred flanks

spotted breast

yellow-green legs

juvenile

SPOTTED CRAKE

Type	rail-like
Size	22–24cm (9–10in)
Habitat	freshwater marshes
Behaviour	wades, takes off from water or ground
Flocking	solitary
Flight	laboured
Voice	far-carrying *quip-quip-quip*, repeated for long periods

IDENTIFICATION

Adult	
Crown	brown
Upperparts	brown, streaked black
Rump	brown
Tail	brown, undertail creamy buff; short and pointed
Throat	grey
Breast	grey; white spots on sides
Belly	grey
Bill	yellow, red base; short and thin
Legs	yellow-green; long

BREEDING

Nest	cup of grasses over water
Eggs	8–12; buffy, blotched red
Incubation	18–21 days ♂ ♀
Young	active; downy
Fledging	25 + days
Broods	2; May–July
Food	invertebrates, vegetation
Population	0–14 pairs

Decidedly rare, skulking and highly elusive bird. Spends most of its time hidden among dense marshland vegetation; usually noted only when it calls late on warm, summer evenings. Call often likened to drip-drip-drip of tap into half-empty barrel. Upperparts brown, heavily streaked black; face grey with dark mark through lores. Underparts grey. Resembles small, short-billed Water Rail but has prominent white spots on sides of breast and pattern of brown, black and white bars on flanks less clear-cut and zebra-like than Water Rail. Undertail coverts are creamy, not white.
Status: summer visitor from April–October; probably breeds in tiny numbers every year. Scarce migrant.
Similar Species: Corn Crake (p.109) and much smaller, rarer, crakes.

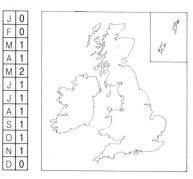

J	0
F	0
M	1
A	1
M	2
J	1
J	1
A	1
S	1
O	1
N	1
D	0

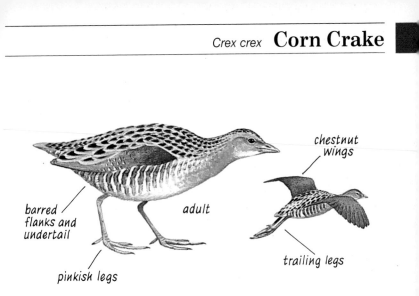

chestnut
wings

barred
flanks and
undertail

adult

trailing legs

pinkish legs

Secretive summer visitor to hay and cereal fields. More often heard than seen, uttering harsh, rasping call; in some areas walks openly and even perches to call. When flushed, bold, chestnut wings and trailing legs diagnostic. Upperparts have black feather-centres edged with buffy brown, producing 'scalloped' effect. In summer, male has pale grey face and upper breast; less grey in winter. Underparts buff, barred chestnut, including undertail coverts; latter often obvious as bird walks away. *Status:* summer visitor April–September. Once widespread, now decidedly scarce; still relatively numerous in Ireland and Hebrides. *Similar Species:* short-billed rails, especially Spotted Crake (p.108) and rare Little and Baillon's Crake.

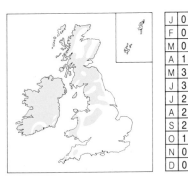

J	0
F	0
M	0
A	1
M	3
J	3
J	2
A	2
S	2
O	1
N	0
D	0

CORN CRAKE

Type	rail-like
Size	25–28cm (10–11in)
Habitat	fields and hedgerows
Behaviour	walks, takes off and lands on ground
Flocking	solitary
Flight	laboured; legs trailing
Voice	grating *crek-crek*, repeated

IDENTIFICATION

Ad.♂ summer	
Crown	black and brown
Upperparts	black, brown feather margins; wings chestnut
Rump	buff and black
Tail	buff and black, undertail buff, barred chestnut; short and pointed
Throat	white
Breast	grey
Belly	buff, barred chestnut
Bill	yellow; short and pointed
Legs	pink; long
Ad.♂ winter	less grey on breast (like ♀ and juvenile)

BREEDING

Nest	platform hidden on ground
Eggs	8–12; greenish, blotched brown
Incubation	15–18 days ♀
Young	active; downy
Fledging	5 weeks
Broods	1; May–June
Food	invertebrates, plants
Population	less than 100 pairs

Moorhen *Gallinula chloropus*

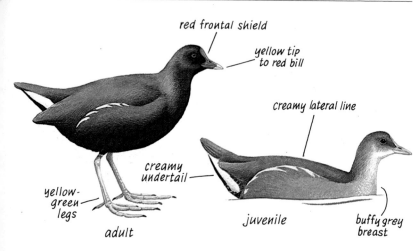

red frontal shield

yellow tip to red bill

creamy lateral line

creamy undertail

yellow-green legs

adult

juvenile

buffy grey breast

MOORHEN	
Type	rail-like
Size	31–35cm (12–14in)
Habitat	freshwater, fields and hedges
Behaviour	swims, wades, walks, takes off and lands on water or ground
Flocking	1–15
Flight	laboured; legs trailing
Voice	loud *currick*; high-pitched *kik-kik-kik-kik*

IDENTIFICATION

Adult	
Crown	dark grey
Upperparts	dark brown, white lateral line
Rump	brown
Tail	brown, undertail black and white; short and pointed
Throat	dark grey
Breast	dark grey
Belly	dark grey
Bill	red, tip yellow; short and pointed
Legs	yellow-green; long
Juvenile	brown, whitish throat and foreneck; lateral line creamy; bill dull green

BREEDING

Nest	cup near ground
Eggs	5–11; buff, spotted
Incubation	19–22 days ♂ ♀
Young	active; downy
Fledging	6–7 weeks
Broods	2–3; Mar–Aug
Food	aquatic insects, molluscs, seeds, plants
Population	300,000 pairs

Common bird of ponds, rivers, canals and marshes; most often seen walking waterside banks with jerking, chicken-like movements of head. On land, long legs and toes obvious, as is white, cocked tail. In adult, white lateral line separates dark grey underparts from dark brown wings. Juvenile brown with whitish chin and foreneck; lateral line creamy; bill and legs dullish green. Swims well but flies laboriously with legs trailing after lengthy pattering take-off. Dives rarely. Seldom found in flocks.

Status: widespread resident except for higher hills; winter visitors arrive from September onwards.

Similar Species: Common Coot (p.111) is all black with white frontal shield and often forms large winter flocks.

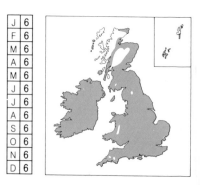

J	6
F	6
M	6
A	6
M	6
J	6
J	6
A	6
S	6
O	6
N	6
D	6

white frontal
shield and bill

adult

grey-green
legs

juvenile

whitish
foreparts

Bulky, sooty black waterbird distinguished by white bill and frontal shield. Juvenile brownish with whitish face and foreneck; lacks frontal shield. Swims buoyantly and frequently dives for food; also up-ends in shallow water. Walks well and often feeds on splashy grassland, though always adjacent to open water. Forms large winter flocks tightly packed together. Evades danger by running over water surface rather than flying. Once airborne, flies strongly on broad, rounded wings with long legs trailing behind.
Status: widespread resident; winter visitors arrive from the Continent October–April.
Similar Species: Moorhen (p.110) has red bill and white undertail.

COMMON COOT

Type	duck-like
Size	36–40cm (14–16in)
Habitat	open freshwater, estuaries
Behaviour	swims, dives, wades, walks, takes off and lands on water
Flocking	1–1000
Flight	laboured; legs trailing
Voice	explosive *kook* or *teuk*

IDENTIFICATION

Adult	
Crown	black; white frontal shield
Upperparts	black
Rump	black
Tail	black; short and pointed
Throat	black
Breast	black
Belly	black
Bill	white; short and pointed
Legs	grey-green; medium length
Juvenile	brownish with whitish foreparts; lacks frontal shield

BREEDING

Nest	bulky cup among aquatic vegetation or adjacent bush
Eggs	6–9; buff, spotted black
Incubation	21–24 days ♂ ♀
Young	active; downy
Fledging	6–8 weeks
Broods	2; mid Mar–June
Food	mostly plants but omnivorous
Population	10,000–100,000 pairs

J	6
F	6
M	6
A	6
M	6
J	6
J	6
A	6
S	6
O	6
N	6
D	6

Oystercatcher *Haematopus ostralegus*

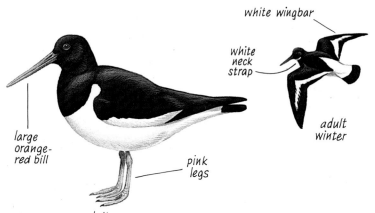

white wingbar

white neck strap

adult winter

large orange-red bill

pink legs

adult summer

OYSTERCATCHER

Type	wader-like
Size	41–45cm (16–18in)
Habitat	marshes, estuaries and shores, fields
Behaviour	wades, walks, perches openly, takes off and lands on water or ground
Flocking	1–several thousand
Flight	strong and powerful; direct
Voice	loud, penetrating *kleep*; also *kleep-a-kleep*

IDENTIFICATION

Ad.summer	
Crown	black
Upperparts	black
Rump	white 'V'
Tail	white, black band; medium length, square
Throat	black
Breast	black, forming breast band
Belly	white
Bill	orange; long and thick
Legs	pink; long
Ad.winter	brownish black upperparts; white chin bar
Juvenile	browner upperparts than Ad.winter; legs grey

BREEDING

Nest	scrape
Eggs	3; buff, blotched black
Incubation	24–27 days ♂ ♀
Young	active; downy
Fledging	34–37 days
Broods	1; mid Apr–June
Food	molluscs, worms
Population	c30,000 pairs, c300,000 winter

Large, striking black and white bird with long, thick, orange-red bill and long, pink legs. Eyes red with bright orange-red eye ring. In winter, adult has brownish wash over black upperparts and white half collar. Juvenile as adult winter but browner above with only rudimentary half collar. Typically a bird of rocky and sandy shores; often gathers in large flocks on favoured estuaries. Highly vocal with loud piping calls; flies strongly, often low along shoreline. Frequently feeds on wet grasslands and freshwater marshes near sea; also along banks of shingle rivers.
Status: widespread coastal resident; winter visitors arrive August–April. Some British breeders migrate to France and Spain.
Similar Species: none.

J	6
F	6
M	6
A	6
M	6
J	6
J	6
A	6
S	6
O	6
N	6
D	6

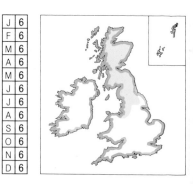

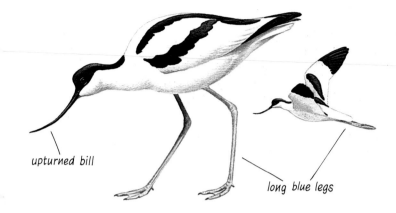

upturned bill

long blue legs

Large, elegant, black and white wader with long legs and distinctly upcurved bill. At rest, black areas form a white-filled oval pattern on wings. Scarce, seen mostly on coasts and marshes, mainly in south and east England. Feeds head-down with regular side-to-side scything movements of head and bill. Generally occurs in small groups; sometimes in much larger winter flocks. Often rather noisy.
Status: two regular breeding colonies in Suffolk, plus irregular breeding in other parts of East Anglia. Winters in Tamar Estuary, Devon. Elsewhere scarce passage migrant along south and east coasts in spring and autumn.
Similar Species: Oystercatcher (p.112) has more black plus straight orange-red bill.

AVOCET

Type	wader-like
Size	41–45cm (16–18in)
Habitat	freshwater marshes, estuaries
Behaviour	wades, takes off and lands on water or ground
Flocking	1–100
Flight	strong and powerful; direct; legs trailing
Voice	loud *kloo-eet*

IDENTIFICATION

Adult	
Crown	black
Upperparts	black and white stripes
Rump	white
Tail	white; medium length, square
Throat	white
Breast	white
Belly	white
Bill	black; long, thin and upturned
Legs	blue-grey; very long
Juvenile	dark brown where adult black

BREEDING

Nest	bare scrape on ground, often on low island
Eggs	4; buff, spotted and blotched black
Incubation	22–24 days ♂ ♀
Young	active; downy
Fledging	6 weeks
Broods	1; Apr–May
Food	insects, crustaceans
Population	450 pairs

J	1
F	1
M	2
A	2
M	3
J	3
J	2
A	2
S	2
O	2
N	1
D	1

Stone-curlew *Burhinus oedicnemus*

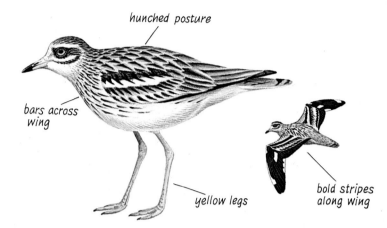

hunched posture

bars across wing

yellow legs

bold stripes along wing

STONE-CURLEW

Type	wader-like
Size	38–43cm (15–17in)
Habitat	heaths, fields
Behaviour	walks, runs, takes off and lands on ground
Flocking	1–2
Flight	strong and powerful; direct
Voice	rippling *coorree*, similar to tin whistle

IDENTIFICATION

Adult

Crown	buff
Upperparts	buff, streaked black; black and white bars across wings
Rump	buff
Tail	buff, black tip; medium length, rounded
Throat	white
Breast	buff, streaked brown
Belly	white
Bill	yellow with black tip; short and pointed
Legs	yellow; long
Juvenile	paler with less marked wingbars

BREEDING

Nest	bare scrape
Eggs	2; creamy, speckled and blotched brown
Incubation	25–27 days ♂ ♀
Young	active; downy
Fledging	6 weeks
Broods	1 occasionally 2; Apr–May
Food	insects, worms
Population	140–150 pairs

Large, plover-like summer visitor to stony or other sparsely vegetated ground, mainly in south-eastern England. Most active at dawn and dusk. When disturbed, prefers to run rather than fly. Buffy brown streaked with black above and on breast; wings have bold horizontal white bar with black border. Complex face pattern of brown and white stripes. Long, yellow legs and penetrating yellow eye. Difficult to pick out at any distance due to cryptic camouflage and hunched attitude; also stands stock-still to merge with background. In flight, shows bold pattern of black and white on long, pointed wings.
Status: scarce summer visitor March–October; winters southern Europe and Africa.
Similar Species: none.

J	0
F	0
M	1
A	2
M	2
J	2
J	2
A	2
S	1
O	1
N	0
D	0

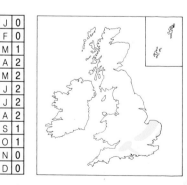

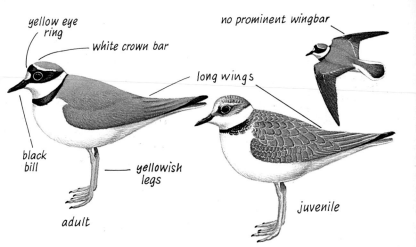

Charadrius dubius **Little Ringed Plover**

yellow eye ring

white crown bar

no prominent wingbar

long wings

black bill

yellowish legs

adult

juvenile

Scarce summer visitor to inland freshwaters (especially gravel pits) of southern and central England. Smaller, slimmer version of Ringed Plover with similar round-headed appearance, short bill and typical 'run-stop' plover behaviour. Adult has white forehead with black band across crown bordered by narrow white line; yellow eye ring. In flight, lacks wingbar; shows white outer tail feathers. Juvenile similar but with darker brown (not black) head markings; breast band often incomplete. *Status:* scarce summer visitor and passage migrant March–October. *Similar Species:* Ringed Plover (p.116) has orange-yellow, not black, bill and shows wingbar in flight. Kentish Plover (p.117) is always paler sandy brown above.

LITTLE RINGED PLOVER

Type	wader-like
Size	14–16cm (5–6in)
Habitat	freshwater
Behaviour	wades, runs, takes off and lands on ground
Flocking	1–2
Flight	strong and powerful; direct
Voice	short, down-slurred *piu*

IDENTIFICATION

Adult	
Crown	white, black and brown
Upperparts	brown
Rump	brown
Tail	black and white; short and square
Throat	white
Breast	white with black band
Belly	white
Bill	black; short and pointed
Legs	dull pink or yellow; medium length
Juvenile	brownish above; head and breast bands brownish, incomplete

BREEDING

Nest	bare scrape on ground
Eggs	4; buffish, spotted and streaked brown
Incubation	24–26 days ♂ ♀
Young	active; downy
Fledging	21–24 days
Broods	1 or 2; Mar–June
Food	insects, molluscs
Population	400–500 pairs

Month	Value
J	0
F	0
M	0
A	3
M	3
J	3
J	2
A	3
S	3
O	2
N	0
D	0

Ringed Plover *Charadrius hiaticula*

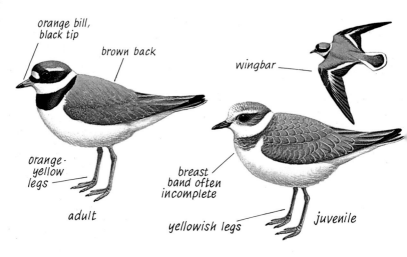

orange bill, black tip

brown back

wingbar

orange-yellow legs

adult

breast band often incomplete

yellowish legs

juvenile

RINGED PLOVER

Type	wader-like
Size	18–20cm (7in)
Habitat	freshwater marshes, estuaries and shores
Behaviour	wades, runs, takes off and lands on water and ground
Flocking	1–100
Flight	strong and powerful; direct
Voice	melodic *tu-lee*

IDENTIFICATION

Adult	
Crown	black and brown
Upperparts	brown
Rump	brown
Tail	black and white; short and square
Throat	white
Breast	white with black band
Belly	white
Bill	orange; short and pointed
Legs	orange-yellow; medium length
Juvenile	brown head with creamy forehead and eyebrow; incomplete breast band; bill black; legs yellowish

BREEDING

Nest	bare scrape on ground
Eggs	4; buff, spotted brown
Incubation	23–26 days ♂ ♀
Young	active; downy
Fledging	25 days
Broods	2 sometimes 3; May–July
Food	invertebrates
Population	9000 pairs; 350,000 winter; more on passage

Typical small 'banded' plover. Rotund shape with rounded head and short, stubby bill. Pattern of black and white on head and breast distinguish from all but two related species – see below. Orange bill and legs in adult; broad white wingbar in flight. Juvenile has brown head with creamy forehead and eyebrow (lacking in Little Ringed Plover) and smudgy, incomplete breast band. Bill black; legs yellowish. Runs fast and stands stock-still like other plovers. Often forms loose flocks and may gather in large numbers at suitable feeding grounds.
Status: resident breeder, passage migrant and winter visitor to coasts and estuaries. Also occurs and breeds inland but never commonly.
Similar Species: Little Ringed Plover (p.115) and Kentish Plover (p.117).

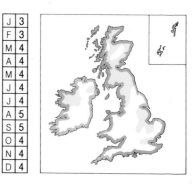

J	3
F	3
M	4
A	4
M	4
J	4
J	4
A	5
S	5
O	4
N	4
D	4

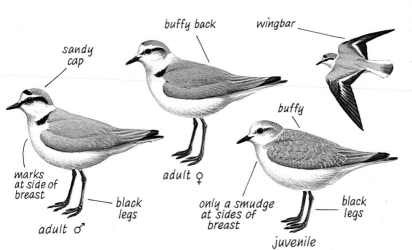

sandy cap

buffy back

wingbar

marks at side of breast

black legs

adult ♂

adult ♀

buffy

only a smudge at sides of breast

black legs

juvenile

Rare migrant along southern and eastern coasts of Britain. Smaller than Ringed Plover with incomplete breast band; bill and legs black. In summer, male has black breast patches and head markings; crown sandy. Winter male, female and juvenile have buffy brown breast patches and head markings; juvenile has only faintest smudge either side of breast. In flight, shows narrow white wingbar and white sides to rump and tail.

Status: rare migrant in spring, and particularly early autumn, to southern and eastern coasts. Formerly bred in Kent; has bred at least once in recent years.

Similar Species: Ringed Plover (p.116) and Little Ringed Plover (p.115) have darker upperparts and complete breast band.

KENTISH PLOVER

Type	wader-like
Size	15–17cm (6–6½in)
Habitat	freshwater marshes, estuaries and shores
Behaviour	wades, runs, takes off and lands on ground
Flocking	1–2
Flight	strong and powerful; direct
Voice	quiet *wit-wit-wit*; melodic *choo-wit*

IDENTIFICATION

Ad.♂summer	
Crown	sandy and black
Upperparts	buff
Rump	buff
Tail	white; short and square
Throat	white
Breast	white; incomplete black band
Belly	white
Bill	black, short and pointed
Legs	black; medium length
Ad.♀summer ♂ winter	crown, head markings and incomplete breast band buffy brown
Juvenile	paler; scaled upperparts; faint buff smudge at sides of breast

BREEDING

Nest	bare scrape on ground
Eggs	3; buff, spotted black
Incubation	24 days ♂ ♀
Young	active; downy
Fledging	25 days
Broods	2; Apr–June
Food	insects
Population	irregular passage migrant

J	0
F	0
M	1
A	1
M	1
J	1
J	1
A	1
S	1
O	0
N	0
D	0

Dotterel *Charadrius morinellus*

eyebrows meet at nape

no wingbar

cleaner cut breast pattern

breast band

adult ♂

adult ♀

DOTTEREL

Type	wader-like
Size	20–23cm (8–9in)
Habitat	moors, fields
Behaviour	runs, takes off and lands on ground
Flocking	1–15
Flight	strong and powerful; direct
Voice	quiet *peep-peep* in flight; *titi-ri-titti-ri* repeated

IDENTIFICATION

Ad.summer	
Crown	black
Upperparts	grey; wings brown and black
Rump	buff and brown
Tail	buff and brown; short and rounded
Throat	white
Breast	grey, white band
Belly	chestnut
Bill	black; short and thin
Legs	yellow; medium length
Ad.winter and juvenile	grey above and below, good white eyebrow, indistinct breast band

BREEDING

Nest	hollow on ground
Eggs	3; buffy, spotted blackish brown
Incubation	21–26 days ♂
Young	active; downy
Fledging	4 weeks
Broods	1; May–June
Food	insects
Population	60–100 pairs; very scarce migrant

Small, rotund plover; easily overlooked on stony mountain-top habitat where well camouflaged among lichens and mosses. Summer adults have distinctive grey breast and chestnut underparts separated by white band. Prominent white eyebrows meet on nape. In winter and juvenile plumages, becomes greyish; marked only by white eyebrow and indistinct breast band. Plain wings and no distinctive tail pattern in flight. Runs and stops in typical plover manner.
Status: rare summer visitor; breeds on high stony ground on a few Scottish and Lakeland mountain-tops. Otherwise scarce passage migrant occurring most regularly in East Anglia in May.
Similar Species: none.

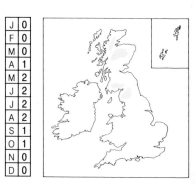

J	0
F	0
M	0
A	1
M	2
J	2
J	2
A	2
S	1
O	1
N	0
D	0

Pluvialis apricaria # European Golden Plover

adult northern summer

more black on face

narrow wingbar

adult winter

black belly

little streaking on buffy breast

adult southern summer

adult winter

Medium-sized plover with typically rotund body, round head, short bill and long legs. Upperparts spangled black and gold. In winter, underparts whitish with buffy breast markings. In summer, southern sub-species has black belly extending to central breast stripe and grey face. Northern sub-species has more black on belly and breast with black face. In flight, shows faint wingbar and plain barred tail pattern. Found among hills in summer and in substantial flocks on marshes and grassland in winter.
Status: widespread and numerous winter visitor; breeds in most mountain districts.
Similar Species: similarly shaped Grey Plover (p.120) frequents estuaries and shores, and is spangled grey and black above; shows black 'arm pits' in flight.

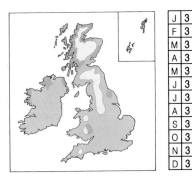

J	3
F	3
M	3
A	3
M	3
J	3
J	3
A	3
S	3
O	3
N	3
D	3

EUROPEAN GOLDEN PLOVER

Type	wader-like
Size	27–29cm (10–11in)
Habitat	moors, heaths, fields, marshes
Behaviour	walks, runs, takes off and lands on ground
Flocking	1–1000
Flight	strong and powerful; direct
Voice	whistled *tlui*

IDENTIFICATION

Ad.summer	
Crown	black and gold
Upperparts	spangled black and gold
Rump	black and gold
Tail	black and gold; short and square
Throat	black
Breast	black, white margins
Belly	black, white margins
Bill	black; short and thin
Legs	grey; long
Ad.winter	lacks black face and underparts; buffy breast markings

BREEDING

Nest	scrape on ground
Eggs	4; buff, blotched brown
Incubation	27–28 days, mainly ♀
Young	active; downy
Fledging	4 weeks
Broods	1; Apr–June
Food	worms, insects
Population	30,000 pairs; 700,000 winter

Grey Plover *Pluvialis squatarola*

black and pale grey

black face and belly

adult summer

winter

black 'armpits'

little streaking on white breast

winter

GREY PLOVER

Type	wader-like
Size	28–31cm (11–12in)
Habitat	estuaries, shores
Behaviour	wades, walks, takes off and lands on water or ground
Flocking	1–1000
Flight	strong and powerful; direct
Voice	plaintive whistled *tlee-oo-ee*

IDENTIFICATION

Ad.summer

Crown	grey and black
Upperparts	spangled grey and black
Rump	white
Tail	black and white; short and square
Throat	black
Breast	black, white margins
Belly	black
Bill	black; short and thin
Legs	black; long
Ad.winter	grey above, white below

BREEDING

Nest	hollow on ground
Eggs	4; buff, spotted
Incubation	23 days ♂ ♀
Young	active; downy
Fledging	?
Broods	1; June–July
Food	invertebrates, worms
Population	20,000 winter

Similar to European Golden Plover, but larger and confined to coasts, estuaries and adjacent marshes. Upperparts spangled grey and black. In winter, underparts white with grey speckling on breast. In summer, belly, breast and face black, with white margins on sides of breast and head. In flight, shows wingbar, white rump and black axillaries (arm pits). Legs longer than European Golden Plover and extend just beyond tip of tail in flight. Found in large flocks on favoured estuaries and shorelines. *Status:* common winter visitor and passage migrant to all coasts. *Similar Species:* European Golden Plover (p.119).

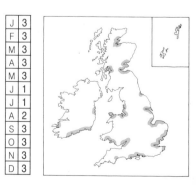

J	3
F	3
M	3
A	3
M	3
J	1
J	1
A	2
S	3
O	3
N	3
D	3

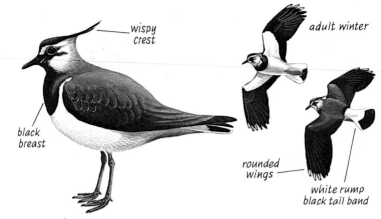

wispy crest

adult winter

black breast

rounded wings

white rump
black tail band

adult summer

Common throughout Britain and Ireland. Looks black and white at any distance; distinctive crest. Close approach reveals upperparts have glossy green and purple sheen. Head white with intricate pattern of black markings; throat black, widening into black breast band. In winter, throat and upper breast become white. Gregarious outside breeding season. *Status:* widespread and numerous breeding bird; huge winter influx from the Continent.
Similar Species: none.

LAPWING

Type	wader-like
Size	29–32cm (11–12in)
Habitat	freshwater marshes, moors, estuaries, fields
Behaviour	wades, walks, takes off and lands on ground
Flocking	1–1000
Flight	laboured; direct; aerial dive
Voice	plaintive *pee-wit*

IDENTIFICATION

Adult

Crown	black and white; wispy crest
Upperparts	green-black
Rump	white
Tail	black and white, undertail pale brown; short and square
Throat	black and white
Breast	black
Belly	white
Bill	black; short and thin
Legs	dark red; long

BREEDING

Nest	hollow on ground
Eggs	4; buff, blotched black
Incubation	24–29 days, mainly ♀
Young	active; downy
Fledging	33 days
Broods	1; Mar–Apr
Food	invertebrates
Population	200,000 pairs; 1,000,000+ winter

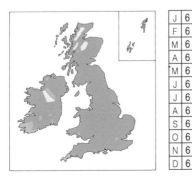

J	6
F	6
M	6
A	6
M	6
J	6
J	6
A	6
S	6
O	6
N	6
D	6

Knot *Calidris canutus*

short straight bill

eyebrow

chestnut underparts

wingbar

adult summer

adult winter

grey rump

KNOT

Type	wader-like
Size	24–27cm (9–10in)
Habitat	estuaries and shores
Behaviour	wades, takes off and lands on water or ground
Flocking	1–20,000
Flight	strong and powerful; direct
Voice	low *knut*

IDENTIFICATION

Ad.winter	
Crown	grey
Upperparts	grey
Rump	grey
Tail	grey; short and square
Throat	white
Breast	grey
Belly	white
Bill	black; straight and thin
Legs	dark green; medium length
Ad.summer	face and underparts chestnut-red; mantle spangled black and chestnut; wings grey and black

BREEDING

Nest	lined hollow
Eggs	4; pale green, spotted brown
Incubation	20–25 days ♂ ♀ ?
Young	active; downy
Fledging	20 days ?
Broods	1; June
Food	molluscs, crustaceans, worms
Population	200,000–400,000 winter

Medium-sized, stocky shorebird similar to Dunlin, but considerably larger, with shorter bill and legs. Highly gregarious at all seasons with majority concentrated at relatively few favoured estuaries. In winter, grey above with pale feather margins; underparts white with faint speckling on breast and flanks; well marked eye stripe and eyebrow. In summer, mantle spangled black and chestnut; face and underparts chestnut; wings grey and black. In flight, shows faint wingbar and distinctive white rump; tail has grey terminal band.
Status: abundant, though localized, winter visitor and regular passage migrant.
Similar Species: winter Dunlin (p.128) but Knot much larger with proportionately shorter bill.

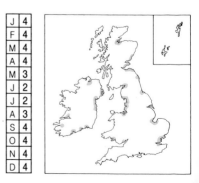

J	4
F	4
M	4
A	4
M	3
J	2
J	2
A	3
S	4
O	4
N	4
D	4

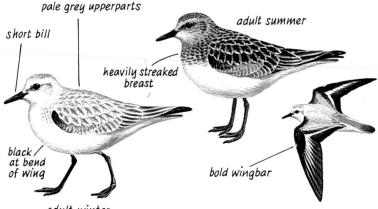

Calidris alba **Sanderling**

pale grey upperparts

short bill

adult summer

heavily streaked breast

black at bend of wing

bold wingbar

adult winter

Palest of the shorebirds with light grey upperparts and white below; prominent black mark at bend of wing. Gregarious, forms small flocks that characteristically feed in fast, running motion up and down beaches with movement of waves. In summer, head, breast and back spangled black and chestnut for brief period. Summer birds (especially juveniles) away from shoreline, may provoke thoughts of other, rarer, species or even juvenile Dunlin.

Status: widespread winter visitor and numerous passage migrant; confined to coasts and sometimes adjacent marshes.

Similar Species: no other wader runs up and down beach with the waves or is so pale in winter plumage.

	SANDERLING
Type	wader-like
Size	19–22cm (7–8½in)
Habitat	shores
Behaviour	wades, runs, takes off and lands on water or ground
Flocking	1–100
Flight	strong and powerful; direct
Voice	*quit-quit*, repeated

IDENTIFICATION

Ad.winter	
Crown	grey
Upperparts	grey; black at bend of wing
Rump	black and white
Tail	black and white; short and square
Throat	white
Breast	white
Belly	white
Bill	black; short and straight
Legs	black; medium length
Ad.summer	head, back and breast spangled black and chestnut

BREEDING

Nest	neat hollow on ground
Eggs	4; greenish, spotted brownish
Incubation	23–24 days ♂ ♀
Young	active; downy
Fledging	23–24 days
Broods	1; June–July
Food	molluscs, crustaceans
Population	12,000 winter; 30,000 May

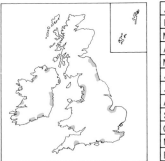

Month	
J	3
F	3
M	3
A	3
M	3
J	1
J	0
A	2
S	2
O	3
N	3
D	3

Little Stint *Calidris minuta*

short bill

rufous back

double white 'V' on back

narrow wingbar

juvenile

black legs

adult summer

a little breast streaking

adult winter

LITTLE STINT

Type	wader-like
Size	14–15cm (5½in)
Habitat	marshes, estuaries
Behaviour	wades, walks, takes off from water or ground
Flocking	1–10
Flight	strong and powerful; direct
Voice	sharp *tyit*

IDENTIFICATION

Juvenile	
Crown	brown and black
Upperparts	brown and black; two white 'V's on back
Rump	black and white
Tail	black and white; short and square
Throat	white
Breast	buff; streaked on sides
Belly	white
Bill	black; short and straight
Legs	black; short
Ad.winter	grey above, white below, lacks 'V' on back
Ad.summer	spangled chestnut and black above, buffy breast

BREEDING

Nest	neat cup on ground
Eggs	4; pale olive, speckled brownish
Incubation	? mainly ♂
Young	active; downy
Fledging	?
Broods	1; June–July
Food	molluscs, crustaceans, worms
Population	less than 30 winter; 200+ September

Small version of Dunlin with short, straight bill and non-stop feeding habits. In winter, grey above, white below. In summer, crown and upperparts warm brown with black feather centres and brown speckling at sides of breast. Juveniles (most numerous visitors) brown with black feather centres, double white 'V' on back, and buffy streaking at sides of breast. In flight, shows narrow white wingbar and black tail centre. Favours marshes but also often found on estuaries.
Status: scarce winter visitor, regular spring migrant and numerous, though variable, autumn migrant.
Similar Species: Temminck's Stint (p.125); also vagrant American 'peeps', especially Semi-palmated or Least Sandpiper.

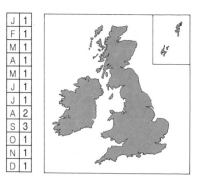

J	1
F	1
M	1
A	1
M	1
J	1
J	1
A	2
S	3
O	1
N	1
D	1

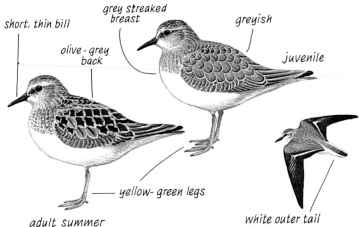

Calidris temminckii **Temminck's Stint**

short, thin bill

grey streaked breast

greyish

olive-grey back

juvenile

yellow-green legs

adult summer

white outer tail

Marginally smaller than Little Stint and much more grey and uniformly marked. Winter adult and juvenile grey above, with slightly paler feather margins. White below with grey breast. In summer, upperparts olive-grey with black streaks. Shortish legs and extended body shape, together with picking feeding action, recall Common Sandpiper rather than Dunlin or Little Stint. Prefers fresh marshes with emergent vegetation. *Status:* scarce, but regular, double passage migrant. Breeds regularly in small numbers in Scotland. *Similar Species:* Little Stint (p.124); Temminck's is more uniform and less 'contrasting' in all plumages.

TEMMINCK'S STINT

Type	wader-like
Size	13–15cm (5–5½in)
Habitat	freshwater marshes
Behaviour	wades, walks, takes off from water or ground
Flocking	1 or 2
Flight	strong and powerful; direct; flitting
Voice	high-pitched *trrrr-trrrr*

IDENTIFICATION

Ad.winter and juvenile	
Crown	grey
Upperparts	grey
Rump	black and white
Tail	black and white; short and square
Throat	white
Breast	grey
Belly	white
Bill	black; short, straight and thin
Legs	yellow green; medium length
Ad.summer	upperparts olive-grey, speckled black; breast grey, streaked

BREEDING

Nest	hollow on ground
Eggs	4; pale olive, speckled brownish
Incubation	21–22 days, mainly ♂
Young	active; downy
Fledging	15–18 days
Broods	1; June
Food	insects
Population	rare breeder; scarce passage migrant

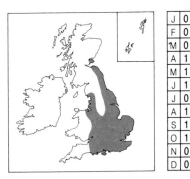

J	0
F	0
M	0
A	1
M	1
J	1
J	0
A	1
S	1
O	1
N	0
D	0

Curlew Sandpiper *Calidris ferruginea*

decurved bill

long neck, rounded head

juvenile

square white rump

longish legs

adult winter

adult summer

buffy unstreaked breast

juvenile

CURLEW SANDPIPER

Type	wader-like
Size	18–20cm (7–8in)
Habitat	freshwater marshes, estuaries and shores
Behaviour	wades, walks, takes off and lands on ground
Flocking	1–15
Flight	strong and powerful; direct
Voice	*churrip*

IDENTIFICATION

Juvenile

Crown	grey
Upperparts	grey and buff
Rump	white
Tail	white, grey tip; short and square
Throat	white
Breast	buff-white
Belly	white
Bill	black, long and decurved
Legs	black; long
Ad.winter	grey above, white below; unmarked breast
Ad.summer	chestnut head and underparts; grey wings

BREEDING

Nest	hollow on ground
Eggs	3–4; olive, blotched brown
Incubation	?; ♂ ♀
Young	active; downy
Fledging	?
Broods	1; June–July
Food	insects, molluscs, crustaceans
Population	variable; 100 to several thousand August–September; a few in spring

Double passage migrant, mostly in autumn. Shape distinctive; long legs, long neck, decurved bill. White rump diagnostic. Adults constitute first wave of autumn birds (July–August); most show some chestnut feathers on breast. Later autumn wave (August–September) mainly juveniles; grey above with buffy feather margins giving scaled appearance. Buff wash over unstreaked breast. Some late adult migrants (September–October) are grey above and unstreaked white below. In spring, chestnut head and body contrast with grey wings.
Status: regular in autumn, mostly August–September. Scarce in spring, mostly May–early June.
Similar Species: Dunlin (p.128) is slightly smaller, shorter-necked and less elegant.

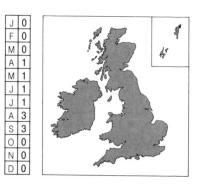

J	0
F	0
M	0
A	1
M	1
J	1
J	1
A	3
S	3
O	0
N	0
D	0

Calidris maritima **Purple Sandpiper**

orange-red base to bill

uniform grey back

spotted breast

brown feather margins

adult summer

narrow wingbar

winter

yellow legs

adult winter

The most maritime of all shorebirds, seldom found away from rocky shorelines. Stockily-built, short-legged wader with bill about same length as head; base of bill orange-red. Few distinguishing features apart from shape and general dark coloration. In winter, head and breast dark grey with white eye ring and throat. Upperparts black with dark grey feather margins. Belly white with dark spots. In summer, back and wings dark with broad, brown edges to feathers. Head, neck, breast and belly heavily streaked. Feeds busily among rocks and seaweed, often in company with Turnstones (p.143).
Status: winter visitor to most suitable coastlines (October–April). Few in summer but has bred in Scotland.
Similar Species: no waders are as dark.

PURPLE SANDPIPER

Type	wader-like
Size	20–22cm (7½–8½in)
Habitat	coasts
Behaviour	walks, wades, perches openly, takes off and lands on water or ground
Flocking	1–20
Flight	strong and powerful; direct
Voice	mostly silent; occasional *weet-weet*

IDENTIFICATION

Ad.winter	
Crown	dark grey
Upperparts	black and grey
Rump	black and white
Tail	black and white, short and rounded
Throat	white
Breast	dark grey
Belly	white, dark spots
Bill	black, orange base; straight and thin
Legs	yellow; short
Ad.summer	black and buff above; heavily streaked breast

BREEDING

Nest	leaf-lined hollow
Eggs	4; pale greenish, blotched brown
Incubation	21–22 days, mainly ♂
Young	active; downy
Fledging	3–4 weeks
Broods	1; June–July
Food	molluscs, crustaceans
Population	1 pair breeds; 25,000 winter

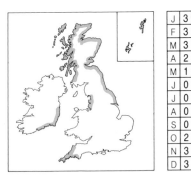

J	3
F	3
M	3
A	2
M	1
J	0
J	0
A	0
S	0
O	2
N	3
D	3

Dunlin *Calidris alpina*

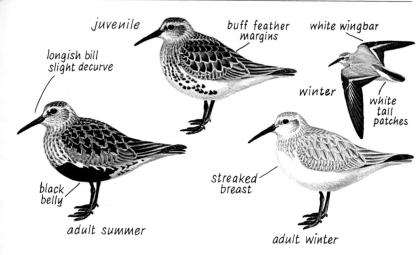

juvenile

buff feather margins

white wingbar

longish bill slight decurve

winter

white tail patches

black belly

streaked breast

adult summer

adult winter

	DUNLIN
Type	wader-like
Size	16–19cm (6–8in)
Habitat	marshes, estuaries and shores, moors
Behaviour	walks, wades, takes off from water and ground
Flocking	1–10,000
Flight	strong and powerful; direct
Voice	rasped *schreep*

IDENTIFICATION

Ad.winter	
Crown	grey
Upperparts	grey
Rump	black and white
Tail	black and white; short and square
Throat	white
Breast	white, streaked grey
Belly	white
Bill	black; long and thin, decurved at tip
Legs	black; medium length
Ad.summer	brown above; black belly patch
Juvenile	brown above, buff breast heavily streaked

BREEDING

Nest	hollow on ground
Eggs	4; greenish, blotched brown
Incubation	21–22 days ♂ ♀
Young	active; downy
Fledging	25 days
Broods	1; May–June
Food	molluscs, crustaceans
Population	4000–8000 pairs; 650,000 winter

Most widespread and abundant small wader, found in enormous flocks on estuaries and shorelines; also in small numbers on inland moors. Dumpy little bird that feeds busily and generally adopts a hunched-up attitude. In winter, upperparts grey with paler feather margins; underparts white with grey streaks on breast. In summer, chestnut and black on crown and back; breast streaked, black belly patch. In autumn many adults retain partial black belly. Juvenile brown above with narrow buff margins; buff breast heavily streaked.
Status: widespread moorland breeder. Double passage migrant and abundant winter visitor to all coasts and floods.
Similar Species: standard small wader from which all other small waders have to be distinguished.

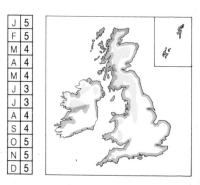

J	5
F	5
M	4
A	4
M	4
J	3
J	3
A	4
S	4
O	5
N	5
D	5

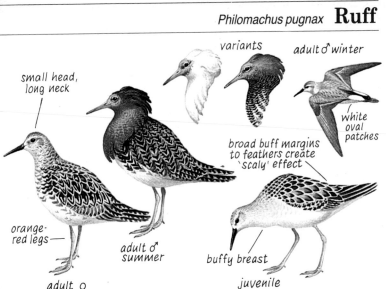

variants

adult ♂ winter

small head, long neck

white oval patches

broad buff margins to feathers create 'scaly' effect

orange-red legs

adult ♂ summer

buffy breast

adult ♀

juvenile

Rare breeder but relatively common double passage migrant and increasing winter visitor. Male (Ruff) much larger than female (Reeve). Male in summer, even on passage, boasts elaborate multi-coloured plumes on head and neck and has wattled, bare red face. Females, juveniles and males at other times have long necks, small heads, fine, medium-length, pointed bills and longish red, pink, yellow or green legs. Back always scalloped with buff margins to brown feathers.
Status: scarce breeder in East Anglia and north-west England; regular double passage migrant; scarce winter visitor.
Similar Species: Common Redshank (p.138) also has reddish legs but shape quite different. Juveniles may be confused with rare Buff-breasted Sandpiper.

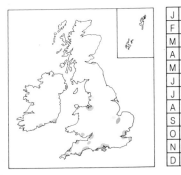

J	2
F	2
M	2
A	2
M	2
J	1
J	1
A	3
S	3
O	2
N	2
D	2

RUFF

Type	wader-like
Size	♂ 27–31cm (10–12in); ♀ 22–25cm (8–9in)
Habitat	freshwater marshes, flooded grassland
Behaviour	wades, walks, takes off from water or ground
Flocking	1–100
Flight	strong and powerful; direct
Voice	*chuck-uck*

IDENTIFICATION

Ad.♂winter and ♀	
Crown	buff
Upperparts	buff and brown, 'scalloped'
Rump	black and white
Tail	black and white; short and square
Throat	white
Breast	buff, speckled
Belly	white
Bill	black; straight and thin
Legs	pinkish red or yellowish; long
Ad.♂summer	elaborate head and neck plumes
Juvenile	uniformly buff below

BREEDING

Nest	hollow on ground
Eggs	4; olive, blotched brown
Incubation	20–21 days ♀
Young	active; downy
Fledging	?
Broods	1; Apr–May
Food	insects, invertebrates
Population	20+ Reeves; 1400 winter; several thousand passage

Jack Snipe *Lymnocryptes minimus*

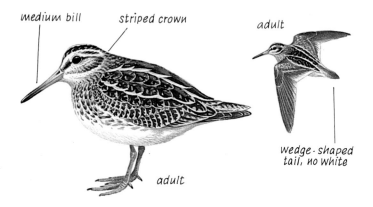

medium bill · striped crown · adult

wedge-shaped tail, no white

adult

adult

JACK SNIPE

Type	wader-like
Size	18–20cm (7–8in)
Habitat	freshwater and marshes, fields and hedges
Behaviour	wades, walks, runs, takes off and lands on water or ground
Flocking	1–2
Flight	strong and powerful; direct
Voice	usually silent

IDENTIFICATION

Adult	
Crown	white with black stripe
Upperparts	brown and black, streaked
Rump	brown and black
Tail	brown and black; short and rounded
Throat	white
Breast	buff and brown, streaked
Belly	white
Bill	brown; straight and thin
Legs	green; medium length

BREEDING

Nest	lined cup on ground
Eggs	4; green, blotched brown
Incubation	17–24 days ♀
Young	active; downy
Fledging	?
Broods	1; June–July
Food	molluscs, worms, insects
Population	winter ?

Smaller, shorter-billed version of Common Snipe but much less common and more elusive, keeping itself well hidden in cover. Frequents freshwater marshes and flooded ground. Usually seen only when flushed; flies when in danger of being trodden on. Silent take-off and brief, low, straight flight with no towering or zig-zagging. No white on tail margins.
Status: passage migrant and winter visitor from September–April.
Similar Species: Common Snipe (p.131) is larger, with longer bill, zig-zag flight and harsh flight note.

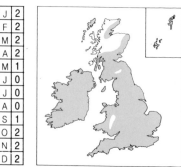

J	2
F	2
M	2
A	2
M	1
J	0
J	0
A	0
S	1
O	2
N	2
D	2

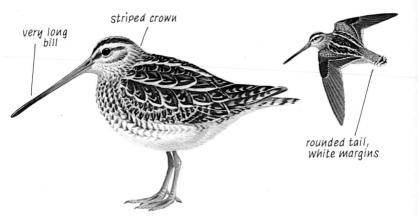

very long bill

striped crown

rounded tail, white margins

Heavily streaked, well camouflaged wader with long, straight bill. Mottled brown and black above with bold, buff stripes on back forming 'V'. Buff crown stripe and eyebrow plus dark eye stripe and dark margins to ear coverts produce distinctive striped pattern. Found mostly on freshwater marshes and flooded fields; generally gregarious. Tends to keep to cover but also feeds quite openly when not alarmed. If disturbed, flies off with pronounced zig-zagging, often towering into the air. Distinctive harsh flight note; also produces bleating sound in aerial diving display.
Status: widespread resident and abundant winter visitor.
Similar Species: Jack Snipe (p.130) smaller and usually silent with low, straight flight.

COMMON SNIPE

Type	wader-like
Size	25–27cm (9½–10½in)
Habitat	freshwater marshes, moors, fields
Behaviour	wades, walks, runs, takes off from water and ground
Flocking	1–100
Flight	strong and powerful, flitting, aerial dive
Voice	harsh *scarp*, repeated *chirper-chirper*; aerial 'drumming'

IDENTIFICATION

Adult	
Crown	dark brown with buff stripe
Upperparts	brown and black, streaked
Rump	brown and black
Tail	brown and black, edged white; short and rounded
Throat	white
Breast	buff and brown, streaked
Belly	white
Bill	brown; very long, thin and straight
Legs	green; long

BREEDING

Nest	lined hollow on ground
Eggs	4; pale green, blotched brown
Incubation	18–20 days ♀
Young	active; downy
Fledging	19–20 days
Broods	1, 2?; Apr–May
Food	worms, insects
Population	80,000–110,000 pairs; many hundreds of thousands winter

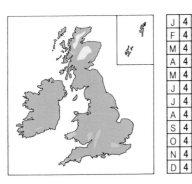

J	4
F	4
M	4
A	4
M	4
J	4
J	4
A	4
S	4
O	4
N	4
D	4

Woodcock · *Scolopax rusticola*

long bill

barred crown

barred back

rounded wings

rotund shape

WOODCOCK

Type	wader-like
Size	32–36cm (12–14in)
Habitat	forest and woods
Behaviour	walks, takes off or lands on ground
Flocking	solitary
Flight	strong and powerful; direct
Voice	shrill *tssick* flight note when roding

IDENTIFICATION

Adult	
Crown	buff, transverse black bars
Upperparts	dark brown and buff, bars and stripes
Rump	brown and black
Tail	brown and black; short and rounded
Throat	buff
Breast	buff and brown, barred
Belly	buff and brown, barred
Bill	buff; very long and thin
Legs	pink; short and stout

BREEDING

Nest	leaf-lined hollow on ground
Eggs	4; buff, blotched brown
Incubation	20–23 days ♀
Young	active; downy
Fledging	5–6 weeks
Broods	2; Mar–May
Food	worms, insects
Population	10,000–50,000 pairs

Bulky, Snipe-like wader of moist, open woodland. Well camouflaged by brown and buff bars creating a 'dead leaves' effect. Hardly ever seen on ground but occasional bird may be flushed from nest. In flight, bulky shape, long, down-pointed bill and broad, rounded wings diagnostic. Mainly nocturnal. Territorial display flight (roding) at dawn and dusk.

Status: resident virtually throughout Britain and Ireland; some immigration from the Continent in winter.

Similar Species: Common Snipe (p.131) has longer bill, is smaller and slimmer and lives in different habitat.

J	2
F	2
M	2
A	2
M	3
J	3
J	2
A	2
S	2
O	2
N	2
D	2

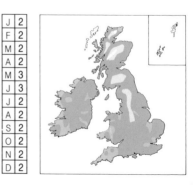

Limosa limosa **Black-tailed Godwit**

long straight bill

uniform greyish upperparts

bold black and white wings

adult winter

black tail bar

legs extend in flight

chestnut breast

chestnut ends at breast, white belly

adult summer

adult winter

Large, long-legged, long-billed wader of freshwater marshes, flooded fields and estuaries. In summer, adult has chestnut head, neck and breast with white chin and white eyebrow. Back spangled black and chestnut; wings grey. Belly white, barred black and brown. In winter, grey back and wings with no prominent streaking. Breast pale grey; belly white. Juvenile brown and buff; upperparts 'scalloped'. In flight, shows black band at tip of white tail and broad white wingbar.
Status: double passage migrant and winter visitor. Returned to breed in 1952 after lengthy absence; now breeds regularly in small numbers.
Similar Species: Bar-tailed Godwit (p.134) is smaller, has shorter legs and shorter, upturned bill; lacks wingbar.

	BLACK-TAILED GODWIT
Type	wader-like
Size	38–43cm (14½–16½in)
Habitat	marshes, estuaries, fields
Behaviour	wades, walks, takes off and lands on water or ground
Flocking	1–200
Flight	strong and powerful; direct
Voice	loud *reeka-reeka-reeka*

IDENTIFICATION

Ad.winter	
Crown	grey
Upperparts	grey
Rump	white
Tail	white with black band; short and square
Throat	white
Breast	pale grey
Belly	white
Bill	dark with pink base; very long, straight and thin
Legs	black; very long
Ad.summer	chestnut foreparts; barred white belly
Juvenile	upperparts dark brown and buff, scalloped; breast buff

BREEDING

Nest	lined hollow on ground
Eggs	4; green, blotched brown
Incubation	22–24 days ♂ ♀
Young	active; downy
Fledging	4 weeks
Broods	1; Apr–June
Food	worms, molluscs, insects
Population	60–70 pairs; 12,000–15,000 winter

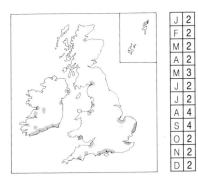

J	2
F	2
M	2
A	2
M	3
J	2
J	2
A	4
S	4
O	2
N	2
D	2

Bar-tailed Godwit *Limosa lapponica*

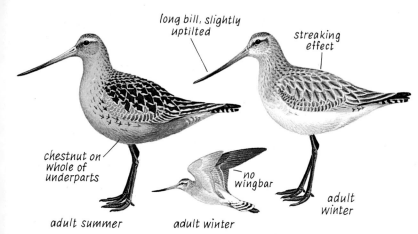

long bill, slightly uptilted

streaking effect

chestnut on whole of underparts

no wingbar

adult summer

adult winter

adult winter

	BAR-TAILED GODWIT
Type	wader-like
Size	36–40cm (14–16in)
Habitat	estuaries and shores, freshwater marshes
Behaviour	wades, walks, takes off from water and ground
Flocking	1–1000
Flight	strong and powerful; direct
Voice	*kirrick-kirrick*

IDENTIFICATION

Ad.winter	
Crown	buff and brown
Upperparts	buffy grey, streaked black
Rump	white
Tail	barred black; short and square
Throat	white
Breast	buff
Belly	white
Bill	dark with pink base; very long and thin, upturned
Legs	black; long
Ad.summer	chestnut head and all underparts
Juvenile	heavily streaked and mottled black and buff above; breast buff with clear streaking

BREEDING

Nest	lined hollow on ground
Eggs	4; olive, blotched brown
Incubation	20–21 days ♂ ♀
Young	active; downy
Fledging	?
Broods	1; May–June
Food	molluscs, worms
Population	58,000 winter

Large, long-legged, long-billed wader of estuaries and shorelines; occasionally roosts in coastal freshwater marshes. In summer, males have chestnut underparts extending to undertail. Back spangled black and chestnut; wings grey. Summer females paler than males. In winter, upperparts buffy grey, heavily streaked black; underparts white. Juvenile streaked buff and black. In flight, appears uniformly greyish with white 'V' extending upwards from rump; feet barely extend beyond tail. *Status:* double passage migrant and numerous winter visitor.
Similar Species: larger Black-tailed Godwit (p.133) shows bold pattern of black and white in flight (feet extend well beyond tail) and has barred white belly and white undertail in summer.

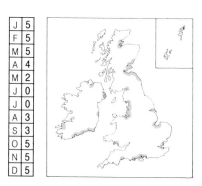

J	5
F	5
M	5
A	4
M	2
J	0
J	0
A	3
S	3
O	5
N	5
D	5

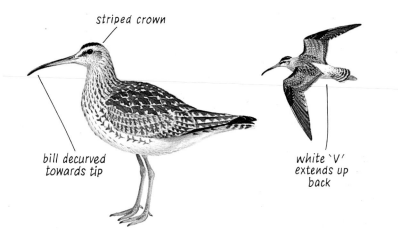

striped crown

bill decurved
towards tip

white 'V'
extends up
back

Smaller version of Eurasian Curlew that breeds in small numbers in northern Scotland but is otherwise double passage migrant. Central crown stripe, pale bordered black; pale eyebrow. Bill decurved towards tip. Upperparts greyish brown with dark centres and pale edges to feathers. Neck and breast buff with dark streaking. In flight, shows white 'V' up back; feet just protrude beyond tail. Distinctive call.

Status: scarce breeder in Scotland; regular double passage migrant April–June, July–October.

Similar Species: Eurasian Curlew (p136) lacks crown stripe and has longer, more decurved bill. (Beware young Eurasian Curlews with short bills in autumn.) Also several other 'curlews' – all extremely rare.

WHIMBREL

Type	wader-like
Size	39–43cm (15–17in)
Habitat	freshwater marshes, estuaries, moors
Behaviour	wades, walks, takes off from water and ground
Flocking	1–15
Flight	strong and powerful; direct
Voice	rapidly whistled *whi-whi-whi-whi-whi-whi-whi*

IDENTIFICATION

Adult	
Crown	pale central stripe, bordered black
Upperparts	greyish brown, dark feather centres
Rump	white
Tail	black and white; short and square
Throat	buff and brown
Breast	buff, brown streaks
Belly	white
Bill	black; long and decurved near tip
Legs	grey; long

BREEDING

Nest	hollow on ground
Eggs	4; olive-green, blotched brown
Incubation	24–28 days ♂ ♀
Young	active; downy
Fledging	5–6 weeks
Broods	1; May–June
Food	molluscs, crabs
Population	less than 200 pairs; over 2000 spring; less than 2000 autumn

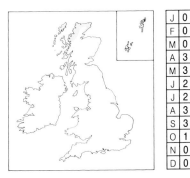

J	0
F	0
M	0
A	3
M	3
J	2
J	2
A	3
S	3
O	1
N	0
D	0

Eurasian Curlew *Numenius arquata*

very long, curved bill

no crown stripes

white 'V' extends up back

EURASIAN CURLEW

Type	wader-like
Size	51–61cm (20–24in)
Habitat	freshwater marshes, estuaries and shores, moors and heaths, fields
Behaviour	wades, walks, takes off and lands on water or ground
Flocking	1–1000
Flight	strong and powerful; direct
Voice	drawn out *coor-lee*; bubbling call summer

IDENTIFICATION

Adult	
Crown	buff and brown
Upperparts	buff and brown
Rump	white
Tail	buff and brown; short and square
Throat	buff and brown, streaked
Breast	buff and brown, streaked
Belly	white
Bill	black; very long and decurved
Legs	dark green; long

BREEDING

Nest	lined hollow on ground
Eggs	4; olive, blotched brown
Incubation	26–30 days, mainly ♀
Young	active; downy
Fledging	5–6 weeks
Broods	1; Apr–June
Food	worms, molluscs, crabs
Population	40,000–70,000 pairs; 200,000 winter

Large shorebird with long legs and very long, decurved bill. Upperparts brown with buffy feather margins; underparts heavily streaked brown on neck and breast. In flight, shows uniform wings and white 'V' extending up rump. Generally gregarious, forming large flocks on estuaries, marshes and adjacent fields.

Status: widespread breeding bird, mainly in northern and western hill districts; also on lowland heaths and marshes. Numerous winter visitor and passage migrant.

Similar Species: Whimbrel (p.135) has striped crown, marked eyebrow and shorter bill with downward curve nearer the tip. Juvenile Eurasian Curlew has shorter bill than adult and may be confused with Whimbrel.

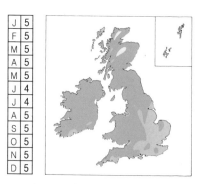

J	5
F	5
M	5
A	5
M	5
J	4
J	4
A	5
S	5
O	5
N	5
D	5

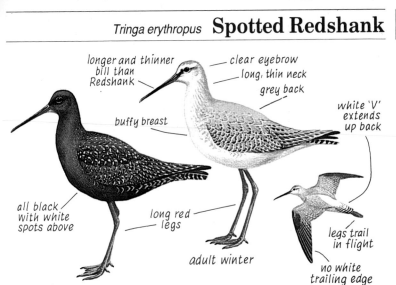

Tringa erythropus **Spotted Redshank**

longer and thinner bill than Redshank

clear eyebrow

long, thin neck

grey back

buffy breast

white 'V' extends up back

all black with white spots above

long red legs

legs trail in flight

adult winter

no white trailing edge

adult summer

A more delicate and graceful version of Common Redshank with longer, darker bill and longer legs. In summer, adult is completely black above and below with white spangling on wings and back. In winter, upperparts grey; wing feathers spotted black with white margins. In late spring and early autumn, adults often show traces of black in plumage. Juveniles resemble Common Redshank more closely but brown upperparts finely spotted black and white. In flight white rump extends up back in a 'V'; no wingbar. Feet trail beyond tip of tail.
Status: regular double passage migrant and winter visitor in smaller numbers to south and east coasts.
Similar Species: Common Redshank (p.138) is less elegant.

	SPOTTED REDSHANK
Type	wader-like
Size	29–32cm (11–12½in)
Habitat	freshwater marshes, estuaries
Behaviour	wades, walks, takes off from water or ground
Flocking	1–50
Flight	strong and powerful; direct
Voice	loud *choo-it*

IDENTIFICATION

Ad.winter	
Crown	grey
Upperparts	grey; wing feathers white margins, spotted black
Rump	white
Tail	black and white; short and square
Throat	white
Breast	grey
Belly	white
Bill	red; long and thin
Legs	red; long
Ad.summer	uniformly black with white speckling on upperparts
Juvenile	upperparts brown, spotted black and white; underparts white, barred brown

BREEDING

Nest	hollow on ground
Eggs	4; olive, blotched blackish
Incubation	?; ♂
Young	active; downy
Fledging	?
Broods	1; May–June
Food	molluscs, crustaceans
Population	80–200 winter; 700 Sept

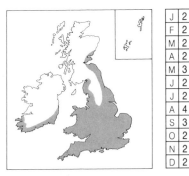

J	2
F	2
M	2
A	2
M	3
J	2
J	2
A	4
S	3
O	2
N	2
D	2

Common Redshank *Tringa totanus*

shorter bill than Spotted Redshank

brown back

red legs

adult summer

adult winter

white trailing edge

COMMON REDSHANK	
Type	wader-like
Size	26–30cm (10–11½in)
Habitat	freshwater marshes, estuaries and shores, fields
Behaviour	wades, walks, takes off from water and ground
Flocking	1–1000
Flight	strong and powerful; direct
Voice	melodic *tyew-yew-yew*; and repeated *twek*

IDENTIFICATION

Adult	
Crown	brown
Upperparts	brown
Rump	white
Tail	black and white; short and square
Throat	white, heavy brown streaking
Breast	white, heavy brown streaking
Belly	white
Bill	dark brown, base red; long and thin
Legs	red; long

BREEDING

Nest	lined hollow on ground
Eggs	4; buff, blotched blackish
Incubation	23–24 days ♂ ♀
Young	active; downy
Fledging	30 days
Broods	1; Apr–June
Food	worms, molluscs, crustaceans
Population	40,000–50,000 pairs; 95,000 winter

Common and widespread wader of coasts, estuaries, inland marshes and wetlands. In winter, large flocks found on favoured estuaries; also occurs along rocky and muddy shores. Upperparts brown, paler and more uniform in winter. Underparts white with heavy streaking, particularly in summer. Legs and base of bill bright red. In flight shows broad white trailing edge to wing.
Status: breeds over large areas, particularly in north and west Britain and Ireland. Abundant passage migrant and winter visitor, mainly to coasts and estuaries.
Similar Species: Spotted Redshank (p.137) and beware red-legged Ruff (p. 129).

J	5
F	5
M	5
A	5
M	4
J	4
J	4
A	5
S	5
O	5
N	5
D	5

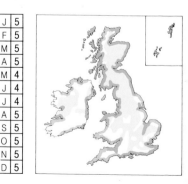

grey, uptilted bill

grey and black back

grey back

no white on wing

green legs

adult summer

adult winter

legs trail in flight

white extends in 'V' up back

Long-legged, long-billed, greyish wader of marshes and estuaries. Upperparts grey, marked with streaks of black in summer. Underparts mainly white, speckled grey in summer. Long green legs and long, grey, slightly upturned bill. Always appears graceful and elegant. In flight, wings uniformly dark grey with white rump extending in 'V' up back; feet extend beyond tip of tail.
Status: scarce breeder in Scottish Highlands and Islands and western Ireland. Double passage migrant, most numerous in autumn; scarce winter visitor to south-west England and Wales and coast of Ireland.
Similar Species: none.

GREENSHANK

Type	wader-like
Size	29–32cm (11–12½in)
Habitat	freshwater marshes, moors, estuaries
Behaviour	wades, walks, takes off and lands on water or ground
Flocking	1–15
Flight	strong and powerful; direct
Voice	loud *tu-tu-tu*

IDENTIFICATION

Ad.winter	
Crown	grey
Upperparts	grey
Rump	white
Tail	grey; short and square
Throat	white
Breast	grey
Belly	white
Bill	grey; long and thin
Legs	green; long
Ad.summer	black streaks on upperparts; underparts speckled grey

BREEDING

Nest	hollow on ground
Eggs	4; buff, blotched brown
Incubation	24–25 days, mainly ♀
Young	active; downy
Fledging	4 weeks
Broods	1; May–June
Food	worms, molluscs, crustaceans
Population	800–900 pairs; 1000–1500 winter; 2000 September

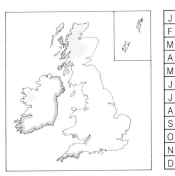

J	1
F	1
M	1
A	3
M	3
J	2
J	2
A	3
S	3
O	2
N	1
D	1

Green Sandpiper *Tringa ochropus*

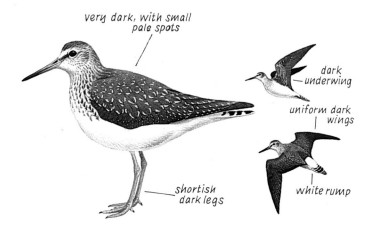

very dark, with small pale spots

shortish dark legs

dark underwing

uniform dark wings

white rump

GREEN SANDPIPER

Type	wader-like
Size	22–24cm (8½–9in)
Habitat	freshwater marshes
Behaviour	wades, walks, takes off from water and ground
Flocking	1–10
Flight	strong and powerful, direct
Voice	rising *tluit-weet-wit* of alarm

IDENTIFICATION

Adult	
Crown	black and brown
Upperparts	dark brown
Rump	white
Tail	black and white, barred; short and square
Throat	white
Breast	white, brown streaks
Belly	white
Bill	black; straight and thin
Legs	dark green; medium length

BREEDING

Nest	disused bird's nest in tree
Eggs	4; olive, spotted reddish brown
Incubation	20–23 days, mainly ♀
Young	active; downy
Fledging	4 weeks
Broods	1; Apr–June
Food	molluscs, crustaceans, insects
Population	very rare breeder; several hundred passage; 500–1000 winter

Medium-sized wader; dark brown above and white below but always appears black and white at any distance. Speckled on breast; short white eyebrow. In flight, shows uniformly dark wings and back, white rump and barred tail. Generally solitary or in small groups on freshwater marshes, particularly along dykes and ditches. Bobs head and tail. *Status:* double passage migrant but never numerous. Has bred in Scotland. *Similar Species:* Wood Sandpiper (p.141) is paler brown above and has longer, paler legs and shorter, thicker bill

J	1
F	1
M	1
A	2
M	2
J	1
J	1
A	2
S	3
O	1
N	1
D	1

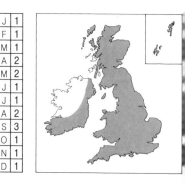

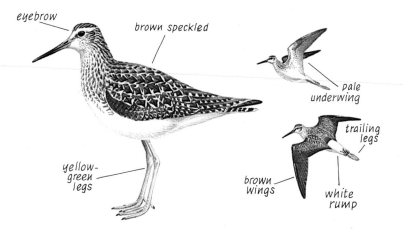

Tringa glareola **Wood Sandpiper**

eyebrow

brown speckled

pale underwing

trailing legs

yellow-green legs

brown wings

white rump

Similar to Green Sandpiper but always browner above with heavily speckled plumage and more pronounced eyebrow. Slimmer build and longer, pale legs produce a more elegant impression. Generally occurs singly or in small groups on freshwater marshes, often where vegetation emerges above the water. In flight, shows white rump, barred tail and uniform wing, but never appears black and white like Green Sandpiper.
Status: regular double passage migrant, most numerous in autumn. Rare breeder in Scotland.
Similar Species: Green Sandpiper (p.140). Speckled upperparts may produce similar pattern to small female Ruff (p.129).

WOOD SANDPIPER

Type	wader-like
Size	19–21cm (7–8in)
Habitat	freshwater marshes
Behaviour	wades, walks, takes off and lands on water or ground
Flocking	1–15
Flight	strong and powerful; direct
Voice	flat *chi-chi-chi*

IDENTIFICATION

Adult	
Crown	brown
Upperparts	brown, speckled buff and white
Rump	white
Tail	black and white; short and square
Throat	white
Breast	buff, faint streaks
Belly	white
Bill	black; straight and thin
Legs	yellow-green; long

BREEDING

Nest	hollow on ground
Eggs	4; pale green, blotched brown
Incubation	22–23 days, mainly ♀
Young	active; downy
Fledging	?
Broods	1; May–June
Food	molluscs, crustaceans, insects
Population	less than 5 pairs; passage 1000 or more?

J	0
F	0
M	0
A	2
M	2
J	1
J	1
A	3
S	3
O	1
N	0
D	0

Common Sandpiper *Actitis hypoleucos*

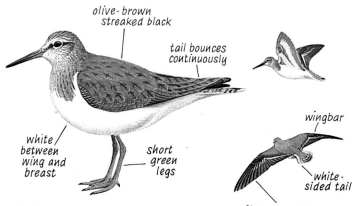

olive-brown streaked black

tail bounces continuously

white between wing and breast

short green legs

wingbar

white-sided tail

fluttering flight

COMMON SANDPIPER

Type	wader-like
Size	18–21cm (7–8in)
Habitat	freshwater marshes, estuaries
Behaviour	wades, walks, takes off and lands on water or ground
Flocking	1–2
Flight	direct; flitting
Voice	whistled *sweeswee-swoo*

IDENTIFICATION

Adult	
Crown	brown
Upperparts	olive-brown
Rump	buff
Tail	buff; short and square
Throat	white
Breast	white, streaked buff on sides
Belly	white
Bill	black; straight and thin
Legs	green; short

BREEDING

Nest	hollow on ground
Eggs	4; buff, speckled brown
Incubation	20–23 days ♂ ♀
Young	active; downy
Fledging	13–21 days
Broods	1; May–June
Food	molluscs, crustaceans, insects
Population	50,000 pairs; 100 winter

Distinctive sandpiper with brown upperparts and white below. Brown streaking at sides of breast forms clear line above bend of wing; distinctive white wedge between the two. Clear-cut eye stripe and eyebrow. Short green legs accentuate long body; folded wings do not reach tip of tail. Continuous wagging motion when feeding and at rest. Flickering, shallow wing beats produce characteristic flight, usually low over water. Prefers margins of streams, dykes and ponds to open marshes; usually solitary.
Status: breeding summer visitor to hill districts of north and west. Common double passage migrant elsewhere.
Similar Species: Wood Sandpiper (p.141) and Green Sandpiper (p.140) also 'bob' but not continuously like Common Sandpiper.

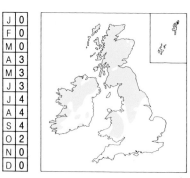

J	0
F	0
M	0
A	3
M	3
J	3
J	4
A	4
S	4
O	2
N	0
D	0

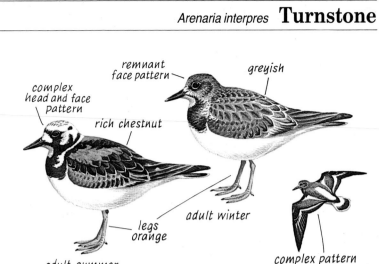

remnant face pattern

greyish

complex head and face pattern

rich chestnut

legs orange

adult winter

adult summer

complex pattern of bars and stripes

Stocky, short-legged, stubby-billed wader of coastal pools and beaches, especially rocky shores. Generally gregarious. Characteristic habit of turning stones in search of food; also picks and probes at surface. In summer, upperparts rich chestnut marked with black and buff. Head and neck white with intricate black markings extending to broad black breast band. Remaining underparts white. In winter, same overall pattern but in shades of grey. In flight, wingbar and wing patch combine with white rump and double tail bands to produce unmistakable pattern.
Status: common double passage migrant and winter visitor.
Similar Species: none.

TURNSTONE

Type	wader-like
Size	22–24cm (8–9in)
Habitat	estuaries and shores
Behaviour	wades, walks, perches openly, takes off from water and ground
Flocking	1–300
Flight	strong and powerful; direct
Voice	distinctive rattling *tukatuk*

IDENTIFICATION

Ad.winter and juvenile	
Crown	grey and black
Upperparts	grey and black
Rump	white
Tail	white, two black bands; short and square
Throat	white
Breast	grey
Belly	white
Bill	black; short and thin
Legs	orange; short
Ad.summer	rich chestnut above with bold black and white face pattern

BREEDING

Nest	scrape on ground
Eggs	4; greenish, blotched brown
Incubation	22–23 days ♂ ♀
Young	active; downy
Fledging	?
Broods	1; May–July
Food	invertebrates
Population	50,000 winter

J	4
F	4
M	4
A	2
M	3
J	3
J	1
A	2
S	2
O	4
N	4
D	4

Red-necked Phalarope *Phalaropus lobatus*

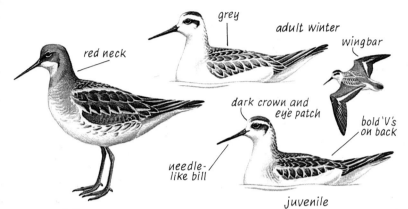

grey

adult winter

wingbar

red neck

dark crown and eye patch

bold 'V's on back

needle-like bill

juvenile

adult ♀ summer

RED-NECKED PHALAROPE

Type	wader-like
Size	17–19cm (6½–7in)
Habitat	freshwater marshes, sea
Behaviour	swims, wades, takes off from water and ground
Flocking	1–15
Flight	strong and powerful; direct
Voice	quiet *tyit*

IDENTIFICATION

Ad.♀summer	
Crown	grey
Upperparts	grey and buff; wings black and buff
Rump	black and white
Tail	black and white; short and square
Throat	white chin, red neck
Breast	orange-red
Belly	white
Bill	black; straight and fine
Legs	black; medium length
Ad.♂summer	as ♀ but paler
Ad.winter	grey above with eye mark
Juvenile	dark brown on crown and back; dark eye mark

BREEDING

Nest	neat cup in marsh
Eggs	4; pale green, blotched brown
Incubation	18–20 days ♂
Young	active; downy
Fledging	18–22 days
Broods	1; June–July
Food	insects, crustaceans
Population	16–20 pairs; variable autumn migration

Delicate little wader that spends most of its time swimming. In summer, breeds on a few marshy pools in north of Scotland and western Ireland; winters at sea, often in large flocks. In breeding season, female has grey crown, nape, lower breast and back; the latter is marked by two buffy 'V's. Wings sooty black with buffy margins. Chin white, neck and upper breast orange-red. Male duller. In winter, grey above and white below; small dark comma extends behind eye. Juvenile slate grey with buffy feather margins, two buff 'V's on back and dark crown. Shows broad wingbar in flight. *Status:* passage migrant (usually storm-driven) mostly in autumn. Rare breeder in Scotland and Ireland. *Similar Species:* Grey Phalarope (p.145) has thicker bill.

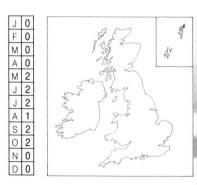

J	0
F	0
M	0
A	0
M	2
J	2
J	2
A	1
S	2
O	2
N	0
D	0

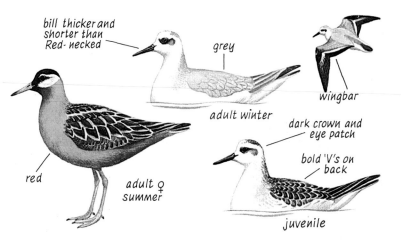

bill thicker and shorter than Red-necked

grey

wingbar

adult winter

dark crown and eye patch

bold 'V's on back

red

adult ♀ summer

juvenile

Similar to Red-necked Phalarope but slightly larger and decidedly more bulky, with stouter and proportionately shorter bill. In breeding plumage, rust-red on neck and underparts. Back is black with double buffy 'V' and broad buffy margins to wings. Crown, forehead and chin black, face white. Bill has yellow base. Winter and juvenile birds similar to Red-necked and best separated by stocky shape and thicker bill.
Status: autumn passage migrant in variable numbers, mostly storm-driven.
Similar Species: Red-necked Phalarope (p.144), see above.

	GREY PHALAROPE
Type	wader-like
Size	19–21cm (7–8in)
Habitat	freshwater, sea, estuaries
Behaviour	swims, wades, takes off from water and ground
Flocking	1–2
Flight	strong and powerful; direct
Voice	high-pitched *twit*

IDENTIFICATION

Ad.winter	
Crown	grey
Upperparts	grey
Rump	black and white
Tail	black and white; short and square
Throat	white
Breast	white
Belly	white
Bill	black, yellow base; straight and thin
Legs	yellow; medium length
Ad.summer	chestnut red underparts; white face
Juvenile	dark brown on crown and back; dark eye mark

BREEDING

Nest	hollow among vegetation in marsh
Eggs	4; pale green, blotched brown
Incubation	19 days ♂
Young	active; downy
Fledging	16–21 days
Broods	1; June–July
Food	insects, molluscs, crustaceans
Population	variable, autumn migrant

J	0
F	0
M	0
A	1
M	1
J	0
J	0
A	1
S	2
O	2
N	1
D	0

Pomarine Skua *Stercorarius pomarinus*

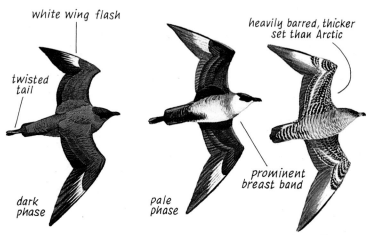

white wing flash

twisted tail

dark phase

pale phase

heavily barred, thicker set than Arctic

prominent breast band

juvenile

POMARINE SKUA

Type	gull-like
Size	43–53cm (16–21in)
Habitat	open sea; estuaries and shores
Behaviour	swims, takes off and lands on water
Flocking	1–10
Flight	strong and powerful; direct; glides, aerial dive
Voice	silent at sea

IDENTIFICATION

Ad.pale	
Crown	black
Upperparts	brown
Rump	brown
Tail	brown; rounded; central feathers long and twisted
Throat	yellow
Breast	buff; smudgy breast band
Belly	white
Bill	buff; short and thin
Legs	brown; medium length
Ad.dark	uniformly brown; white wing flashes
Juvenile	heavily barred; lacks long central tail feathers

BREEDING

Nest	hollow on ground
Eggs	2; buff, spotted brown
Incubation	27–28 days ♂ ♀
Young	semi-helpless; downy
Fledging	5–6 weeks
Broods	1; June–July
Food	fish
Population	scarce passage migrant, mainly spring

Like Arctic Skua, occurs in two phases – light and dark. Both phases show white wing flashes, but pale phase has smudgy breast band (more prominent than pale Arctic). Spring adults easily separated from Arctic by broad, twisted, central feathers extending well beyond rest of tail. In autumn and juveniles, structure more important than plumage details; Pomarine always heavier and more bulky than Arctic. Juvenile heavily barred above and below. Generally seen offshore during extended sea-watches in spring and autumn.
Status: regular but scarce passage migrant in first half of May and August–October off southern and western headlands.
Similar Species: Arctic Skua (p.147), see above.

J	0
F	0
M	0
A	1
M	2
J	1
J	0
A	1
S	1
O	1
N	1
D	0

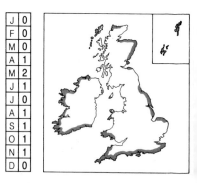

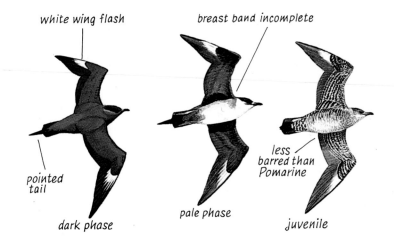

white wing flash

breast band incomplete

pointed tail

dark phase

less barred than Pomarine

pale phase

juvenile

Most commonly seen of the four skua species and the 'base' from which others must be differentiated. Fast, highly agile, dashing flight reminiscent of Peregrine. Pursues other seabirds. Occurs in two phases – light and dark – both of which show white wing flashes. Pale phase has dark cap and upperparts; underparts pale with indistinct dark breast band. Dark phase uniformly brown. Spring adults have two central tail feathers extended; absent in juveniles and (usually) autumn adults.
Status: summer visitor to far north; regular passage migrant to all coasts, especially in autumn.
Similar Species: lighter and more agile than Pomarine Skua (p.146) and heavier and less tern-like than Long-tailed Skua (p.148).

ARCTIC SKUA	
Type	gull-like
Size	38–48cm (14½–18½in)
Habitat	sea, moors, estuaries
Behaviour	swims, perches openly, takes off from water and ground
Flocking	1–15
Flight	strong and powerful; direct; glides, aerial dive
Voice	high *kee-ow*; silent at sea

IDENTIFICATION

Ad.pale	
Crown	black
Upperparts	brown
Rump	brown
Tail	black; long central feathers
Throat	yellow
Breast	white; indistinct band
Belly	white
Bill	black; short and thin
Legs	brown; medium length
Ad.dark	uniformly brown; white wing flashes, as pale phase
Juvenile	heavily barred; lacks long central tail feathers

BREEDING

Nest	unlined hollow on ground
Eggs	2; greenish, blotched brown
Incubation	24–28 days ♂ ♀
Young	semi-helpless; downy
Fledging	30 days
Broods	1; May–June
Food	fish
Population	1000 pairs; regular passage migrant, mostly autumn

J	0
F	0
M	0
A	2
M	3
J	3
J	3
A	3
S	3
O	1
N	0
D	0

Long-tailed Skua *Stercorarius longicaudus*

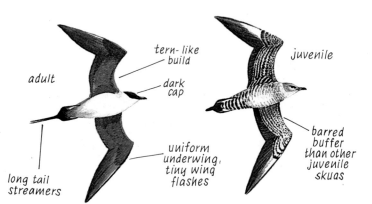

adult

tern-like build

dark cap

long tail streamers

uniform underwing, tiny wing flashes

juvenile

barred buffer than other juvenile skuas

LONG-TAILED SKUA

Type	gull-like
Size	38–56cm (14½–21in)
Habitat	sea, estuaries
Behaviour	swims, takes off and lands on water
Flocking	1–2
Flight	strong and powerful; direct; glides, aerial dive
Voice	silent at sea

IDENTIFICATION

Adult

Crown	black
Upperparts	grey
Rump	grey
Tail	black; long central feathers
Throat	white
Breast	white
Belly	buff
Bill	black; short and thin
Legs	brown; medium length
Juvenile	heavily barred; lacks long central tail feathers and cap

BREEDING

Nest	unlined hollow on ground
Eggs	2; olive, blotched brown
Incubation	23 days ♂ ♀
Young	semi-helpless; downy
Fledging	3 weeks
Broods	1; June
Food	fish
Population	rare, passage migrant

Rarest of the skuas, occurring only in pale phase. Spring adults have very long central tail feathers, usually lacking in autumn and sub-adult birds. Upperparts greyish, not brown; underparts pure white. Dark cap more contrasting than in other pale phase skuas; wing flashes less pronounced. Juvenile barred as other skuas, but less rufous.
Status: scarce passage migrant to all coasts in spring and autumn.
Similar Species: pale phase Arctic Skua (p.147). Long-tailed lighter built than Arctic with more buoyant flight.

J	0
F	0
M	0
A	0
M	1
J	1
J	0
A	1
S	1
O	1
N	0
D	0

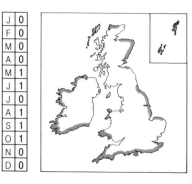

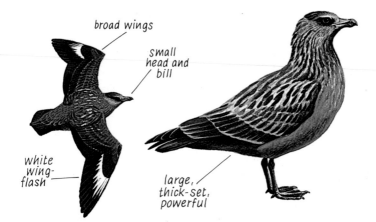

broad wings

small head and bill

white wing-flash

large, thick-set, powerful

Largest of the skuas with uniformly dark brownish plumage and bold white wing flashes. Wings much broader than other skuas and flight less agile. Smaller head and bill than large gulls and easier, dashing flight, especially in pursuit of other seabirds.
Status: scarce breeder in far north of Britain; passage migrant to all other coasts.
Similar Species: often said to resemble large immature gull but not really confusable once seen.

GREAT SKUA

Type	gull-like
Size	56–61cm (22–24in)
Habitat	sea, estuaries, moors
Behaviour	swims, perches openly, takes off and lands on water or ground
Flocking	1–2
Flight	strong and powerful; direct; glides, aerial dive
Voice	harsh *uk-uk-uk*; nasal *skeerr*

IDENTIFICATION

Adult	
Crown	brown and black
Upperparts	dark brown, streaked buff
Rump	dark brown, streaked buff
Tail	dark brown and buff; medium length, rounded
Throat	buff and brown, streaked
Breast	buff and brown, streaked
Belly	buff and brown, streaked
Bill	black; stout
Legs	brown; medium length

BREEDING

Nest	unlined hollow on ground
Eggs	2; olive, spotted brown
Incubation	28–30 days ♂ ♀
Young	semi-helpless; downy
Fledging	6–7 weeks
Broods	1; May–June
Food	fish, eggs, birds
Population	3800 pairs; scarce passage migrant

J	0
F	0
M	1
A	3
M	3
J	3
J	3
A	3
S	2
O	0
N	0
D	0

Mediterranean Gull *Larus melanocephalus*

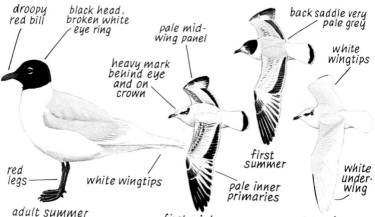

droopy red bill

black head, broken white eye ring

pale mid-wing panel

heavy mark behind eye and on crown

back saddle very pale grey

white wingtips

red legs

white wingtips

adult summer

first summer

pale inner primaries

first winter

white under-wing

adult winter

	MEDITERRANEAN GULL
Type	gull-like
Size	37–40cm (14–15in)
Habitat	freshwater marshes, sea, estuaries and shores
Behaviour	swims, wades, walks, perches openly, takes off from water and ground
Flocking	1–3
Flight	soars, glides; strong and powerful; direct
Voice	plaintive *kee-ow*

IDENTIFICATION

Ad.winter	
Crown	white, streaked hind crown
Upperparts	grey
Rump	white
Tail	white; medium length, square
Throat	white
Breast	white
Belly	white
Bill	red; short and thin
Legs	red; medium length
Ad.summer	black hood, white eye ring
Juvenile	brown across wings, pale central wing patch

BREEDING

Nest	lined hollow near water
Eggs	3; creamy, spotted black
Incubation	23–25 days ♂ ♀
Young	partly-active; downy
Fledging	35–40 days
Broods	1; May–June
Food	invertebrates, fish
Population	15–23 pairs; 100–150 winter

Very pale gull with heavy, droopy, red bill and red legs. Adult in summer has black, not brown, head with prominent broken white eye ring. Back and wings pale grey, with white primaries and white underwing. In winter, black head replaced by dark smudge behind eye and streaked hind crown. Uniform white primaries and underwing of adult facilitate identification at considerable range.

Status: rare breeder; scarce passage migrant and winter visitor.

Similar Species: adult Black-headed Gull (p.153). Juvenile more like Common Gull (p.151) than Black-headed, but with paler and more contrasting central wing panel. First winter Mediterranean and Common Gulls similar, but Common Gull has pale grey (not white) 'saddle' on back.

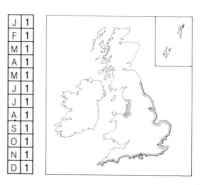

J	1
F	1
M	1
A	1
M	1
J	1
J	1
A	1
S	1
O	1
N	1
D	1

buffy inner primaries

central wing panel greyish

small, rounded head and bill

yellow

adult

yellow

adult summer

first winter

black tips, white mirrors

adult winter

Abundant inland and along coasts in winter, but virtually confined to north and north-west in summer. Grey upperparts with black wingtips and white 'mirrors' create similar pattern to Herring Gull (p.154), but head and bill significantly smaller, giving more gentle look. Thin, yellow bill lacks red spot. Juvenile and first winter birds show dark trailing edge to secondaries and pale mid-wing panel.
Status: breeds inland in north and west Britain and Ireland; abundant winter visitor.
Similar Species: Kittiwake (p.159) has similar benign look; first winter Mediterranean Gull (p.150) separated from first winter Common Gull with care.

COMMON GULL	
Type	gull-like
Size	38–43cm (14–16½in)
Habitat	towns, freshwater marshes, moors, sea, estuaries, shores, fields
Behaviour	swims, wades, walks, perches openly, takes off from water or ground
Flocking	1–1000
Flight	soars, glides; strong and powerful; direct
Voice	high *kee-aa*

IDENTIFICATION	
Adult	
Crown	white
Upperparts	grey; black wingtips with white 'mirrors'
Rump	white
Tail	white; medium length, square
Throat	white
Breast	white
Belly	white
Bill	yellow; short and thin
Legs	yellow-green; medium length
Juvenile	brown wings, grey 'saddle'

BREEDING	
Nest	lined hollow on ground
Eggs	3; blotched brown
Incubation	22–27 days ♂ ♀
Young	partly-active; downy
Fledging	4 weeks
Broods	1; May
Food	worms, insects, molluscs
Population	50,000 pairs; 700,000 winter

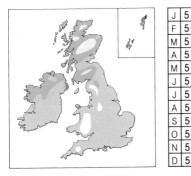

J	5
F	5
M	5
A	5
M	5
J	5
J	5
A	5
S	5
O	5
N	5
D	5

Little Gull *Larus minutus*

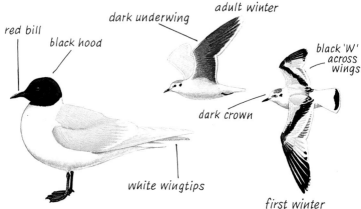

red bill

black hood

dark underwing

adult winter

black 'W' across wings

dark crown

white wingtips

first winter

adult summer

LITTLE GULL

Type	gull-like
Size	27–29cm (10–11in)
Habitat	freshwater marshes, sea, estuaries and shores
Behaviour	swims, wades, walks, perches openly, takes off from water or ground
Flocking	1–100
Flight	soars, glides, flitting; strong and powerful
Voice	repeated *ka-ee* and low *ka-ka-ka*

IDENTIFICATION

Ad.winter

Crown	white, dark hind crown
Upperparts	grey
Rump	white
Tail	white; medium length, square
Throat	white
Breast	white
Belly	white
Bill	black; short and thin
Legs	black; short
Ad.summer	black hood, red bill
Juvenile	'W' across upperwing

BREEDING

Nest	reeds and rushes
Eggs	3; pale green, blotched black
Incubation	20–21 days ♂ ♀
Young	partly-active; downy
Fledging	21–24 days
Broods	1; May–June
Food	invertebrates, fish, insects
Population	double-passage migrant; scarce winter visitor

Small, dainty, tern-like gull, most often seen feeding in flight, picking insects from surface of water like a marsh tern. Adult has uniformly pale grey wings lacking black tips; underwing dark grey. In summer, head black, tiny bill red. In winter, hood replaced by dark hind crown and spot behind eye. Juvenile and first winter birds have inverted black 'W' across upperwings in flight – like Kittiwake (p.159) of same age; Kittiwake is larger.
Status: has bred. Regular passage migrant and scarce winter visitor; may gather in good numbers at a few particularly favoured spots.
Similar Species: smaller size precludes confusion.

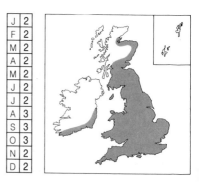

J	2
F	2
M	2
A	2
M	2
J	2
J	2
A	3
S	3
O	3
N	2
D	2

Larus ridibundus **Black-headed Gull**

red bill

white forewing

adult winter

pale grey back

red legs

adult summer

hint of white in forewing

first winter

Most common and widespread gull, equally at home inland and along shorelines. In all plumages distinguished by white outer primaries creating a white forewing. Outer underwing dark. Adult in summer has chocolate hood, red bill and red legs. In winter, hood reduced to spot behind eye. First winter birds have pale grey backs with brown markings across wings. Gregarious, forming huge nocturnal roosts.
Status: widespread and numerous colonial breeder; abundant winter visitor.
Similar Species: Mediterranean Gull (p.150) and Little Gull (p.152).

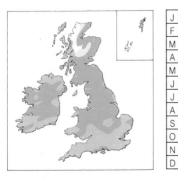

J	6
F	6
M	6
A	6
M	6
J	6
J	6
A	6
S	6
O	6
N	6
D	6

BLACK-HEADED GULL

Type	gull-like
Size	35–38cm (13–14½in)
Habitat	towns, marshes, moors, sea, shoreline, fields
Behaviour	swims, wades, walks, perches openly, takes off from water or ground
Flocking	1–40,000
Flight	soars, glides; strong and powerful; direct
Voice	repeated *kuk-kuk*; angry *kee-ar*

IDENTIFICATION

Ad.winter	
Crown	white
Upperparts	grey
Rump	white
Tail	white; medium length, square
Throat	white
Breast	white
Belly	white
Bill	red; short and thin
Legs	red; medium length
Ad.summer	chocolate hood
Juvenile	brown on head and back

BREEDING

Nest	scrape or cup of vegetation in marsh
Eggs	3; buffy, spotted black
Incubation	21–27 days ♂ ♀
Young	partly-active; downy
Fledging	5–6 weeks
Broods	1; Apr–May
Food	invertebrates, seeds
Population	150,000–300,000 pairs; 3,000,000 winter

Herring Gull *Larus argentatus*

yellow bill, red spot

streaked head

black tips, white mirrors

pale grey (saddle) back

adult winter

pale inner primaries

second winter

pink legs

first winter

dark trailing edge

adult summer

	HERRING GULL
Type	gull-like
Size	53–59cm (20–23in)
Habitat	towns, freshwater marshes, moors, sea, sea-cliffs, estuaries, shores
Behaviour	swims, wades, walks, perches openly, takes off from water or ground
Flocking	1–10,000
Flight	soars, glides; strong and powerful; direct
Voice	loud ringing *kyow-kyow*

IDENTIFICATION

Adult

Crown	white
Upperparts	grey; black wingtips with white 'mirrors'
Rump	white
Tail	white; medium length, square
Throat	white
Breast	white
Belly	white
Bill	yellow, red spot; straight and thick
Legs	pink; medium length
Juvenile	speckled brown above

BREEDING

Nest	cup of vegetation on cliff, dunes, marsh, building
Eggs	2–3; pale green, blotched brown
Incubation	25–33 days, mainly ♀
Young	partly-active; downy
Fledging	6 weeks
Broods	1; Apr–May
Food	virtually anything
Population	over 300,000 pairs

Most common and familiar of the larger gulls. Grey back; grey wings with black tips and white 'mirrors'. Large yellow bill with red spot; flesh coloured legs. In winter, head variably streaked black. Immatures must be separated with care from Lesser Black-backed Gulls of same age. Juvenile Herring Gulls have wider pale margins to upperparts and pale inner primaries that break up hind wing pattern. First summer birds invariably have pale creamy upperparts, much paler than Lesser Black-backed. Second winter birds have pale grey 'saddles'.
Status: widespread resident and winter visitor; breeds along most coasts.
Similar Species: adult Common Gull (p.151) and immature Lesser Black-backed Gull (p.155) as above.

J	6
F	6
M	6
A	6
M	6
J	6
J	6
A	6
S	6
O	6
N	6
D	6

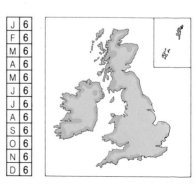

Larus fuscus **Lesser Black-backed Gull**

yellow bill, red spot

all dark back

adult winter

more marked trailing edge than Herring

second winter

yellow legs

narrow pale feather margins

lacks pale inner primaries

first winter

adult summer

Large, dark-backed gull with yellow legs and yellow bill with red spot. Scandinavian sub-species, *L.f. fuscus*, nearly as black on back as Great Black-backed, but considerably smaller. Like other large gulls, takes three years to acquire adult plumage but has slate-grey 'saddle' by second summer. Younger birds separated from Herring Gulls of similar age by narrower, paler margins to upperparts and bolder spots on underparts.
Status: widespread breeder mostly around coasts; passage migrant and increasing winter visitor.
Similar Species: adult Herring Gull (p.154) has lighter grey back and pink, not yellow, legs; immatures similar, see above. Adult Great Black-backed Gull (p.158) is much larger, almost black on back and has pale pink legs.

LESSER BLACK-BACKED GULL

Type	gull-like
Size	51–56cm (20–22in)
Habitat	marshes, moors, sea, estuaries, shores, fields
Behaviour	swims, wades, walks, perches openly, takes off from water and ground
Flocking	1–1000
Flight	soars, glides; strong and powerful; direct
Voice	variety of loud calls such as *kyow-kyow, kee-aa*

IDENTIFICATION

Adult

Crown	white
Upperparts	slate-grey; black wingtips with white 'mirrors'
Rump	white
Tail	white; medium length, square
Throat	white
Breast	white
Belly	white
Bill	yellow with red spot; straight and thick
Legs	yellow; medium length
Juvenile	speckled brown above, buff below

BREEDING

Nest	lined hollow on flat ground
Eggs	3; olive, blotched blackish
Incubation	25–29 days ♂ ♀
Young	partly-active; downy
Fledging	35–40 days
Broods	1; Apr–June
Food	virtually anything
Population	50,000 pairs; 70,000 winter

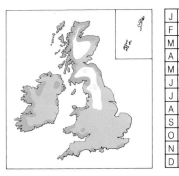

J	4
F	4
M	5
A	5
M	5
J	5
J	5
A	5
S	5
O	5
N	4
D	4

Iceland Gull *Larus glaucoides*

small yellow bill, red spot

small, rounded head

pale back

first winter

buffy

white wingtips

adult winter

adult winter

	ICELAND GULL
Type	gull-like
Size	51–57cm (20–22in)
Habitat	sea, estuaries and shores
Behaviour	swims, wades, walks, perches openly, takes off and lands on water or ground
Flocking	solitary
Flight	soars, glides; strong and powerful; direct
Voice	shrill *kyow*

IDENTIFICATION

Adult	
Crown	buff
Upperparts	very pale grey
Rump	white
Tail	white; medium length, square
Throat	white
Breast	white
Belly	white
Bill	yellow with red spot; straight and thick
Legs	pink; medium length
Juvenile	buff with white primaries

BREEDING

Nest	vegetation on cliffs or islands
Eggs	2–3; ?
Incubation	?
Young	?
Fledging	?
Broods	1; June
Food	fish
Population	70–300 winter

Decidedly scarce winter visitor; most common in the north but may occur along any shoreline. Adult has very pale grey back and wings with white primaries. First year birds are buffy; second year birds are pale creamy above and below – both have white primaries. Smaller, more rounded head, coupled with smaller bill and more benign expression are most reliable means of separating this bird from larger Glaucous Gull.

Status: scarcer than Glaucous Gull everywhere; winter visitor in variable numbers.

Similar Species: Glaucous Gull (p.157) is larger and has bigger head – see also above.

J	2
F	2
M	1
A	1
M	1
J	0
J	0
A	0
S	1
O	1
N	1
D	1

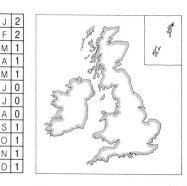

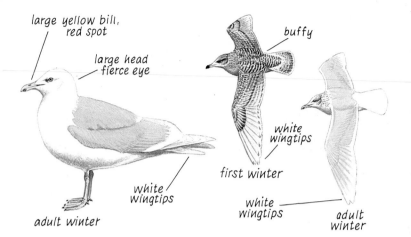

large yellow bill, red spot

large head
fierce eye

buffy

white
wingtips

first winter

white
wingtips

adult winter

white
wingtips

white
wingtips

**adult
winter**

Large, pale grey-backed gull – almost
as large as Great Black-backed (p.158).
Similar to Herring Gull (p.154) but
lacks black tips in white primaries.
Can be confused with much rarer
Iceland Gull (p.156) but bill much
longer and more powerful and head
flatter with more fierce expression.
Pink legs and yellow bill with red spot.
Immatures pass through similar
pattern of changes to Iceland Gull – all
have white primaries.
Status: scarce; regular winter visitor to
most coasts. More numerous in north.
Similar Species: Iceland Gull (p.156) as
above.

GLAUCOUS GULL	
Type	gull-like
Size	58–69cm (22–27in)
Habitat	sea, estuaries
Behaviour	swims, wades, walks, perches openly, takes off and lands on water or ground
Flocking	1–2
Flight	soars, glides; strong and powerful; direct
Voice	harsh *kyow* like other large gulls

IDENTIFICATION	
Adult	
Crown	white
Upperparts	grey
Rump	white
Tail	white; medium length, square
Throat	white
Breast	white
Belly	white
Bill	yellow with red spot; straight and thick
Legs	pink; medium length
Juvenile	buff with white primaries

BREEDING	
Nest	bulky cup of vegetation on cliff or small island
Eggs	2–3; pale olive, blotched blackish
Incubation	27–30 days ♂ ♀
Young	partly-active; downy
Fledging	40–50 days ?
Broods	1; May–June
Food	fish, invertebrates, carrion
Population	200–500 winter

J	2
F	2
M	1
A	1
M	1
J	1
J	1
A	1
S	1
O	1
N	1
D	2

Great Black-backed Gull *Larus marinus*

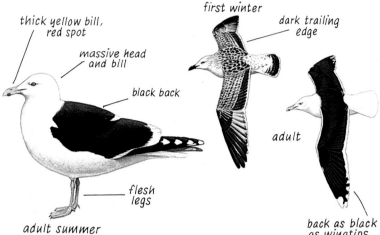

first winter

dark trailing edge

thick yellow bill, red spot

massive head and bill

black back

adult

flesh legs

adult summer

back as black as wingtips

	GREAT BLACK-BACKED GULL
Type	gull-like
Size	63–69cm (24½–27in)
Habitat	sea, estuaries, marshes
Behaviour	swims, wades, walks, perches openly, takes off from water or ground
Flocking	1–100s
Flight	soars, glides; strong and powerful; direct
Voice	harsh *owk*; also *uk-uk-uk*

IDENTIFICATION

Adult

Crown	white
Upperparts	black; black wingtips with white 'mirrors'
Rump	white
Tail	white; medium length, square
Throat	white
Breast	white
Belly	white
Bill	yellow with red spot; large and thick
Legs	pink; medium length
Juvenile	buff brown with dark trailing edge to wing

BREEDING

Nest	large mass of sticks and seaweed on ground on island or rock
Eggs	2–3; olive, speckled brown
Incubation	26–30 days ♂ ♀
Young	partly-active; downy
Fledging	7–8 weeks
Broods	1; Apr–May
Food	seabirds, offal, rubbish
Population	25,000 pairs

Massive gull that stands larger than Herring and Lesser Black-backed Gulls in all plumages. Sheer size of bird picks it out from any mixed gull flock. Adult has black back and wings, huge head and large, deep bill. Immatures have almost white margins to dark brown feathers of upperparts and are much more contrasted than Herring and Lesser Black-backed Gulls of similar age. Mainly marine, but penetrates inland in winter, mostly to rubbish tips and reservoirs.
Status: breeds along most western coasts; winter visitor elsewhere.
Similar Species: adult Lesser Black-backed Gull (p.155), especially Scandinavian sub-species *fuscus*, is as black above but smaller with less massive head and bill.

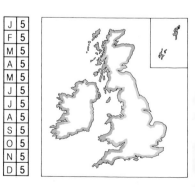

J	5
F	5
M	5
A	5
M	5
J	5
J	5
A	5
S	5
O	5
N	5
D	5

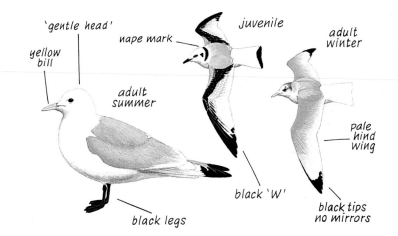

'gentle head'

nape mark

juvenile

adult winter

yellow bill

adult summer

pale hind wing

black 'W'

black tips no mirrors

black legs

Totally maritime gull about same size as Common Gull and superficially similar. Both species have small head, short yellow bill and benign expression. Kittiwake has shorter legs and longer, narrower wings; black wingtips lack white 'mirrors'. Immatures show black inverted 'W' across upperwings in flight (like much smaller Little Gull p.152) and black neck bar. Spends most of time at sea flying lightly and buoyantly; breeds on cliffs, forming large colonies.
Status: breeds on most cliff-bound shores, especially numerous in north and west.
Similar Species: Common Gull (p.151), as above.

KITTIWAKE

Type	gull-like
Size	38–43cm (15½–16½in)
Habitat	sea, cliffs
Behaviour	swims, perches openly, takes off and lands on water or ground
Flocking	1–1000s
Flight	soars, glides; strong and powerful; direct
Voice	repeated *kitti-week*

IDENTIFICATION

Adult	
Crown	white
Upperparts	grey; black wingtips
Rump	white
Tail	white; medium length, square
Throat	white
Breast	white
Belly	white
Bill	yellow; short and thin
Legs	black; short
Juvenile	black 'W' across wings, black tail band, black bill

BREEDING

Nest	neat cup of seaweed on tiny cliff ledge
Eggs	2; creamy, speckled brown
Incubation	25–30 days ♂ ♀
Young	partly-active; downy
Fledging	43 days
Broods	1; May–June
Food	fish
Population	c 500,000 pairs

J	4
F	4
M	4
A	4
M	4
J	4
J	4
A	4
S	4
O	4
N	4
D	4

Sandwich Tern *Sterna sandvicensis*

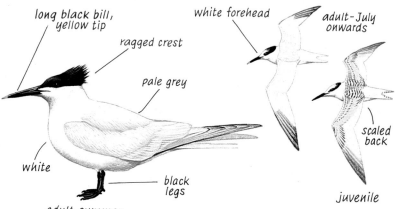

long black bill, yellow tip

ragged crest

pale grey

white

black legs

adult summer

white forehead

adult – July onwards

scaled back

juvenile

SANDWICH TERN	
Type	tern-like
Size	38–43cm (14–17in)
Habitat	sea, estuaries and adjacent marshes
Behaviour	swims, dives from air, perches openly, takes off from water or ground
Flocking	1–1000s
Flight	hovers, aerial dive; strong and powerful; direct
Voice	loud *ker-rik*

IDENTIFICATION

Ad.summer	
Crown	black, with ragged crest
Upperparts	whitish grey
Rump	white
Tail	white; long and forked
Throat	white
Breast	white
Belly	white
Bill	black with yellow tip; straight and thin
Legs	black; short
Ad.winter and juvenile	greyer above, white forehead and crown; black hind crown; juvenile barred 'saddle'

BREEDING

Nest	bare scrape; highly colonial
Eggs	2; buffy, speckled brown
Incubation	20–24 days ♂ ♀
Young	partly-active; downy
Fledging	35 days
Broods	1; Apr–May
Food	fish
Population	*c*12,000 pairs

Largest of the terns with typical buoyant flight on long, narrow wings. Sandwich is much paler than other terns and has black legs and long, black bill with yellow tip. Black cap forms ragged crest on hind crown. Confined to coastlines where dives into sea for food. Forms dense colonies.
Status: summer visitor like other terns; breeds very locally along all coasts. Passage migrant away from colonies.
Similar Species: no terns are as large, as white or have black bills.

J	0
F	0
M	2
A	4
M	4
J	4
J	4
A	4
S	3
O	2
N	0
D	0

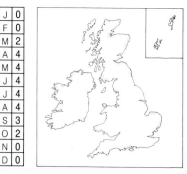

adult summer

pale wings

dark forehead

almost spotted back

black bill

paler grey than Common or Arctic

white / not grey (pinkish Spring)

adult summer

long tail streamers

juvenile

Rarest of the breeding terns with a few isolated colonies, mostly on islands, holding bulk of population. Elsewhere decidedly rare or overlooked. A small tern somewhere between Common and Little Tern in size but with long tail streamers boosting measured length. Best picked out from more abundant Common and Arctic Terns by paler colour – almost white above and below. Identification confirmed by black bill (some Common Terns have almost complete black bill) and tail streamers (may become broken). In spring has pink flush on breast.
Status: rare summer visitor and passage migrant; arrives later than other terns.
Similar Species: Common Tern (p.162) and Arctic Tern (p.163).

ROSEATE TERN	
Type	tern-like
Size	32–40cm (12–15in)
Habitat	sea, estuaries and adjacent marshes
Behaviour	swims, dives from air, perches openly, takes off and lands on water or ground
Flocking	1–100
Flight	hovers; strong and powerful; direct
Voice	*kee-a, pee-pee-pee,* similar to Common Tern

IDENTIFICATION	
Ad.summer	
Crown	black
Upperparts	whitish grey
Rump	white
Tail	white; long and forked
Throat	white
Breast	white, pink flush in spring
Belly	white
Bill	black; short and thin
Legs	red; short
Ad.winter and juvenile	white forehead; juvenile scaled upperparts

BREEDING	
Nest	unlined hollow
Eggs	1–2; creamy, speckled brown
Incubation	21–26 days ♂ ♀
Young	partly-active; downy
Fledging	27–30 days
Broods	1; June
Food	fish
Population	100–500 pairs

J	0
F	0
M	0
A	1
M	2
J	2
J	2
A	2
S	1
O	0
N	0
D	0

Common Tern *Sterna hirundo*

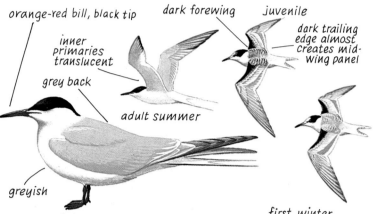

orange-red bill, black tip

dark forewing

juvenile

dark trailing edge almost creates mid-wing panel

inner primaries translucent

grey back

adult summer

greyish

adult summer

first winter

	COMMON TERN
Type	tern-like
Size	30–36cm (11–14in)
Habitat	sea, estuaries, inland freshwater
Behaviour	swims, dives from air, perches openly, takes off and lands on water or ground
Flocking	1–1000
Flight	hovers, aerial dive; strong and powerful; direct
Voice	harsh *key-arr*, *kirri-kirri*

IDENTIFICATION

Ad.summer	
Crown	black
Upperparts	pale grey
Rump	white
Tail	white; long and forked
Throat	white
Breast	white
Belly	white
Bill	red with black tip; short and thin
Legs	red; short
Ad.winter and juvenile	white forehead; juvenile barred brownish on upperparts

BREEDING

Nest	unlined hollow
Eggs	2–3; creamy, blotched black
Incubation	20–23 days, mainly ♀
Young	partly-active; downy
Fledging	28 days
Broods	1, 2?; May–June
Food	fish
Population	15,000–20,000 pairs

Common and widespread summer visitor. Essentially pale grey above and white below but underparts have pale greyish wash. Black cap; red legs. Bill usually red with black tip but sometimes pure red or almost black. (Beware separating Common Terns from Arctic or Roseate Terns by bill colour alone.) Deeply forked tail; light and buoyant flight. Dives for food; also picks food from surface of water like Black Tern. Autumn adults and juveniles have black leading edge to wing that forms bar when wing is folded.

Status: summer visitor; breeds along most coasts in concentrated colonies, also inland in smaller numbers.

Similar Species: Arctic Tern (p.163) and Roseate Tern (p.161).

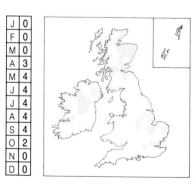

J	0
F	0
M	0
A	3
M	4
J	4
J	4
A	4
S	4
O	2
N	0
D	0

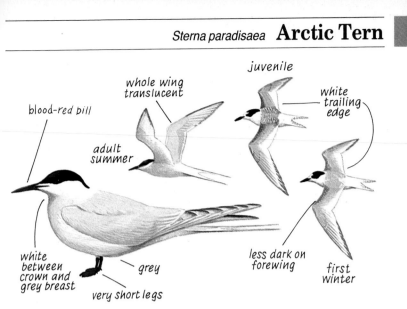

juvenile

whole wing translucent

white trailing edge

blood-red bill

adult summer

white between crown and grey breast

grey

very short legs

less dark on forewing

first winter

Like Common Tern but with shorter, darker red bill (without black tip), longer tail and fully translucent wing when seen from below. Common Tern has translucent patch only on inner primaries. Generally greyer below with white cheeks standing out pure white. More confined to coast than Common Tern. Juveniles have less black on leading edge of wing than Common Tern and prominent white trailing edge to secondaries.
Status: summer visitor mainly to northern coasts; passage migrant in south.
Similar Species: Common Tern (p.162) as above.

ARCTIC TERN

Type	tern-like
Size	30–39cm (11–15in)
Habitat	sea, estuaries, freshwater marshes
Behaviour	swims, dives from air, perches openly, takes off and lands on water and ground
Flocking	1–1000
Flight	hovers, aerial dive; strong and powerful, direct
Voice	*key-rrr*, similar to Common Tern but briefer

IDENTIFICATION

Ad.summer	
Crown	black
Upperparts	grey
Rump	white
Tail	white; long and forked
Throat	white
Breast	whitish grey
Belly	whitish grey
Bill	red; short and thin
Legs	red; short
Ad.winter and juvenile	white forehead

BREEDING

Nest	bare scrape
Eggs	2; buffy, blotched brown
Incubation	20–22 days ♂ ♀
Young	partly-active; downy
Fledging	20–22 days
Broods	1; May–June
Food	fish
Population	*c* 40,000 pairs

Month	Value
J	0
F	0
M	0
A	3
M	4
J	4
J	4
A	4
S	4
O	2
N	0
D	0

Little Tern *Sterna albifrons*

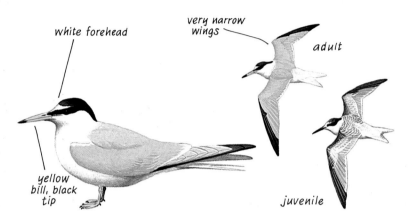

white forehead

very narrow wings

adult

yellow bill, black tip

juvenile

LITTLE TERN

Type	tern-like
Size	23–26cm (9–10in)
Habitat	sea, estuaries and adjacent freshwater
Behaviour	swims, dives from air, perches openly, takes off from water and ground
Flocking	1–50
Flight	hovers, aerial dive; strong and powerful; direct
Voice	various chatterings; high-pitched, sharp *kitik*

IDENTIFICATION

Ad.summer

Crown	black with white forehead
Upperparts	grey; black wingtips
Rump	white
Tail	white; medium length, forked
Throat	white
Breast	white
Belly	white
Bill	yellow, black tip; short and thin
Legs	yellow; short
Ad.winter and juvenile	more white on crown; juvenile sandy buff above, 'saddle' barred

BREEDING

Nest	bare scrape near sea
Eggs	2–3; olive, blotched brown
Incubation	19–22 days ♂ ♀
Young	partly-active; downy
Fledging	15–17 days
Broods	1; May–June
Food	fish
Population	c1800 pairs

Tiny, fast flying tern. Long, narrow wings, almost Swift-like in shape, flicker in fast wing beats. Essentially marine, feeding close inshore, diving for small fish; breeds along shingle beaches. Legs and bill yellow, the latter with black tip. Black cap always incomplete; forehead white.
Status: declining due to disturbance of breeding grounds; summer visitor to coasts.
Similar Species: small size separates from most other terns.

J	0
F	0
M	0
A	3
M	3
J	3
J	3
A	3
S	2
O	1
N	0
D	0

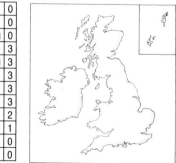

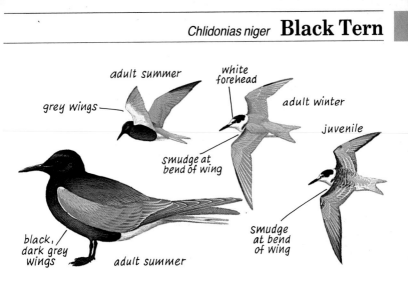

adult summer

grey wings —

white forehead

adult winter

juvenile

smudge at bend of wing

black, dark grey wings

adult summer

smudge at bend of wing

Summer adult all black with dark grey wings. Juvenile and winter adult grey above and white below, with black cap, white forehead and black smudge at sides of breast. Tail notched rather than forked. Black Terns feed by taking insects from surface of water in flight. Flight easy but erratic as they twist and swoop over the water. *Status:* regular double passage migrant through southern and eastern England; more numerous in autumn than spring. Has bred on occasion. *Similar Species:* other terns and Little Gull (p.152) feed in similar way, but Black Terns always smaller and darker.

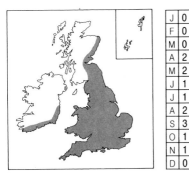

J	0
F	0
M	0
A	2
M	2
J	1
J	1
A	2
S	3
O	1
N	1
D	0

BLACK TERN

Type	tern-like
Size	23–26cm (9–10in)
Habitat	freshwater marshes, sea, estuaries
Behaviour	swims, dives from air, perches openly, takes off from water and ground
Flocking	1–15
Flight	hovers, flitting; aerial dive; undulating
Voice	high-pitched *kik*

IDENTIFICATION

Ad.summer	
Crown	black
Upperparts	black; dark grey wings
Rump	dark grey
Tail	grey; medium length, notched
Throat	black
Breast	black
Belly	black
Bill	black; short and thin
Legs	red-brown; short
Ad.winter and juvenile	grey above, white below, white forehead, dark smudge at sides of breast

BREEDING

Nest	mound of vegetation in marshy lagoon
Eggs	3; buffy, spotted brown
Incubation	14–17 days, mainly ♀
Young	partly-active; downy
Fledging	4 weeks
Broods	1; May
Food	insects
Population	very rare breeder; several 100s spring and autumn

Guillemot *Uria aalge*

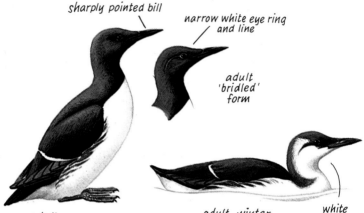

sharply pointed bill

narrow white eye ring and line

adult 'bridled' form

adult summer

adult winter

white face

	GUILLEMOT
Type	auk-like
Size	40–44cm (15–17in)
Habitat	sea and cliffs
Behaviour	swims, dives from surface, perches openly, takes off and lands on water and ground
Flocking	1–1000s
Flight	laboured; direct
Voice	various growling and moaning notes

IDENTIFICATION

Ad.summer

Crown	blackish brown
Upperparts	blackish brown
Rump	blackish brown
Tail	blackish brown; short and rounded
Throat	blackish brown
Breast	white
Belly	white
Bill	black; short and thin, pointed
Legs	black; short
Ad.winter	white throat and sides of face

BREEDING

Nest	bare cliff ledge
Eggs	1; highly variable, blotched black
Incubation	28–35 days ♂ ♀
Young	helpless; downy
Fledging	18–25 days
Broods	1; May–June
Food	fish, crustaceans, molluscs
Population	1,000,000 pairs

Strictly marine, Guillemots swim and dive offshore, sometimes at considerable distances from land. Usually found in flocks, they come to land only to breed and when forced to do so by storms. Also driven to land if feathers 'oiled' by pollution at sea. On land, they stand upright. Form dense colonies on cliff edges. Upperparts blackish brown; underparts white. Head and neck blackish brown; bill sharply pointed. In winter, neck and sides of face white. A percentage of Guillemots have white eye ring and white line extending across ear coverts – known as bridled form. *Status:* breeds mainly in north and west; widespread offshore at other times.
Similar Species: Razorbill (p.167) and Puffin (p.169).

J	2
F	2
M	3
A	4
M	4
J	4
J	4
A	3
S	2
O	2
N	2
D	2

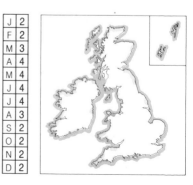

squarer bill than
Guillemot

longish pointed
tail

adult winter

white
face

adult summer

Similar to Guillemot; often forms mixed flocks. Generally blacker above. Bill shape much deeper than Guillemot, with distinctive vertical white line. In flight at sea, pointed tail particularly useful feature; gives bird elongated silhouette. Like Guillemot black neck lost in winter. Nests in rock crevices rather than on open cliff ledges.
Status: breeds in north and west, often on same cliffs as Guillemot.
Similar Species: Guillemot (p.166) and Puffin (p.169).

RAZORBILL

Type	auk-like
Size	39–43cm (15–16½in)
Habitat	sea and cliffs
Behaviour	swims, dives from surface, perches openly, takes off and lands on water and ground
Flocking	1–100
Flight	laboured; direct
Voice	growls and grunts

IDENTIFICATION

Ad.summer	
Crown	black
Upperparts	black
Rump	black
Tail	black; short and pointed
Throat	black
Breast	white
Belly	white
Bill	black, vertical white line; short and thin
Legs	black; short
Ad.winter	throat and sides of face white

BREEDING

Nest	crevice or hole in cliff
Eggs	1; variable, blotched brown
Incubation	25–35 days ♂ ♀
Young	helpless; downy
Fledging	14–24 days
Broods	1; May–June
Food	fish, crustaceans, molluscs
Population	c144,000 pairs

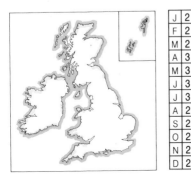

J	2
F	2
M	2
A	3
M	3
J	3
J	3
A	2
S	2
O	2
N	2
D	2

Little Auk *Alle alle*

tiny, stubby bill

white face

Summer

winter

LITTLE AUK

Type	auk-like
Size	20–22cm (7½–8½in)
Habitat	sea, estuaries
Behaviour	swims, dives from surface, takes off and lands on water or ground
Flocking	1–2
Flight	laboured; direct
Voice	silent at sea

IDENTIFICATION

Ad.winter

Crown	black
Upperparts	black
Rump	black
Tail	black; short and square
Throat	white
Breast	white
Belly	white
Bill	black; short and stubby
Legs	grey; short

BREEDING

Nest	hole among rocks, often inland
Eggs	1; blue, spotted brown
Incubation	24 days ♂ ♀
Young	helpless; downy
Fledging	3–4 weeks
Broods	1; June–July
Food	crustaceans
Population	variable (less than 1000) autumn and winter

Tiny, Starling-sized auk that is autumn and winter visitor in variable numbers, most often after severe storms. Upperparts black, underparts white. Throat and breast black in summer, white in winter. Bill short and stubby. Flies fast on whirring wings. Tiny size and rapid flight best features at sea.
Status: rare; storm-driven in late autumn and winter
Similar Species: none.

J	2
F	2
M	1
A	0
M	0
J	0
J	0
A	0
S	1
O	2
N	2
D	2

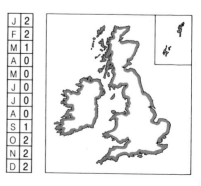

white face

multi-coloured bill

reduced bill

adult winter

less white face

adult summer

Small, comical seabird; forms colonies on offshore islands and sea stacks in north and west. Upperparts black; underparts white; face white. Outstanding feature is large parrot-like bill vertically striped in yellow and red. Size of bill reduced (horny plates at base shed) and colours paler in winter and juvenile plumages. At sea, short, rapidly whirring wings and white face are best features. Nests in burrows, but off-duty birds form groups that loaf around cliff-tops.
Status: locally abundant resident, especially in north and west; some winter wandering.
Similar Species: Guillemot (p.166) and Razorbill (p.167).

PUFFIN

Type	auk-like
Size	29–31cm (11–12in)
Habitat	sea and cliffs
Behaviour	swims, dives from surface, walks, perches openly, takes off and lands on water or ground
Flocking	1–1000
Flight	laboured; direct
Voice	deep *arr-arr*

IDENTIFICATION

Ad.summer	
Crown	black and white
Upperparts	black
Rump	black
Tail	black; short and square
Throat	black
Breast	white
Belly	white
Bill	blue-grey, red and yellow, striped; short and stubby
Legs	red; short
Ad.winter	bill smaller with paler colours
Juvenile	bill smaller and all dark

BREEDING

Nest	burrow
Eggs	1; white
Incubation	40–43 days ♀ only
Young	helpless; downy
Fledging	47–51 days
Broods	1; May
Food	fish, crustaceans, molluscs
Population	*c* 500,000 pairs

J	1
F	1
M	3
A	3
M	3
J	3
J	3
A	3
S	1
O	1
N	1
D	1

Black Guillemot *Cepphus grylle*

white wing patch

white wing patch

adult summer   red legs   **adult winter**

BLACK GUILLEMOT

Type	auk-like
Size	33–35cm (12½–13½in)
Habitat	sea and cliffs
Behaviour	swims, dives from surface, perches openly, takes off and lands on water or ground
Flocking	1–15
Flight	laboured; direct
Voice	whistling cries

IDENTIFICATION

Ad.summer	
Crown	black
Upperparts	black with white patches on wings
Rump	black
Tail	black; short and square
Throat	black
Breast	black
Belly	black
Bill	black; short and thin
Legs	red; short
Ad.winter	white below, grey above; black wings retain white oval patches

BREEDING

Nest	hole among boulders
Eggs	2; white, spotted blackish
Incubation	21–25 days ♂ ♀
Young	helpless; downy
Fledging	34–40 days
Broods	1; May–June
Food	fish, crustaceans, molluscs
Population	16,000–25,000 pairs

Scarce seabird most often seen on water below nesting cliffs. In summer, plumage all black with bold white oval patch on wings. Feet and inside of mouth bright red. In winter, mottled greyish all over, with darker wings still marked by whitish ovals.
Status: scarce resident around northern and western cliffs; virtually unknown further south.
Similar Species: none..

J	1
F	1
M	2
A	2
M	2
J	2
J	2
A	2
S	2
O	2
N	1
D	1

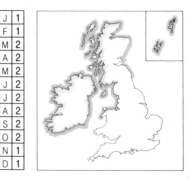

pale grey

wingbars

wingbars

white rump

Columba livia **Rock Dove**

Genuine Rock Doves are now confined to cliffs in extreme north and west. Elsewhere, they have interbred over the centuries with feral pigeons – domesticated Rock Doves escaped from captivity. Pigeons occur in wide variety of plumages, but genuine wild bird is pale grey with patch of irridescent purple and green at sides of neck. Folded wing shows two black bars. Rump white; tail broadly tipped black. Some feral pigeons show close resemblance to this plumage.
Status: highly localized resident in extreme north and west; feral birds widespread and numerous in cities and along cliffs.
Similar Species: Stock Dove (p.172) lacks white rump.

ROCK DOVE

Type	pigeon-like
Size	31–35cm (12–13in)
Habitat	sea cliffs, towns
Behaviour	walks, perches openly, takes off and lands on ground
Flocking	1–100
Flight	glides; strong and powerful; direct
Voice	familiar *oo-roo-coo*, repeated

IDENTIFICATION

Adult	
Crown	grey
Upperparts	grey
Rump	white
Tail	grey, black tip; medium length, square
Throat	grey
Breast	grey
Belly	grey
Bill	black and white; short and thin
Legs	pink; short

BREEDING

Nest	crevices and ledges in cliffs and buildings
Eggs	2; white
Incubation	17–19 days ♂ ♀
Young	helpless; downy
Fledging	30–35 days
Broods	2 or 3; Mar–Sept
Food	seeds, grain
Population	c100,000 pairs

J	3
F	3
M	3
A	3
M	3
J	3
J	3
A	3
S	3
O	3
N	3
D	3

Stock Dove *Columba oenas*

mid-grey

tiny wingbars

no white rump

whole wing bordered black

STOCK DOVE

Type	pigeon-like
Size	31–35cm (12–13in)
Habitat	forests and woods, fields and hedges, gardens, heaths
Behaviour	walks, perches openly, takes off and lands on vegetation and ground
Flocking	1–100
Flight	strong and powerful; direct
Voice	*coo-roo-oo*, repeated monotonously

IDENTIFICATION

Adult	
Crown	grey
Upperparts	grey
Rump	grey
Tail	grey, broad black tip; medium length, square
Throat	grey
Breast	pink
Belly	grey
Bill	red; short and thin
Legs	red; short

BREEDING

Nest	hole in tree or cliff
Eggs	2; white
Incubation	16–18 days ♂ ♀
Young	helpless; downy
Fledging	27–28 days
Broods	2–3; Mar–June
Food	crops, seeds, grain
Population	50,000–60,000 pairs

Grey above and paler grey below, with pale pink breast and less marked double wingbar than Rock Dove. In flight, shows grey wings with broad black borders – quite characteristic once seen. Tail broadly tipped black. Though found in similar areas to Wood Pigeon, can be distinguished by lack of white on neck and wing. *Status:* widespread resident. *Similar Species:* Rock Dove (p.171) and Wood Pigeon (p.173) as above.

J	4
F	4
M	4
A	4
M	4
J	4
J	4
A	4
S	4
O	4
N	4
D	4

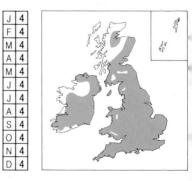

white neck slash

white bars across wing

white wing edge

Largest of the pigeons; marked by white neck flash and broad white bar across open wings. Grey above, pinkish below. In flight, outer wing is black; tail grey with black terminal band. Familiar bird throughout the country, including city-centres.
Status: abundant and widespread resident; abundant winter visitor.
Similar Species: Stock Dove (p.172).

WOOD PIGEON

Type	pigeon-like
Size	39–43cm (15–16½in)
Habitat	forests and woods, fields and hedges, towns, gardens, heaths
Behaviour	walks, perches openly, takes off and lands on vegetation or ground
Flocking	1–1000
Flight	strong and powerful; direct
Voice	*coo-coo-coo-cu-coo*, repeated endlessly

IDENTIFICATION

Adult	
Crown	grey
Upperparts	grey
Rump	grey
Tail	grey with black band; medium length, square
Throat	grey
Breast	pink
Belly	grey
Bill	red; short and thin
Legs	red; short
Juvenile	lacks white neck patch

BREEDING

Nest	twig platform in tree
Eggs	2; white
Incubation	17 days ♂ ♀
Young	helpless; downy
Fledging	29–35 days
Broods	3; Apr–June
Food	crops, seeds, grain
Population	4,800,000 individuals

J	6
F	6
M	6
A	6
M	6
J	6
J	6
A	6
S	6
O	6
N	6
D	6

Collared Dove *Streptopelia decaocto*

black neck slash

buffy

pale, white-edged tail

broad white undertail

COLLARED DOVE

Type	pigeon-like
Size	29–32cm (11–12in)
Habitat	towns and gardens, fields and hedges
Behaviour	walks, perches openly, takes off and lands on vegetation or ground
Flocking	1–50
Flight	glides; strong and powerful; direct
Voice	*coo-cooo-coo* repeated at length; plaintive *weer*

IDENTIFICATION

Adult	
Crown	buff
Upperparts	buff
Rump	buff
Tail	buff with white corners, undertail black with broad white tip; medium length, rounded
Throat	buff
Breast	buff
Belly	buff
Bill	brown; short and thin
Legs	red; short

BREEDING

Nest	platform of twigs in tree
Eggs	2; white
Incubation	14 days ♂ ♀
Young	helpless; downy
Fledging	18 days
Broods	2–5; Mar–Sept
Food	seeds, grain
Population	50,000+ pairs

First nested in Norfolk in 1955 and has since spread throughout the country. Pale buffy above, pinkish below; neat black line (collar) on sides of neck. In flight, undertail has black base and broad white tip. Haunts gardens with conifers as well as grain stores, where may form substantial flocks.
Status: widespread resident, reaches high densities in south-east; continued immigration probable.
Similar Species: Turtle Dove (p.175) is rust-brown on back.

J	5
F	5
M	5
A	5
M	5
J	5
J	5
A	5
S	5
O	5
N	5
D	5

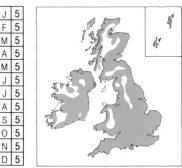

bold black and white
neck slash

dark, white-
edged tail

black and
brown

narrow
white tail
tip

Small, fast-flying dove; purring call is characteristic sound of summer. Grey-brown on head and back; pinkish below. Wing coverts black; each feather broadly edged rust, creating turtle-shell appearance. Shows rufous back and wing coverts in flight. Black tail edged white; smudged black and white neck slash. Forms flocks in autumn.

Status: summer visitor to south and east England.

Similar Species: Collared Dove (p.174) is similar size, but plain buff above.

TURTLE DOVE	
Type	pigeon-like
Size	26–29cm (10–11in)
Habitat	forests and woods, fields and hedges, gardens
Behaviour	walks, perches openly, takes off and lands on vegetation or ground
Flocking	1–50
Flight	strong and powerful; direct
Voice	purring *roor-rr*

IDENTIFICATION

Adult	
Crown	grey
Upperparts	brown and black, 'scalloped'
Rump	brown
Tail	black edged white; medium length, rounded
Throat	pink
Breast	pink
Belly	white
Bill	black; short and thin
Legs	red; short

BREEDING

Nest	platform of twigs in tree
Eggs	2; white
Incubation	13–14 days ♂ ♀
Young	helpless; downy
Fledging	19–21 days
Broods	2; May–June
Food	seeds
Population	c125,000 pairs

J	0
F	0
M	0
A	3
M	5
J	5
J	5
A	5
S	4
O	2
N	1
D	0

Rose-ringed Parakeet *Psittacula krameri*

♀

♂

red

neck ring

long green tail

ROSE-RINGED PARAKEET

Type	parrot-like
Size	37–43cm (14–16½in)
Habitat	towns and gardens, fields and hedges
Behaviour	walks, perches openly, takes off and lands on vegetation or ground
Flocking	1–10
Flight	strong and powerful; direct
Voice	screamed *keeo-keeo*

IDENTIFICATION

Adult	
Crown	green
Upperparts	green
Rump	green
Tail	green; long and pointed
Throat	green
Breast	green
Belly	green
Bill	red; large and hooked
Legs	blue; short
Adult ♂	pink and black neck ring

BREEDING

Nest	tree hole
Eggs	3–4; white
Incubation	25–28 days ♀
Young	helpless; naked
Fledging	8 weeks
Broods	?
Food	seeds, fruit
Population	?

Only parrot at large in Britain; introduced from India in 1960s. Plumage mainly green with blackish outer wings. Extremely long, pointed tail. Large, hooked, red bill. Male has narrow neck ring of pink and black. Often called Ring-necked Parakeet but several Asian parakeets have neck rings; Rose-ringed is the Indian name.
Status: scarce but widespread resident in many areas; increasing and spreading.
Similar Species: none.

J	2
F	2
M	2
A	2
M	2
J	2
J	2
A	2
S	2
O	2
N	2
D	2

Cuculus canorus **Common Cuckoo**

small head and bill

juvenile

juvenile

adult ♀

long narrow wings

grey head and neck

adult

long tail

adult

hepatic phase

barred below

Harbinger of spring and Britain's most familiar bird call. Usually seen in flight when long pointed wings, long tail and small head are reminiscent of a hawk. When perched, often on overhead wire, appears ungainly and off-balance; seems to have difficulty folding wings. Upperparts and breast grey; underparts barred black and white. Juvenile darker; heavily barred above and below. Hepatic female is rare colour phase; chestnut above and white below. All females are heavily barred, like juvenile.
Status: widespread summer visitor.
Similar Species: beware female Sparrowhawk (p.89).

COMMON CUCKOO	
Type	pigeon-like/hawk-like
Size	32–34cm (12–13in)
Habitat	gardens, marshes, moors and heaths, woods, fields and hedges
Behaviour	hops, perches openly, takes off and lands on vegetation or ground
Flocking	1–2
Flight	direct
Voice	*cuc-coo* repeated

IDENTIFICATION

Adult	
Crown	grey
Upperparts	grey
Rump	grey
Tail	grey; long and rounded
Throat	grey
Breast	grey
Belly	black and white, barred
Bill	black; short and thin
Legs	yellow; short
Juvenile	mottled and barred brown, black, buff and white
Hepatic ♀	chestnut and white, heavily barred

BREEDING

Nest	parasitic
Eggs	8–12; highly variable, mimic host
Incubation	12½ days; by host
Young	helpless; naked
Fledging	20–23 days
Broods	not applicable
Food	insects
Population	17,000–35,000 pairs

J	0
F	0
M	1
A	3
M	4
J	4
J	4
A	3
S	3
O	2
N	0
D	0

Barn Owl *Tyto alba*

bold facial disc

white breast

rare dark breasted form

pale rounded wings

flat white face

BARN OWL

Type	owl-like
Size	33–36cm (12½–14in)
Habitat	heaths, woods, fields and hedges
Behaviour	perches openly, takes off and lands on vegetation or ground
Flocking	solitary
Flight	hovers, glides
Voice	variety shrill shrieks, hisses and snoring notes

IDENTIFICATION

Adult

Crown	buffy orange
Upperparts	buffy orange, dark spots
Rump	buffy orange
Tail	buffy orange; short and square
Throat	white
Breast	white
Belly	white
Bill	grey; hooked
Legs	white; medium length

BREEDING

Nest	hole in tree or building
Eggs	4–7; white
Incubation	32–34 days ♀
Young	helpless; naked
Fledging	60 days
Broods	1–2; Mar–May
Food	small mammals, birds
Population	5000–10,000 pairs

The ghost-like, white owl of country folklore. Most often seen quartering fields at dusk when white underparts identify. Upperparts pale orange-buff with darkish spots. Flat-faced appearance with dark ring around facial disc. The dark-breasted form is a rare immigrant from central Europe. *Status:* widespread resident but nowhere common; declining in numbers.
Similar Species: all other owls are brown and buff, except rare Snowy Owl, which is white, mottled black.

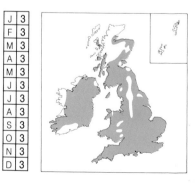

J	3
F	3
M	3
A	3
M	3
J	3
J	3
A	3
S	3
O	3
N	3
D	3

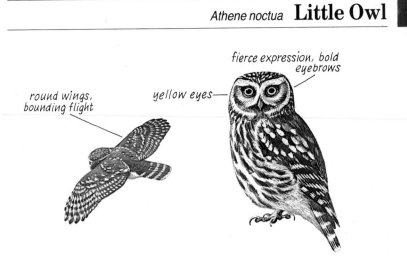

fierce expression, bold eyebrows

yellow eyes

round wings, bounding flight

Small brown and buff owl; most often seen perched openly during daylight. When disturbed, flies away with distinctive bouncing flight, like a woodpecker. Staring yellow eyes and prominent facial disc with bold 'eyebrows' create fierce expression. *Status:* introduced resident England and Wales.
Similar Species: only tiny owl.

LITTLE OWL

Type	owl-like
Size	21–23cm (8–9in)
Habitat	towns and gardens, heaths, woods, fields and hedges
Behaviour	perches openly, takes off and lands on vegetation or ground
Flocking	solitary
Flight	glides; undulating
Voice	plaintive *keeoo*

IDENTIFICATION

Adult	
Crown	brown and buff, spotted
Upperparts	brown and buff, spotted
Rump	brown and buff, spotted
Tail	brown and buff; short and square
Throat	brown and buff, streaked
Breast	brown and buff, streaked
Belly	white, streaked brown
Bill	grey; hooked
Legs	white; medium length

BREEDING

Nest	hole in tree or building
Eggs	3–5; white
Incubation	28–29 days ♀
Young	helpless; downy
Fledging	4–5 weeks
Broods	1, 2 ?; Apr–May
Food	insects, small mammals, small birds
Population	7000–14,000 pairs

J	3
F	3
M	3
A	3
M	3
J	3
J	3
A	3
S	3
O	3
N	3
D	3

Short-eared Owl *Asio flammeus*

rounded head, yellow eyes

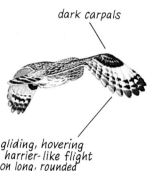

dark carpals

gliding, hovering harrier-like flight on long, rounded wings

SHORT-EARED OWL	
Type	owl-like
Size	36–39cm (14–15in)
Habitat	freshwater marshes, moors, estuaries
Behaviour	perches openly, takes off and lands on ground
Flocking	1–2
Flight	hovers, glides; laboured
Voice	high-pitched *kee-aw*; deep *boo-boo-boo*

IDENTIFICATION

Adult	
Crown	buff
Upperparts	brown and buff, barred
Rump	brown and buff, barred
Tail	brown and buff; short and square
Throat	brown and buff, streaked
Breast	brown and buff, streaked
Belly	pale buff
Bill	black; hooked
Legs	white; medium length

BREEDING

Nest	hollow on ground
Eggs	4–8; white
Incubation	24–28 days ♀
Young	helpless; downy
Fledging	22–27 days
Broods	1 (sometimes 2); Apr–June
Food	small mammals
Population	1000+ pairs

Diurnal owl, associated with marshes and moorland; the owl most frequently seen hunting during daylight. Flat head and long, rounded wings with dark carpal patches above. Pale, almost white, below with dark wingtips and carpal patches. Quarters territory like a harrier – weaves, hovers and glides with wings held in shallow 'V'.
Status: resident mainly in north and along east coast of Britain; passage migrant and winter visitor elsewhere.
Similar Species: only regular diurnal owl of moors and marshes.

J	3
F	3
M	3
A	3
M	3
J	3
J	3
A	3
S	3
O	3
N	3
D	3

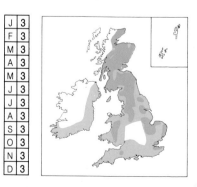

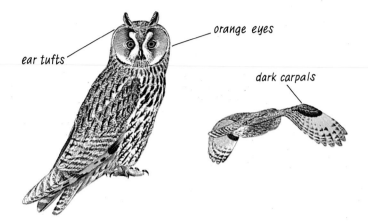

ear tufts

orange eyes

dark carpals

Medium-sized owl with striking orange eyes, prominent facial disc and conspicuous ear tufts. Upperparts mottled buff and brown; underparts buffy, streaked brown. Scarce and secretive owl, lacking obviously distinctive voice. Mainly found in old conifers; sometimes forms communal roosts in winter.

Status: widespread, but patchy, throughout Britain and Ireland. Continental immigrants in winter.

Similar Species: Tawny Owl (p.182) also occurs in woodlands.

LONG-EARED OWL

Type	owl-like
Size	34–37cm (13–14in)
Habitat	forests and woods, heaths
Behaviour	takes off and lands on vegetation or ground
Flocking	solitary
Flight	glides; laboured; direct
Voice	low *oo-oo-oo*, juvenile a rusty-hinge contact squeak

IDENTIFICATION

Adult

Crown	buff and brown, mottled
Upperparts	buff and brown, mottled
Rump	buff and brown, mottled
Tail	buff and brown; short and square
Throat	buff, streaked brown
Breast	buff, streaked brown
Belly	buff, streaked brown
Bill	black; hooked
Legs	buff; medium length

BREEDING

Nest	old nest of different species in tree
Eggs	4–5; white
Incubation	25–30 days ♀
Young	helpless; downy
Fledging	23–24 days
Broods	1 (rarely 2); Feb–May
Food	small mammals
Population	3000–10,000 pairs; 10,000–35,000 winter

J	2
F	2
M	2
A	2
M	2
J	2
J	2
A	2
S	2
O	2
N	2
D	2

Tawny Owl *Strix aluco*

large rounded head

dark eyes

flat head

broad rounded wings

TAWNY OWL

Type	owl-like
Size	36–40cm (14–15½in)
Habitat	towns and gardens, heaths, forests and woods, fields and hedges
Behaviour	perches openly, takes off and lands on vegetation
Flocking	solitary
Flight	glides; direct
Voice	hooted *hoo-hoo-hoo-oo-oo-oo*; harsh *ke-wick*

IDENTIFICATION

Adult

Crown	brown, mottled buff
Upperparts	brown, mottled buff
Rump	brown, mottled buff
Tail	buff and brown; short and square
Throat	buff, streaked brown
Breast	buff, streaked brown
Belly	buff
Bill	grey; hooked
Legs	white; medium length

BREEDING

Nest	hole in tree or building
Eggs	2–4; white
Incubation	28–30 days ♀
Young	helpless; downy
Fledging	32–37 days
Broods	1; Mar–May
Food	small mammals, small birds
Population	50,000–100,000 pairs

The brown owl of the countryside and source of the most familiar owl hoots and shrieks. Although widespread (except Ireland), surprisingly seldom seen. Upperparts brown, mottled buff; underparts buffy, broadly streaked brown. Well-marked facial disc set off by large, dark eyes. In flight, wings long and rounded.

Status: widespread and numerous resident throughout Britain; absent Ireland.

Similar Species: can be confused with much scarcer Long-eared Owl (p.181) but calls completely different.

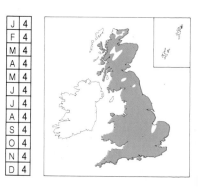

J	4
F	4
M	4
A	4
M	4
J	4
J	4
A	4
S	4
O	4
N	4
D	4

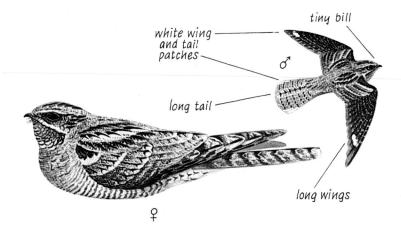

tiny bill

white wing and tail patches

♂

long tail

long wings

♀

Medium-sized nocturnal bird with long wings and tail. Heavily mottled and barred in browns, buffs and greys, creating excellent camouflage when bird nests on ground on open heaths. Male has conspicuous white patches on wings and tail, lacking in female. Best located by distinctive churring call (similar to that made by vibrating tongue in mouth), which continues for long periods. Claps wings in display. *Status:* widespread but scarce and declining summer visitor.
Similar Species: none.

EUROPEAN NIGHTJAR

Type	hawk-like/owl-like
Size	25–28cm (9½–11in)
Habitat	heaths, forests and woods
Behaviour	takes off and lands on vegetation or ground
Flocking	solitary
Flight	glides; flitting
Voice	distinctive churring

IDENTIFICATION

Adult ♂	
Crown	grey
Upperparts	brown, spotted
Rump	brown
Tail	brown, white patches; long and square
Throat	buff and brown, barred
Breast	buff and brown, barred
Belly	buff and brown, barred
Bill	black; short and thin
Legs	buff; short
Adult ♀	lacks white wing and tail patches

BREEDING

Nest	bare hollow
Eggs	2; white, spotted light brown
Incubation	18 days ♂ ♀
Young	partly-active; downy
Fledging	16–18 days
Broods	2; May–July
Food	insects
Population	3000–6000 pairs

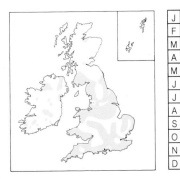

J	0
F	0
M	0
A	1
M	2
J	2
J	2
A	2
S	1
O	1
N	0
D	0

Common Swift *Apus apus*

long narrow wings

torpedo-shaped body

Superficially similar to Swallow and martins but easily distinguished by longer and narrower sickle-shaped wings and all-black coloration. Most aerial of birds, coming to land (buildings and caves) only to lay and incubate eggs and feed young. Flickers wings and forms 'screaming' parties over colonies on summer evenings.
Status: common summer visitor.
Similar Species: Barn Swallow (p.195) and martins (pages 194–6).

COMMON SWIFT

Type	swallow-like
Size	16–17cm (6in)
Habitat	towns, freshwater, moors, heaths, fields and hedges
Behaviour	totally aerial, takes off and lands on buildings
Flocking	1–1000
Flight	glides; strong and powerful; flitting
Voice	high-pitched scream

IDENTIFICATION

Adult

Crown	black
Upperparts	black
Rump	black
Tail	black; short and forked
Throat	grey
Breast	black
Belly	black
Bill	black; short and thin
Legs	black; short

BREEDING

Nest	leaves and debris inside building
Eggs	3; white
Incubation	14–20 days ♂ ♀
Young	helpless; naked
Fledging	5–8 weeks
Broods	1; May–June
Food	insects
Population	*c*100,000 pairs

J	0
F	0
M	0
A	2
M	5
J	6
J	6
A	5
S	2
O	0
N	0
D	0

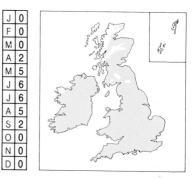

Alcedo atthis **Common Kingfisher**

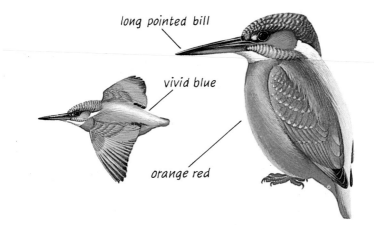

long pointed bill

vivid blue

orange red

Exotic, jewel-like bird, most often seen as a flash of bright blue as it dashes upstream. Confined to small streams, though may move to larger rivers and even coastal marshes during hard weather. Upperparts blue-green with vividly blue rump; underparts bright orange-red. Catches fishes by diving head-first into water.
Status: declining resident, becoming decidedly scarce.
Similar Species: none.

J	3
F	3
M	3
A	3
M	3
J	3
J	3
A	3
S	3
O	3
N	3
D	3

COMMON KINGFISHER

Type	unique
Size	15–16cm (5½–6in)
Habitat	inland freshwater
Behaviour	dives from air, perches openly, takes off and lands in vegetation
Flocking	solitary
Flight	direct; aerial dive
Voice	metallic *chee*, or *chee-kee*, often rapidly repeated

IDENTIFICATION

Adult	
Crown	blue-green, barred black
Upperparts	blue-green; wings barred black
Rump	bright blue
Tail	blue-green; short and square
Throat	white
Breast	orange-red
Belly	orange-red
Bill	black; straight and thin
Legs	red; short

BREEDING

Nest	hole in bank
Eggs	6–7; white
Incubation	19–21 days ♂ ♀
Young	helpless; naked
Fledging	23–27 days
Broods	2; Apr–June
Food	fish
Population	5000–9000 pairs

Hoopoe *Upupa epops*

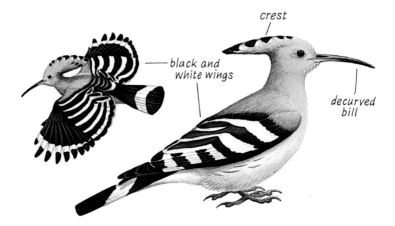

crest

black and white wings

decurved bill

HOOPOE

Type	unique
Size	27–29cm (10–11in)
Habitat	gardens, heaths, woods, fields
Behaviour	perches openly, walks, takes off from vegetation or ground
Flocking	solitary
Flight	laboured; undulating; flitting
Voice	distinctive *poo-poo-poo*, repeated

IDENTIFICATION

Adult	
Crown	sandy fawn; crest tipped black
Upperparts	black with white bars
Rump	black with white bars
Tail	black with white bars; medium length, square
Throat	sandy fawn
Breast	sandy fawn
Belly	white
Bill	black; long and decurved
Legs	grey; short

BREEDING

Nest	hole in tree, building or rocks
Eggs	5–8; greyish
Incubation	16–19 days ♀
Young	helpless; downy
Fledging	20–27 days
Broods	1 (2?); Apr–June
Food	insects
Population	rarely breeds; variable passage migrant

Distinctive at rest and in flight. Sandy fawn above and below, marked by long erectile crest with black margin. Wings and tail black with broad white bars. Short legs and long, black, decurved bill. Spends much time on ground where may be surprisingly inconspicuous; also perches freely in trees.
Status: summer visitor to Mediterranean; overshoots in spring to reach southern England and Ireland. Occasionally stays to breed.
Similar Species: none.

J	0
F	0
M	1
A	1
M	1
J	1
J	1
A	1
S	1
O	0
N	0
D	0

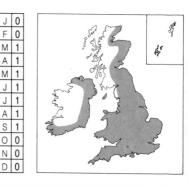

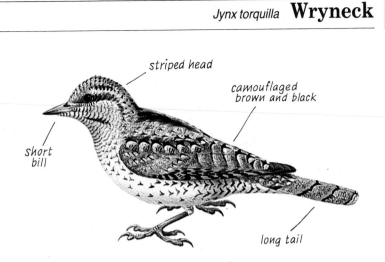

striped head

camouflaged
brown and black

short
bill

long tail

Highly elusive, well-camouflaged relative of the woodpeckers; spends most of its time on the ground or perched inconspicuously in bushes. Does not behave like a woodpecker, although voice similar to Lesser Spotted. Upperparts brown, variously mottled, streaked and barred with black, buff and grey. Short bill, striped head pattern and long tail produce unusual appearance. Name comes from habit of twisting neck right round when startled or handled.
Status: formerly bred southern England; now in process of colonizing Scotland. Regular but scarce passage migrant – especially in autumn on south and east coasts.
Similar Species: none.

WRYNECK

Type	woodpecker-like
Size	15–16cm (5½–6in)
Habitat	gardens, heaths, woods, fields
Behaviour	perches openly, hops, takes off from vegetation or ground
Flocking	solitary
Flight	direct
Voice	far-carrying *kyee-kyee-kyee*, repeated

IDENTIFICATION

Adult	
Crown	buff and brown
Upperparts	brown with black, buff and grey markings
Rump	buff and brown
Tail	grey, barred black; long, square
Throat	buff
Breast	barred buff and brown
Belly	barred buff and brown
Bill	black; short and thin
Legs	brown; short

BREEDING

Nest	hole in tree or wall
Eggs	7–10; white
Incubation	12–14 days, mainly ♀
Young	helpless; naked
Fledging	19–21 days
Broods	1, occasionally 2; May–June
Food	insects
Population	0–10 pairs; passage migrant

J	0
F	0
M	1
A	1
M	1
J	1
J	1
A	1
S	2
O	1
N	0
D	0

Green Woodpecker *Picus viridis*

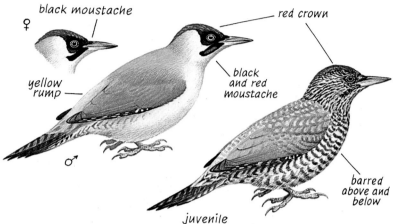

♀ black moustache

red crown

yellow rump

black and red moustache

♂

barred above and below

juvenile

GREEN WOODPECKER

Type	woodpecker-like
Size	30–33cm (11½–13in)
Habitat	gardens, woods, heaths, fields
Behaviour	climbs, hops, takes off from vegetation or ground
Flocking	1–2
Flight	laboured; undulating
Voice	loud, laughing *keu-keu-keu*

IDENTIFICATION

Adult

Crown	red
Upperparts	green
Rump	yellow
Tail	dark brown, barred below; short and pointed
Throat	grey
Breast	grey
Belly	white with greenish wash
Bill	silver-grey; short and thin
Legs	grey; short
Juvenile	face and underparts heavily barred black; less conspicuous moustaches

BREEDING

Nest	bare tree hole
Eggs	5–7; white
Incubation	18–19 days ♂ ♀
Young	helpless; naked
Fledging	18–21 days
Broods	1; Apr–May
Food	insects
Population	15,000–30,000 pairs

Large green and yellow woodpecker which spends much time on ground, feeding. Bright red crown; moustachial stripe red, bordered black in male, pure black in female. Upperparts green, rump yellow, tail dark brown and pointed. Underparts white with faint greenish wash; undertail barred brown. Dagger-like silver-grey bill; grey legs. Typical undulating flight. Unlike other woodpeckers, rarely drums.
Status: widespread resident of woods and heaths in most of Britain except northern Scotland; absent Ireland.
Similar Species: only large green woodpecker to occur in Britain.

J	3
F	3
M	3
A	3
M	3
J	3
J	3
A	3
S	3
O	3
N	3
D	3

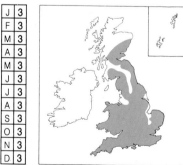

Dendrocopus major Great Spotted Woodpecker

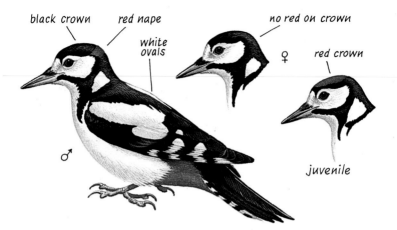

black crown   red nape

white ovals

no red on crown   ♀

red crown

♂

juvenile

Most common and widespread of the three British woodpeckers. Upperparts black broken by white cheeks, neck patch, and two bold white ovals on back. Underparts buffy white; red undertail coverts. Adult male has red patch on hind crown (lacking in female). Juvenile has red crown. Largely confined to woodland; climbs trees easily. Both sexes frequently drum on dead wood producing loud, far-carrying hollow sound. Deeply undulating flight.
Status: widespread resident; absent Ireland.
Similar Species: much smaller and more elusive Lesser Spotted Woodpecker (p.190) lacks red undertail and white ovals on back.

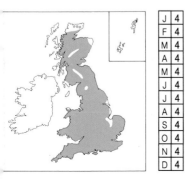

J	4
F	4
M	4
A	4
M	4
J	4
J	4
A	4
S	4
O	4
N	4
D	4

GREAT SPOTTED WOODPECKER

Type	woodpecker-like
Size	22–24cm (8–9in)
Habitat	woods, gardens, hedges
Behaviour	climbs, takes off and lands on vegetation
Flocking	1–2
Flight	laboured; undulating
Voice	loud *tchack*; also far-carrying, hollow drumming

IDENTIFICATION

Adult ♂	
Crown	black; red patch on nape
Upperparts	black and white; bold white ovals on back
Rump	black
Tail	black, undertail red; short and rounded
Throat	white
Breast	buffy white
Belly	buffy white; red on lower belly
Bill	grey; short and thin
Legs	grey; short
Adult ♀	lacks red on nape
Juvenile	red crown

BREEDING

Nest	tree hole
Eggs	4–7; white
Incubation	16 days, mainly ♀
Young	helpless; naked
Fledging	18–21 days
Broods	1; May–June
Food	insects
Population	60,000–80,000 pairs

Lesser Spotted Woodpecker *Dendrocopus minor*

buffy crown

red crown

♀

ladder back

♂

LESSER SPOTTED WOODPECKER

Type	woodpecker-like
Size	14–15cm (5½–6in)
Habitat	heaths, woods, hedgerows, parks
Behaviour	climbs, takes off and lands on vegetation
Flocking	solitary
Flight	undulating
Voice	high-pitched *kee-kee-kee-kee*, repeated; similar to Wryneck

IDENTIFICATION

Adult ♂

Crown	red
Upperparts	black, barred white
Rump	black
Tail	black; short and rounded
Throat	white
Breast	buffy white
Belly	buffy white
Bill	grey; short and thin
Legs	grey; short
Adult ♀	lacks red crown

BREEDING

Nest	tree hole
Eggs	4–6; white
Incubation	14 days ♂ ♀
Young	helpless, naked
Fledging	21 days
Broods	1; May–June
Food	insects
Population	5000–10,000 pairs

Tiny, sparrow-sized, black and white woodpecker; spends most of its time among the woodland canopy where easily overlooked. Agile climber, often on thin twigs near tops of trees. Male has red crown, female buffy white. Upperparts black, boldly barred white across back; white cheeks. Underparts buffy white. Both sexes drum on dead branches producing faster, higher-pitched sound than Great Spotted. Frequently calls early in breeding season. Needs dead and decaying trees for nesting.
Status: resident breeder in England and Wales.
Similar Species: Great Spotted Woodpecker (p.189) is larger and has white shoulder patches and red undertail.

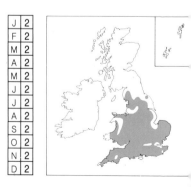

J	2
F	2
M	2
A	2
M	2
J	2
J	2
A	2
S	2
O	2
N	2
D	2

eyebrows meet at nape

white corners to tail

black and white mark at bend of wing

short tail

Small, stockily-built lark; scarce inhabitant of heaths and open woodlands. Favours areas of short grass with scattered trees and shrubs, on which it frequently lands. Similar to Sky Lark but tail obviously shorter and only hint of crest; prominent pale eyebrows meet at nape. Small black and white patch at bend of wing. Upperparts streaked brown and buff; underparts white with brown and buff streaks on breast. Distinctive song uttered from tree-top or in flight; melodic and liquid series of repeated phrases.
Status: fast-declining resident of southern England.
Similar Species: Sky Lark (p.192).

	WOOD LARK
Type	lark-like
Size	14.5–16cm (5½–6in)
Habitat	heaths, woods
Behaviour	walks, takes off and lands on vegetation or ground
Flocking	1–2
Flight	hovers; undulating
Voice	fluty *too-loo-eet*

IDENTIFICATION

Adult	
Crown	buff and brown
Upperparts	buff and brown, streaked
Rump	buff and brown
Tail	buff and brown, tipped white; short and notched
Throat	white
Breast	white, streaked buff
Belly	white
Bill	brown; short and thin
Legs	pink; medium length

BREEDING

Nest	cup on ground
Eggs	3–4; buffy, spotted brown
Incubation	12–16 days ♀
Young	helpless; downy
Fledging	15–17 days?
Broods	2; Mar–May
Food	seeds, insects
Population	60–360 pairs

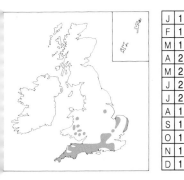

J	1
F	1
M	1
A	2
M	2
J	2
J	2
A	1
S	1
O	1
N	1
D	1

Sky Lark *Alauda arvensis*

small crest

whitish trailing edge

white outer tail

SKY LARK

Type	lark-like
Size	17–18cm (6½–7in)
Habitat	moors, heaths, fields, marshes
Behaviour	walks, takes off and lands on ground
Flocking	1–100
Flight	hovers; undulating
Voice	liquid *chirrup*, also fine warbling song in towering flight

IDENTIFICATION

Adult	
Crown	buff and brown; small crest
Upperparts	buff and brown; heavily-streaked
Rump	buff and brown
Tail	buff and brown, white-edged; long and notched
Throat	white
Breast	buff; streaked brown
Belly	white
Bill	brown; short and thickish
Legs	pinkish; medium length

BREEDING

Nest	cup on ground
Eggs	3–4; greyish, blotched brown
Incubation	11 days ♀
Young	helpless; downy
Fledging	20 days
Broods	2–3; Apr–June
Food	seeds, insects
Population	2,000,000–3,000,000 pairs

Heavily-streaked, ground-dwelling bird of wide variety of habitats; common and widespread at all seasons. Most often seen in towering song flight during spring and early summer. Thickish bill and bulky shape distinguish from pipits; noticeable crest and long, white-edged tail separate from Wood Lark. Gregarious outside breeding season. *Status:* breeds throughout Britain and Ireland; also double passage migrant and winter visitor in large numbers.
Similar Species: Wood Lark (p.191).

J	5
F	5
M	5
A	5
M	5
J	5
J	5
A	5
S	5
O	5
N	5
D	5

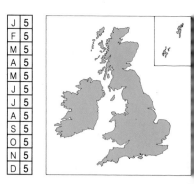

bold face pattern

white outer tail

winter

♂ summer

Scarce autumn and winter visitor to east coast of Britain. Usually confined to shorelines, saltings and shingle with sparse growth of vegetation. Difficult to locate until it flies. Buffy brown above and white below. Shows white outer tail feathers; distinctive black and yellow face pattern and two tiny black 'horns' on top of head. Face pattern subdued in winter but still unmistakable. Usually occurs in small flocks, often in same areas occupied by Snow Buntings.
Status: scarce in autumn, even scarcer in winter. Has bred in Scotland.
Similar Species: none.

SHORE LARK

Type	lark-like
Size	16–17cm (6–6½in)
Habitat	estuaries and shores
Behaviour	walks, takes off and lands on ground
Flocking	1–15
Flight	undulating
Voice	shrill *tseep* or *tseep-seep*, similar to wagtail or pipit

IDENTIFICATION

Adult	
Crown	buff; black 'horns'
Upperparts	buff and brown
Rump	buff
Tail	buff and brown, white outer feathers; medium length, notched
Throat	yellow
Breast	black crescent
Belly	white
Bill	black; short and thin
Legs	black; short
Juvenile	darker above, spotted buff-white; lacks black and yellow face pattern

BREEDING

Nest	cup on ground
Eggs	4; greenish, speckled brown
Incubation	10–14 days ♀
Young	helpless; downy
Fledging	?
Broods	2; May–June
Food	seeds, insects
Population	less than 300 winter

J	2
F	2
M	1
A	0
M	0
J	0
J	0
A	0
S	0
O	2
N	2
D	2

Sand Martin *Riparia riparia*

completely brown upperparts

breast band

SAND MARTIN	
Type	swallow-like
Size	11–12cm (4½–5in)
Habitat	inland freshwater, sea cliffs
Behaviour	aerial, takes off and lands on ground
Flocking	1–100s
Flight	flitting
Voice	continuous twittering, harsh *chirrup*

IDENTIFICATION

Adult	
Crown	sandy brown
Upperparts	sandy brown
Rump	sandy brown
Tail	sandy brown; short and notched
Throat	white
Breast	sandy brown band
Belly	white
Bill	black; short and thin
Legs	black; short

BREEDING

Nest	hole in sand-bank; colonial
Eggs	4–5; white
Incubation	1–12 days ♂ ♀
Young	helpless; downy
Fledging	19 days
Broods	2; May–June
Food	insects
Population	less than 250,000 pairs

Smallest of the swallow-like birds, with shallow, forked tail and sharply angled wings. Erratic flight with less frequent glides than similar species. Upperparts sandy brown; underparts white. Distinctive brown breast band. Always gregarious, forming highly vocal, twittering flocks; frequently gathers to feed over water. Nests in colonies in sand-banks and cliffs. In winter and on passage roosts among dense reeds, often in company with Barn Swallows.
Status: widespread summer visitor, except to northern and western isles. Sharp decline in mid-1980s associated with drought in Africa.
Similar Species: Barn Swallow (p.195) and House Martin (p.196) have blackish upperparts.

J	0
F	0
M	2
A	4
M	4
J	4
J	4
A	4
S	3
O	3
N	0
D	0

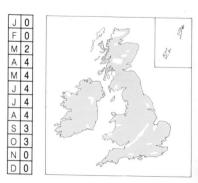

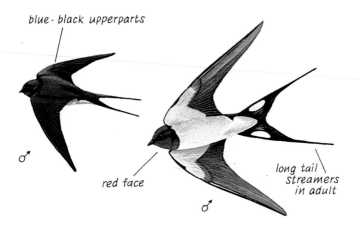

blue-black upperparts

red face

♂

long tail streamers in adult

♂

Summer visitor to farms and gardens; most frequently nests inside barns, sheds, garages and other outbuildings. Fast, highly acrobatic flight in search of flying insects. Long, angled wings and deeply-forked tail streamers in adult; streamers longer in male than female. Spread tail shows row of white spots. Upperparts dark metallic blue; face and throat red, bordered below by narrow, dark breast band. Remaining underparts vary from pale cream to rich pink. Mostly gregarious (save at breeding site), gathering in large numbers to feed over marshes and freshwater and to roost in reed beds. *Status:* common and widespread summer visitor.
Similar Species: House Martin (p.196) and Sand Martin (p.194).

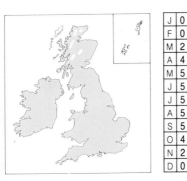

J	0
F	0
M	2
A	4
M	5
J	5
J	5
A	5
S	5
O	4
N	2
D	0

BARN SWALLOW

Type	swallow-like
Size	16–22cm (6½–8½in)
Habitat	gardens, freshwater, marshes, moors, fields
Behaviour	aerial, takes off and lands on buildings
Flocking	1–100s
Flight	glides; flitting
Voice	high-pitched *vit-vit-vit*; song, a twittering trill

IDENTIFICATION

Adult	
Crown	dark metallic blue
Upperparts	dark metallic blue
Rump	dark metallic blue
Tail	blue-black; long and forked
Throat	red
Breast	dark metallic blue; narrow band
Belly	pale cream to rich pink
Bill	black; short and thin
Legs	black; short
Juvenile	lacks tail streamers

BREEDING

Nest	mud cup inside outbuilding
Eggs	4–5; white with reddish spots
Incubation	14–16 days, ♀ alone?
Young	helpless; downy
Fledging	17–24 days
Broods	2–3; May–June
Food	insects
Population	500,000+ pairs

House Martin _Delichon urbica_

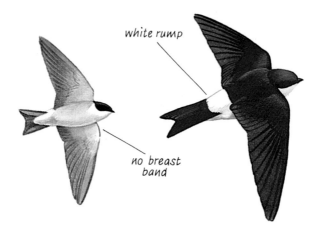

white rump

no breast band

HOUSE MARTIN

Type	swallow-like
Size	12–13cm (4½–5in)
Habitat	towns, inland freshwater
Behaviour	aerial, takes off and lands on buildings
Flocking	1–100
Flight	glides; flitting
Voice	harsh _chirrup_, quite unlike other 'swallows'

IDENTIFICATION

Adult

Crown	blue-black
Upperparts	blue-black, wings black
Rump	white
Tail	black; short and forked
Throat	white
Breast	white
Belly	white
Bill	black; short and thin
Legs	white; short

BREEDING

Nest	mud dome under eaves; colonial
Eggs	4–5; white
Incubation	13–19 days ♂ ♀
Young	helpless; downy
Fledging	19–25 days
Broods	2–3; May–June
Food	insects
Population	300,000–600,000 pairs

Compact, black and white, swallow-like bird. Common summer visitor, nesting mostly under eaves of buildings; usually forms colonies. Requires nearby source of soft mud to construct nearly spherical nest, which is well known in many small towns and villages. Blue-black on crown and back; black wings and tail; prominent white rump and pure white underparts. Usually gregarious but does not join communal roosts of Barn Swallows and Sand Martins in reed beds. Often seen feeding over freshwater.

Status: common and widespread summer visitor.

Similar Species: Barn Swallow (p.195) and Sand Martin (p.194).

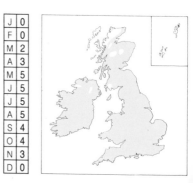

J	0
F	0
M	2
A	3
M	5
J	5
J	5
A	5
S	4
O	4
N	3
D	0

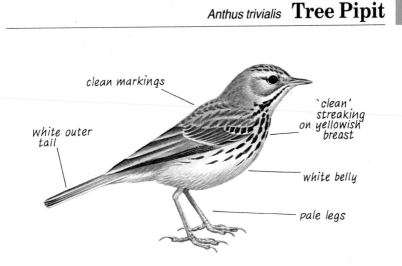

Anthus trivialis **Tree Pipit**

clean markings

`clean' streaking on yellowish breast

white outer tail

white belly

pale legs

Similar to more widespread and abundant Meadow Pipit but summer visitor only, preferring open woodlands and overgrown heaths with plentiful perches. Brown streaks on buff upperparts, buffy yellow breast and white flanks; conspicuous buffy eyebrow. Voice distinct, frequently uttered in song flight starting and terminating on perch.
Status: summer visitor to Britain; absent from Ireland except on passage.
Similar Species: Meadow Pipit (p.198) has (mostly) different habitat and call; streaking less clear and clean. See also Rock Pipit (p.199).

TREE PIPIT

Type	wagtail-like
Size	14–16cm (5½–6½in)
Habitat	heaths, woods
Behaviour	walks, perches openly, takes off from vegetation or ground
Flocking	solitary
Flight	direct; hovers
Voice	harsh *tees*; also a loud descending trill with drawn-out *see-see-see* ending

IDENTIFICATION

Adult

Crown	buff, streaked brown
Upperparts	buff, streaked brown
Rump	buff, streaked brown
Tail	buff, streaked brown, white outer feathers; medium length, notched
Throat	buff
Breast	buffy yellow, streaked brown
Belly	white
Bill	brown; short and thin
Legs	pinkish; medium length

BREEDING

Nest	cup on ground
Eggs	4–6; variable, speckled brown
Incubation	12–14 days ♀
Young	helpless; downy
Fledging	12–13 days
Broods	1–2; May–June
Food	insects
Population	50,000–100,000 pairs

J	0
F	0
M	2
A	3
M	3
J	3
J	3
A	3
S	3
O	2
N	0
D	0

Meadow Pipit *Anthus pratensis*

white outer tail

streaked breast

streaking less contrasting

pale legs

darker/greyer type

MEADOW PIPIT

Type	wagtail-like
Size	14–15cm (5½–6in)
Habitat	marshes, heaths, coasts, estuaries, fields
Behaviour	walks, perches openly, takes off and lands on ground
Flocking	1–50
Flight	direct; hovers
Voice	thin, high-pitched *tissip* or *eest*; also an accelerating trill in parachuting display flight

IDENTIFICATION

Adult

Crown	buff, streaked dark brown
Upperparts	olive-brown or greyish, streaked dark brown
Rump	buff, streaked dark brown
Tail	buff, streaked dark brown, white outer feathers; medium length, notched
Throat	white
Breast	buff, streaked dark brown
Belly	white
Bill	brown; short and thin
Legs	pinkish; medium length

BREEDING

Nest	cup on ground
Eggs	3–5; variable, spotted brown
Incubation	11–15 days ♀
Young	helpless; downy
Fledging	10–14 days
Broods	2; Apr–June
Food	insects
Population	3,000,000+ pairs

Widespread and numerous at all seasons and abundant among shoreline marshes and on beaches in winter. Olive-brown or greyish above with heavy, dark streaking. Buff breast and white belly with dense streaking on breast and flanks. Pinkish brown legs with long hind claw and white outer tail feathers. Forms flocks in favoured areas; usually gregarious on migration.
Status: widespread resident; abundant passage migrant and winter visitor.
Similar Species: in summer, Tree Pipit (p.197); along shorelines and in winter, Rock and Water Pipits (p.199).

J	5
F	5
M	5
A	5
M	5
J	5
J	5
A	5
S	5
O	5
N	5
D	5

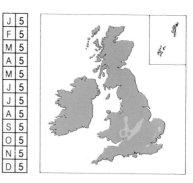

Anthus petrosus Rock Pipit / A. spinoletta Water Pipit

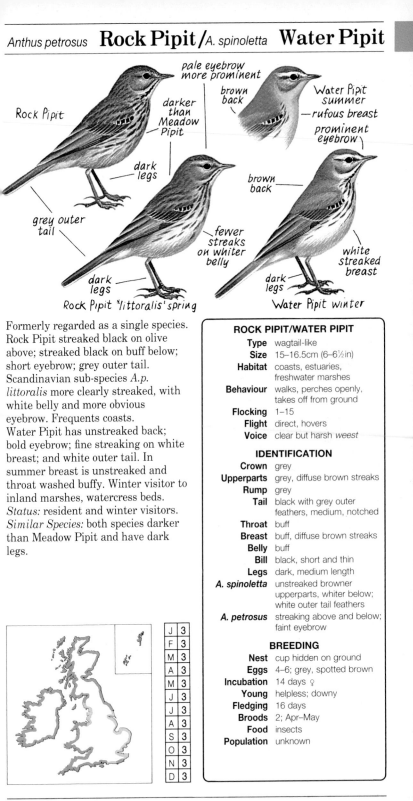

Rock Pipit

pale eyebrow more prominent

darker than Meadow Pipit

dark legs

grey outer tail

brown back

Water Pipit summer
— rufous breast

prominent eyebrow

dark legs

Rock Pipit 'littoralis' spring

fewer streaks on whiter belly

brown back

white streaked breast

dark legs

Water Pipit winter

Formerly regarded as a single species. Rock Pipit streaked black on olive above; streaked black on buff below; short eyebrow; grey outer tail. Scandinavian sub-species *A.p. littoralis* more clearly streaked, with white belly and more obvious eyebrow. Frequents coasts. Water Pipit has unstreaked back; bold eyebrow; fine streaking on white breast; and white outer tail. In summer breast is unstreaked and throat washed buffy. Winter visitor to inland marshes, watercress beds. *Status:* resident and winter visitors. *Similar Species:* both species darker than Meadow Pipit and have dark legs.

ROCK PIPIT/WATER PIPIT

Type	wagtail-like
Size	15–16.5cm (6–6½in)
Habitat	coasts, estuaries, freshwater marshes
Behaviour	walks, perches openly, takes off from ground
Flocking	1–15
Flight	direct, hovers
Voice	clear but harsh *weest*

IDENTIFICATION

Crown	grey
Upperparts	grey, diffuse brown streaks
Rump	grey
Tail	black with grey outer feathers, medium, notched
Throat	buff
Breast	buff, diffuse brown streaks
Belly	buff
Bill	black, short and thin
Legs	dark, medium length
A. spinoletta	unstreaked browner upperparts, whiter below; white outer tail feathers
A. petrosus	streaking above and below; faint eyebrow

BREEDING

Nest	cup hidden on ground
Eggs	4–6; grey, spotted brown
Incubation	14 days ♀
Young	helpless; downy
Fledging	16 days
Broods	2; Apr–May
Food	insects
Population	unknown

J	3
F	3
M	3
A	3
M	3
J	3
J	3
A	3
S	3
O	3
N	3
D	3

Yellow Wagtail *Motacilla flava*

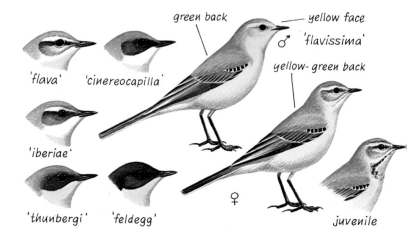

green back

yellow face

♂ 'flavissima'

yellow-green back

'flava'

'cinereocapilla'

'iberiae'

'thunbergi'

'feldegg'

♀

juvenile

YELLOW WAGTAIL

Type	wagtail-like
Size	16–17cm (6½–7in)
Habitat	inland freshwater, marshes, estuaries, fields
Behaviour	walks, perches openly, takes off and lands on ground
Flocking	1–15
Flight	undulating
Voice	loud *see-ip*; also a disjointed warble

IDENTIFICATION

Ad. *flavissima*

Crown	green
Upperparts	green, wings black and white
Rump	green
Tail	black, white-edged; long and notched
Throat	yellow
Breast	yellow
Belly	yellow
Bill	brown; short and thin
Legs	black; medium length
Other sub-sp.	adults vary in head colour

BREEDING

Nest	cup on ground
Eggs	5–6; greyish, speckled brown
Incubation	12–14 days, mainly ♀
Young	helpless; downy
Fledging	17 days
Broods	1–2; May–June
Food	insects
Population	*c* 25,000 pairs

Slim, elegant summer visitor to damp meadows and marshes. Distinguished by yellow underparts, green back and typical wagtail bounce of its long, white-edged, black tail. Spends much time walking. Several distinct subspecies; main difference is head colour – most obvious in spring male. British breeders usually have yellow heads; others have blue, black, grey and black and even white heads. Blue-headed Wagtail regular passage migrant; gregarious on passage.
Status: widespread summer visitor to England, Wales and central Scotland.
Similar Species: Grey Wagtail (p.201) also has yellow underparts but grey back in all plumages.

J	0
F	0
M	2
A	3
M	4
J	4
J	4
A	4
S	3
O	2
N	0
D	0

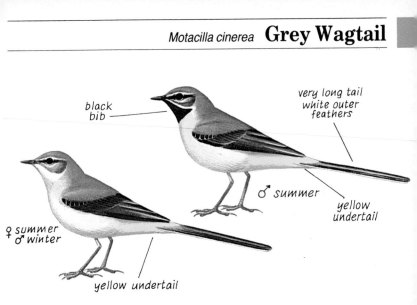

black bib

very long tail
white outer
feathers

♂ summer

yellow
undertail

♀ summer
♂ winter

yellow undertail

Largest of the three British wagtails and the one most closely associated with water, especially fast-running streams. In winter also found near waterfalls, weirs and sometimes lakes, reservoirs, watercress beds and even farmyards. Upperparts grey with white eyebrow, black wings, yellow green rump, and long, white-edged, black tail. Underparts white with yellow undertail coverts and variable amount of yellow on breast. In summer, male has prominent black bib.
Status: widespread and common resident, but winter visitor only to large areas of eastern England; summer visitor to northern Scotland.
Similar Species: Yellow Wagtail (p.200) and Pied Wagtail (p.202).

GREY WAGTAIL

Type	wagtail-like
Size	18–20cm (7–8in)
Habitat	inland freshwater, marshes
Behaviour	walks, perches openly, takes off from vegetation or ground
Flocking	1–2
Flight	undulating
Voice	metallic *tzitzi*; also a warble reminiscent of Blue Tit

IDENTIFICATION

Ad.♂summer	
Crown	grey, white eyebrow
Upperparts	grey, wings black
Rump	yellow-green
Tail	black, white-edged; long and notched
Throat	white; black bib
Breast	yellow
Belly	white
Bill	black; short and thin
Legs	pink; medium length
Ad.♀, winter♂	less yellow below; lacks black bib

BREEDING

Nest	neat cup in crevice beside stream
Eggs	4–6; buffy, mottled greyish
Incubation	11–14 days, mainly ♀
Young	helpless; downy
Fledging	17 days
Broods	1, occasionally 2; Apr–May
Food	insects
Population	25,000–50,000 pairs

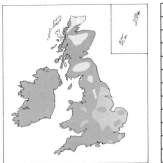

J	3
F	3
M	3
A	3
M	3
J	3
J	3
A	3
S	3
O	3
N	3
D	3

Pied Wagtail *Motacilla alba*

♂ pied winter

♂ pied summer

white chin

black chin

grey back

White ♂ summer

black chin

whit chin

White ♂ winter

black of chin never meets black of crown in White Wagtail

sooty back

pied ♀ summer

juvenile pied

White ♀ summer

PIED WAGTAIL

Type	wagtail-like
Size	17–18cm (6½–7in)
Habitat	inland freshwater, fields, gardens
Behaviour	walks, perches openly, takes off from vegetation or ground
Flocking	1–10
Flight	undulating
Voice	harsh *chis-ick*; also a disjointed twitter

IDENTIFICATION

M.a.yarrellii

Crown	black, white face
Upperparts	black, white-tipped flight feathers
Rump	black
Tail	black, white outer feathers; long and notched
Throat	black bib in summer; white in winter
Breast	black band
Belly	white
Bill	black; short and thin
Legs	black; medium length
M.a.alba	back pale grey at all times

BREEDING

Nest	cup on ground
Eggs	5–6; grey, speckled brown
Incubation	12–14 days, ♀ only ?
Young	helpless; downy
Fledging	13–16 days
Broods	2; Apr–June
Food	insects
Population	*c* 500,000 pairs

Familiar black and white wagtail; widespread resident of open habitats with and without water. Common subspecies in British Isles is *M.a.yarrellii*. Male mainly black above with white face, white margins to flight feathers and white outer tail. Black bib terminates in broad black breast band; remaining underparts white. Female similar but with slate-grey back. Juveniles and first winter birds have grey backs and are similar to Continental sub-species *M.a.alba*, known as the White Wagtail. White Wagtails regularly occur on migration and have uniform grey backs.
Status: widespread resident.
Similar Species: Grey Wagtail (p.201) often lacks almost all yellow on underparts in winter – particularly in first winter plumage.

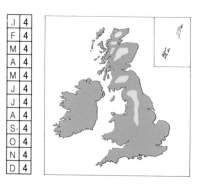

J	4
F	4
M	4
A	4
M	4
J	4
J	4
A	4
S	4
O	4
N	4
D	4

crest

black bib

yellow on wings and tail

Decidedly Starling-like in shape and size, but pinkish brown in colour. Swept-back crest, black lores and chin patch broken by white moustachial streak produce 'cross' expression. Black wings marked by tiny wax-like spots of red and yellow; black banded tail tipped yellow. Irrupts in numbers every five or six years; roams hedgerows and gardens in flocks, sometimes a hundred or more strong; otherwise no more than a rarity. *Status:* irregular autumn and winter visitor from Scandinavia and northern Russia, mainly to east coast; numbers variable.

Similar Species: in flight can be mistaken for Common Starling (p.260).

WAXWING	
Type	unique/starling-like
Size	17–18.5cm (7in)
Habitat	gardens, heaths, hedgerows
Behaviour	perches openly, hops, takes off from vegetation or ground
Flocking	1–100
Flight	direct
Voice	tinkling trill

IDENTIFICATION	
Adult	
Crown	pinkish brown; swept-back crest
Upperparts	pinkish brown; black wings spotted red and yellow
Rump	grey
Tail	grey, black banded, tipped yellow; short and square
Throat	pinkish brown, black bib
Breast	pinkish brown
Belly	pinkish brown
Bill	black; short and thin
Legs	black; medium length

BREEDING	
Nest	cup in conifer
Eggs	5; pale blue, spotted black
Incubation	13–14 days ♀
Young	helpless; naked
Fledging	15–17 days
Broods	1; May–June
Food	berries
Population	variable, up to several hundred in autumn and winter

J	2
F	2
M	2
A	0
M	0
J	0
J	0
A	0
S	0
O	1
N	2
D	2

Dipper *Cinclus cinclus*

white breast

adult

scaly

juvenile

DIPPER

Type	wren-like
Size	17–18.5cm (7in)
Habitat	inland freshwater
Behaviour	swims, dives from surface, wades, walks, perches openly, takes off from water or ground
Flocking	solitary
Flight	direct
Voice	*zit-zit*

IDENTIFICATION

Adult	
Crown	chocolate-brown
Upperparts	black
Rump	black
Tail	black; short and notched
Throat	white
Breast	white
Belly	chestnut-brown
Bill	brown; short and thin
Legs	pinkish; medium length
Juvenile	slate-grey above, scaly patterning on whitish breast

BREEDING

Nest	dome in hole beside stream
Eggs	5; white
Incubation	15–18 days ♀
Young	helpless; downy
Fledging	19–25 days
Broods	2–3; Mar–June
Food	aquatic insects
Population	c 30,000 pairs

Portly, short-tailed, blackish bird marked by bold white gorget; reminiscent of large, white-breasted Wren. Confined to fast-running streams; most often seen from bridges or riverside paths. Spends much time searching for food among tumbling, rock-strewn waters where wades, swims and dives with complete mastery. Usually solitary, often perching openly on rocks; may be quite tame. Territory can be 2 km or more long but only as wide as a river or stream across.

Status: resident in northern and western hilly areas; some immigration of Continental birds in winter.

Similar Species: none.

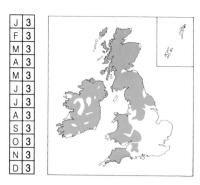

J	3
F	3
M	3
A	3
M	3
J	3
J	3
A	3
S	3
O	3
N	3
D	3

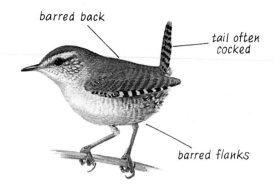

barred back

tail often cocked

barred flanks

One of most widespread and numerous birds of Britain and Ireland, easily recognized by small size and cocked tail. Chestnut above, with clear pale eyebrow and barred back and wings. Underparts buffy; some barring on flanks. Spends much time hunting through dense ground cover, where presence betrayed only by characteristic calls and loud, wheezing song. Quite tame in gardens.
Status: widespread and numerous.
Similar Species: none; wrens are New World birds and this is the only species to have colonized the Old World.

WREN

Type	wren-like
Size	9–10cm (3½–4in)
Habitat	gardens, marshes, heaths, sea cliffs, woods, hedges
Behaviour	flits, hops, perches openly, takes off from vegetation or ground
Flocking	1–2
Flight	laboured; direct
Voice	repeated *tic-tic* and *clink*; also a loud ripping warble ending in wheezing *chur*

IDENTIFICATION

Adult	
Crown	chestnut brown
Upperparts	chestnut brown, darkly barred
Rump	chestnut brown
Tail	chestnut brown; short and square
Throat	buffy
Breast	buffy
Belly	buffy, flanks barred
Bill	brown; short and thin
Legs	brown; medium length

BREEDING

Nest	dome in hole in bank
Eggs	5–8; white, speckled red
Incubation	14–17 days ♀
Young	helpless; downy
Fledging	15–20 days
Broods	1; Apr–May
Food	insects
Population	4,000,000–5,000,000 pairs

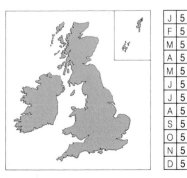

J	5
F	5
M	5
A	5
M	5
J	5
J	5
A	5
S	5
O	5
N	5
D	5

Hedge Accentor *Prunella modularis*

thin bill

grey face

streaked
flanks

adult

HEDGE ACCENTOR

Type	sparrow-like
Size	14–15cm (5½–6in)
Habitat	gardens, heaths, woods, fields and hedges
Behaviour	flits, perches openly, hops, takes off from vegetation and ground
Flocking	1–2
Flight	undulating
Voice	jingling, staccato warble

IDENTIFICATION

Adult	
Crown	grey-brown
Upperparts	brown, streaked black
Rump	dark grey
Tail	brown and black; medium length, notched
Throat	grey
Breast	grey
Belly	whitish grey; brown streaks on flanks
Bill	black; short and thin
Legs	flesh; medium length

BREEDING

Nest	cup in tree or bush
Eggs	4–5; bright blue
Incubation	12–13 days ♀
Young	helpless; downy
Fledging	12 days
Broods	2–3 ?; Apr–May
Food	insects, berries
Population	c 5,000,000 pairs

Tame garden and woodland bird; spends most of its time crouched low on ground searching for food. Seldom moves far from cover; usually perches openly only when singing. Flicks wings more or less continuously. Flies low and briefly in undulating flight. Easily overlooked among House Sparrows but grey foreparts and thin bill separate easily. Back and wings brown, liberally streaked with black; brown streaking on flanks. Juvenile has less grey on head and entire underparts are streaked.

Status: common and widespread resident; some autumn migrants from the Continent stay to winter here.

Similar Species: extremely rare Alpine Accentor.

J	5
F	5
M	5
A	5
M	5
J	5
J	5
A	5
S	5
O	5
N	5
D	5

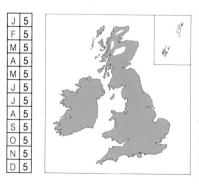

red face and breast

scaled above and below

juvenile

adult

The most familiar and popular of garden and woodland birds; generally confiding with people. Upright, plump little bird; perches openly and hops on the ground. Adult warm olive-brown with red face, chin and breast. Sides of breast pale grey; belly white. Juvenile has brown head, wings and tail with brown barring on buffy back and breast; indistinguishable from adults after moult (June–August).
Status: widespread and numerous resident throughout year. Often large influx of Continental birds in autumn; some northern females also migrate southwards and to the Continent in autumn.
Similar Species: Common Redstart (p.211), Stonechat (p.213), crossbills (pp.272 and 273) and Bullfinch (p.274) all have 'red' breasts but none are orange-red.

ROBIN

Type	chat-like
Size	13–15cm (5–6in)
Habitat	towns and gardens, heaths, woods, hedges
Behaviour	flits, perches openly, hops, takes off from vegetation and ground
Flocking	solitary
Flight	undulating
Voice	thin *tic-tic-tic*, repeated; leisurely warble

IDENTIFICATION

Adult	
Crown	brown
Upperparts	brown
Rump	brown
Tail	brown; medium length, notched
Throat	orange-red
Breast	orange-red, sides pale grey
Belly	white
Bill	brown; short and pointed
Legs	brown; medium length
Juvenile	lacks red breast, scaly above and below

BREEDING

Nest	cup on ground, in tree stump or on bank
Eggs	5–6; white, speckled reddish
Incubation	12–15 days ♀
Young	helpless; downy
Fledging	12–15 days
Broods	2–3; Apr–June
Food	insects
Population	3,500,000 pairs

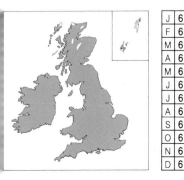

J	6
F	6
M	6
A	6
M	6
J	6
J	6
A	6
S	6
O	6
N	6
D	6

Nightingale *Luscinia megarhynchos*

warm brown

rufous tail

adult

scaled

juvenile

NIGHTINGALE

Type	chat-like
Size	16–17cm (6–6½in)
Habitat	heaths, woods
Behaviour	flits, takes off or lands on vegetation
Flocking	solitary
Flight	direct
Voice	long song of liquid trills with *peeoo* notes at beginning; also harsh *tchak* and *whooeet* contact notes

IDENTIFICATION

Adult

Crown	rufous brown
Upperparts	rufous brown
Rump	rust-red
Tail	rust-red; longish and rounded
Throat	white
Breast	creamy white
Belly	white
Bill	brown; short and pointed
Legs	grey; medium length
Juvenile	paler above and below with scaly markings; rust-red tail

BREEDING

Nest	cup well hidden close to ground
Eggs	4–5; mottled reddish
Incubation	13–14 days ♀
Young	helpless; downy
Fledging	11–12 days
Broods	1; May–June
Food	insects
Population	10,000 pairs

Fabulous songster more often heard than seen. Song a virtuoso performance of liquid trills ending in crescendo; commonly heard well after dark but also frequently during the day. Almost always hidden deep in vegetation; males occasionally perch openly to sing soon after landing. Tail spread in song display. When disturbed, dives into nearest cover showing characteristic rust-red, conspicuously rounded, tail. Adult rufous brown above merging with creamy white underparts. Juvenile marked with scale-like crescents, as juvenile Robin. Rust-red tail remains characteristic.
Status: summer visitor to south-eastern England from late April.
Similar Species: rare Thrush Nightingale is barred like Juvenile.

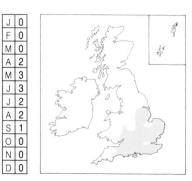

J	0
F	0
M	0
A	2
M	3
J	3
J	2
A	2
S	1
O	0
N	0
D	0

bold eyebrow

♂ summer

white spotted 'cyanecula'

first winter

moustache

blue breast

♂ summer red spotted 'svecica'

♀

rusty tail patches

Scarce passage migrant seen mostly at coastal observatories. Adult male has distinctive cobalt-blue throat and breast with dark blue and red breast bands. Spot in centre of breast is red in *L.s.svecica* and white in *L.s.cyanecula*. Adult female has white throat and breast marked by dark brown breast band extending as moustache to base of bill. Small smudge of red at centre of breast. Most birds passing through Britain are first winter; males have just a hint of blue and red above breast band; females lack both colours on breast. Seldom venture far from dense cover; flit back if disturbed, showing rusty tail patches – best field mark. *Status:* rare migrant; has bred once. *Similar Species:* none.

	BLUETHROAT
Type	chat-like
Size	13–15cm (5–6in)
Habitat	heaths, shores
Behaviour	flits, hops, takes off from vegetation and ground
Flocking	solitary
Flight	undulating
Voice	penetrating *tic-tic*; also thin *hweet*

IDENTIFICATION

Ad.♂ svecica summer	
Crown	brown
Upperparts	brown
Rump	brown
Tail	brown, sides rusty; medium length, notched
Throat	blue
Breast	blue, red spot in centre
Belly	white
Bill	brown; short and thin
Legs	brown; medium length
Ad.♂ cyanecula summer	as above but white spot on breast
Ad.♀ and juv.	as ♂ with less pronounced breast marks

BREEDING

Nest	cup on ground
Eggs	5–7; greenish, speckled reddish
Incubation	14–15 days ♀
Young	helpless; downy
Fledging	14 days
Broods	1–2; May–June
Food	insects
Population	bred once; scarce migrant spring and autumn

J	0
F	0
M	0
A	1
M	1
J	0
J	0
A	1
S	1
O	1
N	0
D	0

Black Redstart *Phoenicurus ochruros*

white wing flash

red tail

♂ summer

♂ winter

♀

red tail

dusky breast

BLACK REDSTART	
Type	chat-like
Size	14–15cm (5½–6in)
Habitat	cliffs, towns and cities
Behaviour	perches openly, takes off from vegetation or ground
Flocking	solitary
Flight	undulating; flitting
Voice	brief *sip* or *tissic*; short warble

IDENTIFICATION

Ad.♂summer	
Crown	black
Upperparts	black; white flash on wings
Rump	rust-red
Tail	rust-red, medium, notched
Throat	black
Breast	black
Belly	grey-black
Bill	black; short and pointed
Legs	black; medium length
Ad.♂winter	greyer above, throat remains black; underparts dirty white
Ad.♀	brown, darker above, paler below; rust-red tail
Juvenile	as ♀, lightly barred

BREEDING

Nest	cup hidden in hole or crevice
Eggs	4–6; white
Incubation	12–16 days ♀
Young	helpless; downy
Fledging	12–19 days
Broods	2–3; Apr–June
Food	insects
Population	c 30–100 pairs

Colonizing summer visitor but still scarce. Favours demolition sites, industrial complexes, power stations and railway sidings; also sea cliffs. Attention often drawn by brief warbling song. Perches openly with rusty tail shimmering. Flies strongly; often feeds on ground. Summer male has black head, back, breast and belly; bold white flash on wings. In winter, black areas become dark grey; black remains on throat; underparts dirty white. Female is brown, darker above, paler below; juvenile as female but lightly barred; both have rust-red tails. *Status:* scarce summer visitor to southern and central England. Passage migrant; most numerous late autumn, some stay through winter.
Similar Species: female and juvenile Common Redstart (p.211) are lighter brown.

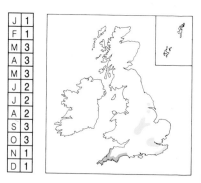

J	1
F	1
M	3
A	3
M	3
J	2
J	2
A	2
S	3
O	3
N	1
D	1

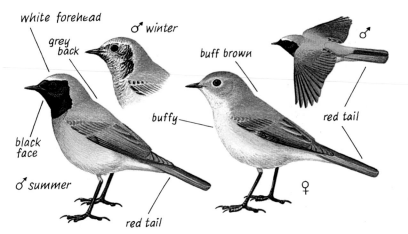

Phoenicurus phoenicurus **Common Redstart**

white forehead
grey back
♂ winter
buff brown
black face
buffy
red tail
♂ summer
red tail
♀

Summer visitor to old woodlands and heaths with scattered trees. Perches on lower branches of trees and bushes and makes pouncing sallies to ground; also flits among vegetation. Orange-red tail frequently shimmered. Summer male has dove-grey crown and back; wings brown. White eyebrows meet on forehead; rest of face black. Underparts orange-red; tail orange-red with darker centre. Female also has orange-red tail but is buffy brown above (darker on wings) and buffy below. Juvenile similar to female but speckled.
Status: widespread summer visitor to Britain, April–October; more common in north and west. Decidedly local in Ireland. Also passage migrant; often numerous in autumn.
Similar Species: Black Redstart (p.210) is darker and has different habitat.

	COMMON REDSTART
Type	chat-like
Size	13.5–14.5cm (5¼–5¾in)
Habitat	woods, heaths, parks
Behaviour	flits, perches openly, hops, takes off from vegetation or ground
Flocking	solitary
Flight	direct; flitting
Voice	*hooeet*, brief warble

IDENTIFICATION

Ad.♂ summer	
Crown	grey
Upperparts	grey; wings brown
Rump	rust-red
Tail	rust-red; medium length, notched
Throat	black
Breast	orange-red
Belly	creamy white
Bill	black; medium length, short and pointed
Legs	black; medium length
Ad.♂ winter	face more greyish; underparts duller orange-red
Ad.♀ summer	buff-brown above, buffy below; rust-red tail

BREEDING

Nest	cup hidden in bank, tree roots or tree hole
Eggs	6–7; pale blue
Incubation	11–14 days ♀
Young	helpless; downy
Fledging	14–20 days
Broods	2; May–June
Food	insects
Population	c 50,000–100,000 pairs

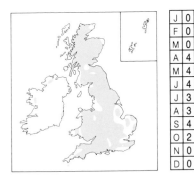

J	0
F	0
M	0
A	4
M	4
J	4
J	3
A	3
S	4
O	2
N	0
D	0

Whinchat *Saxicola rubetra*

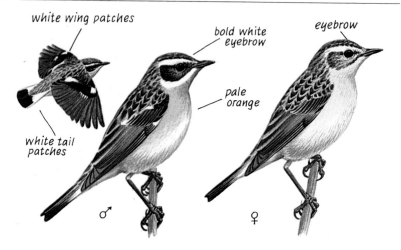

white wing patches

bold white
eyebrow

eyebrow

pale
orange

white tail
patches

♂

♀

WHINCHAT

Type	chat-like
Size	12–13cm (4¾–5in)
Habitat	heaths, downland
Behaviour	perches openly, takes off and lands on vegetation or ground
Flocking	solitary
Flight	direct; flitting
Voice	metallic *tic-tic*; brief warble

IDENTIFICATION

Adult

Crown	brown, streaked black
Upperparts	brown, streaked black; white wing patches
Rump	brown, streaked black
Tail	brown centre, white patches on sides, black band at tip; short and square
Throat	creamy orange
Breast	creamy orange
Belly	creamy orange
Bill	black; short and pointed
Legs	black; medium length

BREEDING

Nest	cup on ground at base of bush
Eggs	5–7; pale blue, finely speckled brown
Incubation	13–14 days ♀
Young	helpless; downy
Fledging	17 days
Broods	1–2; May–June
Food	insects
Population	20,000–40,000 pairs

Widespread summer visitor and passage migrant to open heaths and downland; most often seen perched atop a small bush. Pounces to ground to feed; often returns to same perch. In summer, adult has brown upperparts, heavily streaked black; white flash in closed wing. Prominent, creamy white eyebrow; dark ear coverts. Underparts pale creamy orange. In flight, shows white patch on inner wing and white patches either side of tail. Female a more subdued version of male. In winter, male more like female.
Status: summer visitor April–September. Double passage migrant in good numbers, particularly in autumn.
Similar Species: closely related Stonechat (p.213) lacks prominent eyebrow in all plumages.

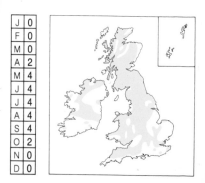

J	0
F	0
M	0
A	2
M	4
J	4
J	4
A	4
S	4
O	2
N	0
D	0

black head, white half collar

grey brown head

♂

white rump

♂

♀

Widespread chat, present throughout year; prefers gorse habitats. Perches prominently on tops of bushes and pounces to ground. Flies low, showing greyish white rump and white patches on wings. In summer, male has black head bordered by prominent white half collar. Back and wings dark brown, streaked black; tail dark brown. Breast orange-red. In winter, male paler with more obviously streaked upperparts and less reddish breast. Female much paler than male with dark, not black, head. Eastern sub-species paler and greyer with little colour on breast. *Status:* resident and winter visitor. *Similar Species:* Whinchat (p.212) is summer visitor, has prominent eyebrow and creamy, not reddish, breast.

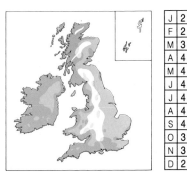

J	2
F	2
M	3
A	4
M	4
J	4
J	4
A	4
S	4
O	3
N	3
D	2

STONECHAT

Type	chat-like
Size	12–13cm (4¾–5in)
Habitat	heaths, grassland
Behaviour	perches openly, hops, takes off and lands on vegetation or ground
Flocking	solitary
Flight	direct; flitting
Voice	metallic *chak-chak* also jingling warble

IDENTIFICATION

Adult ♂	
Crown	black
Upperparts	dark brown, streaked black; white wing patches
Rump	greyish white
Tail	dark brown; medium length, square
Throat	black, white half collar
Breast	orange-red
Belly	white
Bill	black; short and pointed
Legs	black; medium length
Adult ♀	paler, orange-buff breast; lacks black head

BREEDING

Nest	cup on ground at base of bush
Eggs	5–6; pale blue, lightly-speckled brown
Incubation	14–15 days ♀
Young	helpless; downy
Fledging	12–13 days
Broods	2–3; Apr–June
Food	insects, worms
Population	30,000–60,000 pairs

Northern Wheatear *Oenanthe oenanthe*

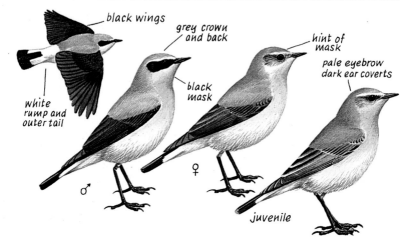

black wings

grey crown and back

white rump and outer tail

black mask

♂

♀

hint of mask

pale eyebrow
dark ear coverts

juvenile

NORTHERN WHEATEAR

Type	chat-like
Size	14–15.5cm (5½–6in)
Habitat	moors, heaths, grassland, beaches
Behaviour	hops, perches openly, takes off from vegetation or ground
Flocking	solitary, small groups on migration
Flight	hovers; strong and powerful; direct; flitting
Voice	harsh *chak-chak*; brief warble

IDENTIFICATION

Adult ♂	
Crown	grey
Upperparts	grey; wings black
Rump	white
Tail	white with black tip; medium length, square
Throat	creamy buff
Breast	creamy buff
Belly	creamy buff
Bill	black; short and pointed
Legs	black; medium length
Ad. ♀ and juv.	browner above; hint of face mask

BREEDING

Nest	untidy cup in hole in rocks or bank
Eggs	5–6; pale blue, unmarked
Incubation	14 days, mainly ♀
Young	helpless; downy
Fledging	15 days
Broods	1–2; Apr–May
Food	insects
Population	c 50,000–100,000 pairs

Widespread summer visitor to open country; seldom perches higher than rock or fence post. Typical upright position with sudden darting movements; frequently 'bobs'. In flight, white rump and tail pattern distinctive. Adult male has grey crown and back with black 'mask'. Wings black; underparts creamy buff. Adult female grey-brown above with only hint of face mask. Juvenile has sandy crown and back with pale margins to dark wing feathers; only hint of mask. Greenland sub-species *O.o.leucorrhoa* larger with longer wings.
Status: common summer visitor March–October; passage migrant.
Similar Species: Three other rare wheatears could be confused with first winter birds; all have browner wings and different rump-tail patterns.

J	0
F	0
M	4
A	4
M	4
J	4
J	4
A	4
S	4
O	3
N	0
D	0

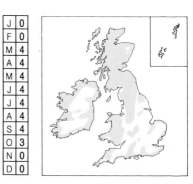

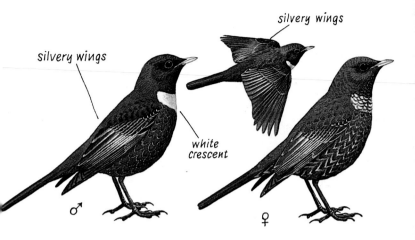

silvery wings

silvery wings

white crescent

♂

♀

Summer visitor to mountains and moorlands with screes and rocky outcrops. Behaviour much as Blackbird but much less confiding. Flies swift and low showing silvery wings. On passage, often skulks in dense cover. In summer, male black with brownish wash; distinctive white crescent across breast. Silvery wing linings form obvious pale panel on folded wing. In winter, male browner with scaly markings; white feathers on breast band have buff, scaly tips. Adult female like winter male. Juvenile brown above with narrow, pale edges to wing feathers; heavily barred below.
Status: widespread summer visitor to north and west. Scarce passage migrant March–November.
Similar Species: Blackbird (p.216) lacks white crescent and silver wings.

	RING OUZEL
Type	thrush-like
Size	23–25cm (9–10in)
Habitat	mountains and moorlands
Behaviour	hops, runs, perches openly, takes off and lands on vegetation or ground
Flocking	solitary, small flocks
Flight	strong and powerful; direct
Voice	harsh *chak-chak*; also a loud *peu-u peu-u*

IDENTIFICATION

Adult ♂	
Crown	black-brown
Upperparts	black-brown; wings have silvery edges
Rump	black-brown
Tail	black-brown; medium length, square
Throat	black-brown
Breast	white crescent
Belly	black-brown
Bill	pale yellow; medium length, pointed
Legs	black, medium length
Adult ♀	subdued colours
Juvenile	scaled; lacks white crescent on breast

BREEDING

Nest	cup on ground
Eggs	4–5; pale blue, blotched brown
Incubation	13–14 days ♂ ♀
Young	helpless, downy
Fledging	13–14 days
Broods	1–2; Apr–May
Food	worms, insects, berries
Population	8,000–16,000 pairs

J	0
F	0
M	0
A	3
M	3
J	3
J	3
A	3
S	3
O	2
N	0
D	0

Blackbird *Turdus merula*

yellow bill

dark breast with faint spots

♂

♀

BLACKBIRD

Type	thrush-like
Size	24–27cm (9½–11in)
Habitat	gardens, heaths, woods, hedges
Behaviour	perches openly, walks, hops, takes off from vegetation or ground
Flocking	1–15
Flight	strong and powerful; direct
Voice	loud harsh chatter of alarm; also a fluty warble

IDENTIFICATION

Adult ♂	
Crown	black
Upperparts	black
Rump	black
Tail	black; medium length, square
Throat	black
Breast	black
Belly	black
Bill	yellow; short and thin
Legs	black; medium length
Adult ♀	underparts mottled grey-brown or rufous brown; brownish bill

BREEDING

Nest	cup in tree or bush
Eggs	4–5; light blue, spotted red
Incubation	11–17 days ♀
Young	helpless; downy
Fledging	12–19 days
Broods	2–3; Mar–May
Food	insects, worms, berries
Population	7,000,000 pairs

One of the most familiar of British birds, common to woodlands, fields and gardens; as much at home in towns as countryside. All-black male has yellow bill and eye ring. Female browner, with subdued speckling on breast varying considerably from rufous brown to greyish brown. First winter males retain dark brown wing feathers; distinguishes from older, black-winged birds. Generally highly territorial, though Continental immigrants often arrive in large autumn flocks.
Status: widespread and numerous resident; common passage migrant and winter visitor throughout Britain and Ireland.
Similar Species: Ring Ouzel (p.215).

J	6
F	6
M	6
A	6
M	6
J	6
J	6
A	6
S	6
O	6
N	6
D	6

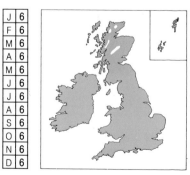

black tail

grey crown

chestnut back

grey rump

buff with speckles

Large, typical thrush with densely speckled breast washed buffy yellow. Head, nape and rump dove-grey – latter particularly useful field mark in flight. Wings and back chestnut-brown; tail black. Pattern of head and face markings produces 'cross' expression. Generally gregarious, forming quite substantial flocks along hedgerows and in fields.

Status: scarce breeder in northern England and Scotland; abundant winter visitor throughout Britain and Ireland.

Similar Species: related Mistle and Song Thrush (pp.220, 218) and Redwing (p.219) have less densely speckled breasts, less chestnut backs, and lack grey crown and rump.

FIELDFARE

Type	thrush-like
Size	24–27cm (9½–11in)
Habitat	heaths, woods, fields and hedges, gardens
Behaviour	perches openly, hops, walks, takes off from vegetation or ground
Flocking	1–100s
Flight	strong and powerful; direct
Voice	harsh *chak-chak*, normally in flight

IDENTIFICATION

Adult	
Crown	dove-grey
Upperparts	chestnut-brown
Rump	dove-grey
Tail	black; medium length, notched
Throat	buffy yellow
Breast	buffy yellow, speckled black
Belly	white, speckled black
Bill	yellow; short and thin
Legs	black; medium length

BREEDING

Nest	cup in fork of tree
Eggs	5–6; pale blue, reddish markings
Incubation	11–14 days ♀
Young	helpless; downy
Fledging	12–16 days
Broods	1–2; Apr–June
Food	worms, insects, berries, fruit
Population	very rare breeder; 1,000,000 winter

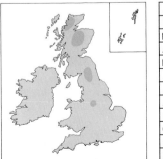

J	5
F	5
M	3
A	3
M	2
J	2
J	2
A	2
S	2
O	3
N	4
D	5

217

Song Thrush *Turdus philomelos*

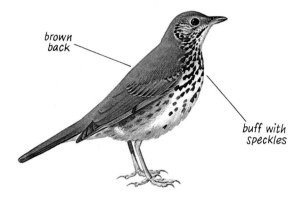

brown back

buff with speckles

SONG THRUSH

Type	thrush-like
Size	22–24cm (8½–9½in)
Habitat	gardens, heaths, woods, fields
Behaviour	perches openly, hops, walks, takes off from vegetation or ground
Flocking	1–15
Flight	strong and powerful; direct
Voice	variety of repeated phrases; *chuk* alarm call

IDENTIFICATION

Adult	
Crown	brown
Upperparts	brown
Rump	brown
Tail	brown; medium length, square
Throat	buff
Breast	creamy yellow, spotted black
Belly	white, spotted black
Bill	black; short and thin
Legs	pink; medium length

BREEDING

Nest	neat cup in tree or bush
Eggs	4–6; pale blue, speckled black
Incubation	11–15 days ♀
Young	helpless; downy
Fledging	12–16 days
Broods	2–3; Mar–June
Food	worms, snails, insects, berries
Population	1,000,000–3,500,000 pairs

Neat, medium-sized thrush found in woods, fields and gardens. Brown above; white neatly spotted with black below; creamy yellow wash on breast. Head has clear eyebrow and moustachial streak. Characteristic habit of repeating song phrase three or four times.
Status: widespread resident throughout Britain and Ireland; passage migrant and winter visitor.
Similar Species: can be confused with Redwing (p.219) in winter and Mistle Thrush (p.220) throughout year.

J	6
F	6
M	6
A	6
M	6
J	6
J	6
A	6
S	6
O	6
N	6
D	6

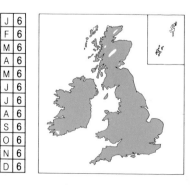

Turdus iliacus **Redwing**

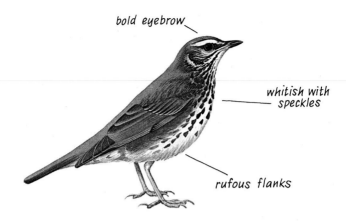

bold eyebrow

whitish with speckles

rufous flanks

Common winter visitor, forming flocks that roam through fields and hedgerows. Brown above, with brown ear coverts separating and accentuating bold eyebrow and double moustachial streak; face markings give distinctly 'cross' look. Whitish underparts spotted in clear streaks, with bold rust-red patch along flanks. Flight fast and direct like Song Thrush; unlike undulating flight of Mistle Thrush.

Status: widespread and abundant winter visitor; recent breeder in northern Scotland.

Similar Species: smaller than Song and Mistle Thrushes (pp.218, 220), which lack rust-red on flanks and prominent face patterns.

REDWING

Type	thrush-like
Size	20–22cm (8–9in)
Habitat	gardens, heaths, woods, fields and hedges
Behaviour	perches openly, hops, walks, takes off from vegetation or ground
Flocking	1–100
Flight	strong and powerful; direct
Voice	soft *seeip* in flight

IDENTIFICATION

Adult	
Crown	brown
Upperparts	brown
Rump	brown
Tail	brown; medium length, square
Throat	whitish
Breast	whitish, streaked brown
Belly	whitish, streaked brown; rust-red flanks
Bill	black; short and thin
Legs	yellow; medium length

BREEDING

Nest	cup against tree trunk
Eggs	4–5; pale blue, speckled brownish
Incubation	11–15 days ♀
Young	helpless; downy
Fledging	10–15 days
Broods	2; Apr–June
Food	berries, worms, insects
Population	30–60 pairs; 1,000,000+ winter

Month	
J	5
F	5
M	5
A	2
M	2
J	1
J	1
A	1
S	2
O	4
N	5
D	5

Mistle Thrush *Turdus viscivorus*

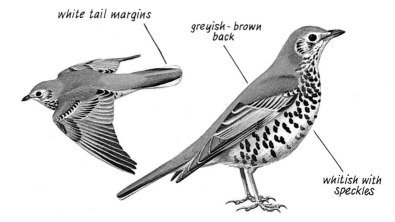

white tail margins

greyish-brown back

whitish with speckles

MISTLE THRUSH

Type	thrush-like
Size	26–28cm (10–11in)
Habitat	gardens, heaths, woods, fields and hedges
Behaviour	perches openly, hops, walks, takes off from vegetation or ground
Flocking	1–15
Flight	strong and powerful; undulating
Voice	loud *tuk-tuk*; a dry, rattling chuckle, Blackbird-like, fluty song, but faster

IDENTIFICATION

Adult	
Crown	grey-brown
Upperparts	grey-brown
Rump	grey-brown
Tail	grey-brown, white corners; medium length, square
Throat	whitish
Breast	whitish, spotted black
Belly	whitish, spotted black
Bill	black; short and thin
Legs	yellow; medium length

BREEDING

Nest	cup in fork of tree
Eggs	4–5; blue, spotted reddish
Incubation	12–15 days ♀
Young	helpless; downy
Fledging	20 days
Broods	2; Mar–May
Food	berries, worms, insects
Population	300,000–600,000 pairs

Largest of the thrushes with distinctly greyer and paler appearance than Song Thrush. Upperparts buffy grey-brown with pale margins to flight feathers. Underparts white, heavily spotted black. In undulating flight, shows grey-brown rump and white corners to tail. Generally less gregarious than other thrushes; forms small, loose groups but seldom large flocks. Song similar to Blackbird but generally with faster delivery.
Status: widespread resident.
Similar Species: Song Thrush (p.218) is smaller and darker, has warm yellowish wash on breast and prominent eyebrow. See also Fieldfare (p.217).

J	5
F	5
M	5
A	5
M	5
J	5
J	5
A	5
S	5
O	5
N	5
D	5

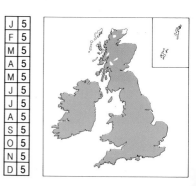

Cettia cetti **Cetti's Warbler**

chestnut-
brown

prominent
rounded tail
often spread

Resident of dense bushy undergrowth, often at edge of reed beds and invariably alongside water. Always secretive and elusive, but presence revealed by uniquely explosive call. Usually sighted as dark brown bird flitting from one bush to another. Clearer views reveal rich chestnut-brown upperparts with clear, pale eyebrow and strongly rounded tail. Underparts whitish. Sometimes cocks tail to reveal barred undertail coverts. *Status:* recent colonizer; scarce resident in southern and eastern England. Serious decline E. Anglia and Kent after bad winters. *Similar Species:* in summer can be confused with Reed, Marsh, and Savi's warblers (pp.224–226); with reasonable views easily distinguished by dark coloration of upperparts.

CETTI'S WARBLER	
Type	warbler-like
Size	13.5–14.5cm (5–5½in)
Habitat	inland freshwater and marshes
Behaviour	flits, takes off and lands on vegetation
Flocking	solitary
Flight	flitting
Voice	explosive *chetti-chetti-chetti*

IDENTIFICATION	
Adult	
Crown	chestnut-brown
Upperparts	chestnut-brown
Rump	chestnut-brown
Tail	chestnut-brown; medium length, rounded
Throat	whitish
Breast	whitish
Belly	whitish
Bill	black; short and thin
Legs	buff; medium length

BREEDING	
Nest	cup in thick vegetation on or near ground
Eggs	4; chestnut
Incubation	♀?
Young	helpless; downy
Fledging	?
Broods	1; Apr–May
Food	insects, seeds
Population	100–240 pairs

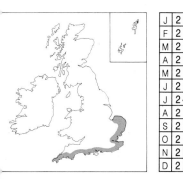

J	2
F	2
M	2
A	2
M	2
J	2
J	2
A	2
S	2
O	2
N	2
D	2

Grasshopper Warbler *Locustella naevia*

streaked back

rounded tail

IDENTIFICATION

Adult	
Crown	buffy brown, dark streaked
Upperparts	buffy brown, dark streaked
Rump	buffy brown, dark streaked
Tail	buffy brown; medium length, rounded
Throat	buff
Breast	buff, faint streaking
Belly	buff
Bill	black; short and thin
Legs	buff; medium length

BREEDING

Nest	cup on or near ground
Eggs	6; white, speckled brownish
Incubation	13–15 days ♂ ♀
Young	helpless; downy
Fledging	10–12 days
Broods	2; May–June
Food	insects
Population	25,000 pairs

Summer visitor to heaths, young conifer plantations, scrub and edges of reed beds. One of 'streaked-back' marshy warblers; upperparts buffy streaked with dark brown; short and inconspicuous pale eyebrow. Underparts buff with faint breast streaking. Most frequently observed at dawn or dusk when produces continuous reeling call – like rewinding of fishing reel.
Status: widespread summer visitor throughout Britain and Ireland.
Similar Species: Sedge Warbler (p.223) has more pronounced streaking above and bold creamy eyebrow. Savi's Warbler (p.226) has similar call, but lower pitched and briefer; lacks streaked back.

J	0
F	0
M	0
A	2
M	3
J	3
J	3
A	3
S	3
O	2
N	0
D	0

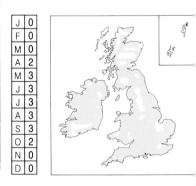

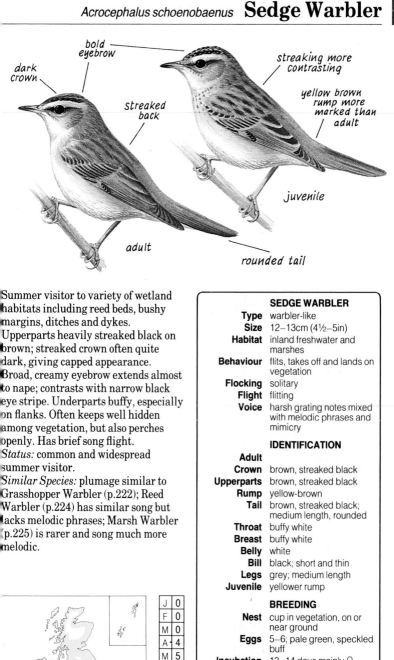

Acrocephalus schoenobaenus **Sedge Warbler**

bold eyebrow

dark crown

streaked back

streaking more contrasting

yellow brown rump more marked than adult

juvenile

adult

rounded tail

Summer visitor to variety of wetland habitats including reed beds, bushy margins, ditches and dykes. Upperparts heavily streaked black on brown; streaked crown often quite dark, giving capped appearance. Broad, creamy eyebrow extends almost to nape; contrasts with narrow black eye stripe. Underparts buffy, especially on flanks. Often keeps well hidden among vegetation, but also perches openly. Has brief song flight.
Status: common and widespread summer visitor.
Similar Species: plumage similar to Grasshopper Warbler (p.222); Reed Warbler (p.224) has similar song but lacks melodic phrases; Marsh Warbler (p.225) is rarer and song much more melodic.

	SEDGE WARBLER
Type	warbler-like
Size	12–13cm (4½–5in)
Habitat	inland freshwater and marshes
Behaviour	flits, takes off and lands on vegetation
Flocking	solitary
Flight	flitting
Voice	harsh grating notes mixed with melodic phrases and mimicry

IDENTIFICATION

Adult	
Crown	brown, streaked black
Upperparts	brown, streaked black
Rump	yellow-brown
Tail	brown, streaked black; medium length, rounded
Throat	buffy white
Breast	buffy white
Belly	white
Bill	black; short and thin
Legs	grey; medium length
Juvenile	yellower rump

BREEDING

Nest	cup in vegetation, on or near ground
Eggs	5–6; pale green, speckled buff
Incubation	13–14 days mainly ♀
Young	helpless; naked
Fledging	10–12 days
Broods	1; May–June
Food	insects
Population	*c* 300,000 pairs

J	0
F	0
M	0
A	4
M	5
J	5
J	5
A	5
S	5
O	4
N	0
D	0

Reed Warbler *Acrocephalus scirpaceus*

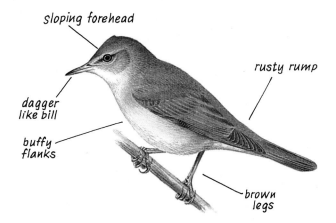

sloping forehead

rusty rump

dagger like bill

buffy flanks

brown legs

	REED WARBLER
Type	warbler-like
Size	12–13cm (4½–5in)
Habitat	inland freshwater and marshes
Behaviour	flits, takes off and lands on vegetation
Flocking	solitary
Flight	flitting
Voice	series of harsh, grating notes – *jag-jag*, *chirrug-chirrug*

IDENTIFICATION

Adult	
Crown	brown
Upperparts	brown
Rump	rufous brown
Tail	brown; medium length, rounded
Throat	white
Breast	whitish
Belly	whitish, flanks buff
Bill	brown; short and thin
Legs	grey-brown, medium length

BREEDING

Nest	deep cup in reeds
Eggs	4; pale green, spotted olive
Incubation	11–12 days ♂ ♀
Young	helpless; naked
Fledging	11–13 days
Broods	1; Apr–June
Food	insects
Population	40,000–80,000 pairs

Summer visitor to reed beds and other waterside vegetation. Tends to skulk in deep cover but will perch on reed-tops, especially while singing. Upperparts warm brown, with distinct rufous wash on rump. Underparts white with buffy flanks. Sloping forehead reaches peak at top of crown, accentuating length of bill.
Status: common summer visitor, mainly to southern England.
Similar Species: call similar to Sedge Warbler (p.223); plumage very similar to Marsh Warbler (p.225).

J	0
F	0
M	0
A	3
M	5
J	5
J	5
A	5
S	4
O	2
N	0
D	0

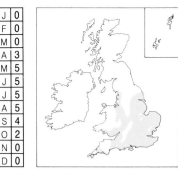

Acrocephalus palustris **Marsh Warbler**

Illustration of Marsh Warbler with labels:
- paler eyebrow than Reed
- steeper forehead
- shorter bill
- uniform underparts
- pale legs
- pale tips to tertials
- longer wings than Reed

Uncommon and extremely elusive summer visitor to southern England. Uniform olive-brown upperparts and buff and white underparts. Very similar to more widespread Reed Warbler, but generally more olive above and whiter below, with flatter crown and slightly longer wings. Prefers areas of willows and rushes near water to stands of pure reed. Best identified by song – a remarkable mimic; harsher notes reminiscent of Greenfinch.

Status: breeds regularly only in West Midlands; elsewhere rare passage migrant.

Similar Species: Reed Warbler (p.224) as above.

MARSH WARBLER

Type	warbler-like
Size	12–13cm (4½–5in)
Habitat	inland freshwaer, marshes, fields
Behaviour	flits, takes off and lands on vegetation
Flocking	solitary
Flight	flitting
Voice	rich phrases, loud trills, harsh notes; mimic

IDENTIFICATION

Adult	
Crown	olive-brown
Upperparts	olive-brown
Rump	olive-brown
Tail	olive-brown; medium length, rounded
Throat	white
Breast	buffy white
Belly	white, flanks creamy
Bill	brown; short and thin
Legs	pinkish; medium length

BREEDING

Nest	cup in dense vegetation, near ground
Eggs	4–5; pale blue
Incubation	12 days ♂ ♀
Young	helpless; naked
Fledging	10–14 days
Broods	1; May–June
Food	insects
Population	10–32 pairs

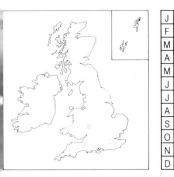

J	0
F	0
M	0
A	0
M	2
J	2
J	2
A	2
S	2
O	2
N	0
D	0

Savi's Warbler *Locustella luscinioides*

lacks dagger-like bill of Reed Warbler

unstreaked back

warm buffy flanks

rounded tail

Summer visitor to southern reed beds, where often perches on reed-tops. Reeling song similar to Grasshopper Warbler, but lower pitched and usually with briefer phrases. Upperparts uniform buff-brown; underparts buff. Barely hint of an eyebrow; distinctly rounded tail. Very similar to Reed Warbler, though lacking its sloping forehead and long bill; song best means of separating.
Status: re-colonized East Anglia and south-east England from 1960s, but declined in 1980s; today decidedly scarce.
Similar Species: plumage similar to Reed and Marsh warblers (pp.224–225); call resembles that of Grasshopper Warbler (p.222).

J	0
F	0
M	0
A	1
M	2
J	2
J	2
A	1
S	1
O	0
N	0
D	0

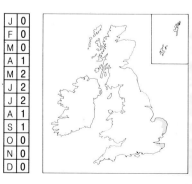

large bill

pale wing panel

long wings

blue legs

square tail

Largish, rather nondescript warbler with long, dagger-like bill and sloping forehead. Olive above, yellowish white below. Short yellow eyebrow, bluish legs, square tail. Summer adults have pale panel in wing formed by margins of inner flight feathers. Long wings with exposed primaries, about a third of overall folded length. Frequents bushy areas; moves about rather awkwardly, crashing through vegetation rather than flitting.
Status: scarce; mainly autumn passage migrant, especially on south and east coasts.
Similar Species: bill and forehead resembles Reed Warbler (p.224) but Icterine is olive and yellow, while Reed is rusty brown and buff. (Migrant Reed Warblers often seen away from aquatic habitats.)

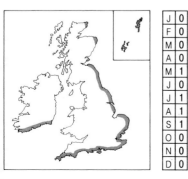

J	0
F	0
M	0
A	0
M	1
J	0
J	1
A	1
S	1
O	0
N	0
D	0

ICTERINE WARBLER

Type	warbler-like
Size	13–14cm (5–5½in)
Habitat	hedgerows, heaths, woods
Behaviour	takes off and lands on vegetation
Flocking	solitary
Flight	flitting
Voice	*churr*, hard *tec*

IDENTIFICATION

Adult	
Crown	olive
Upperparts	olive
Rump	olive
Tail	olive; medium length, square
Throat	yellowish white
Breast	yellowish white
Belly	yellowish white
Bill	brown; short and thin
Legs	bluish; medium length
Juvenile	paler above, whitish below

BREEDING

Nest	cup in bush
Eggs	4–5; pink-purple, spotted black
Incubation	13 days ♂ ♀
Young	helpless; naked
Fledging	13 days
Broods	1; May–June
Food	insects, berries
Population	rare passage migrant

Dartford Warbler *Sylvia undata*

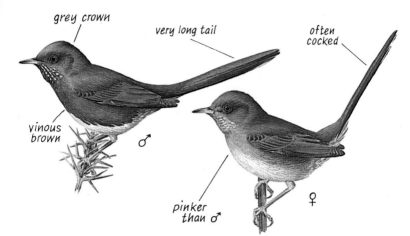

grey crown

very long tail

often cocked

vinous brown

♂

pinker than ♂

♀

DARTFORD WARBLER

Type	warbler-like
Size	12–13cm (4½–5in)
Habitat	heaths
Behaviour	flits, takes off and lands on vegetation
Flocking	solitary
Flight	flitting; undulating
Voice	harsh *chur* or *tic*; also a scratchy warble

IDENTIFICATION

Adult ♂	
Crown	grey
Upperparts	grey-brown
Rump	grey-brown
Tail	black; long and rounded
Throat	vinous brown, white flecked
Breast	vinous brown
Belly	white
Bill	black; short and thin
Legs	yellow; medium length
Adult ♀	underparts pinker
Juvenile	browner above, buffy below

BREEDING

Nest	cup near ground in thick vegetation
Eggs	3–4; white, spotted reddish
Incubation	12–13 days, mainly ♀
Young	helpless; naked
Fledging	11–13 days
Broods	2–3; Apr–June
Food	insects
Population	100–700 pairs

Tiny, elusive warbler generally well hidden in thick cover of dense stands of gorse and heather; most easily seen while singing in early spring.
Upperparts grey-brown, greyer on head; underparts dark vinous brown with sparse white flecking on throat. Outstanding feature is long tail; often cocked when perching. Juveniles browner above and buffy below. Flies on rounded, whirring wings with long tail trailing.
Status: scarce resident, confined to few heathland areas in southern England; suffers population crashes during severe winters.
Similar Species: no other warbler has long tail and dark underparts.

J	2
F	2
M	2
A	2
M	2
J	2
J	2
A	2
S	2
O	2
N	2
D	2

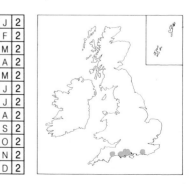

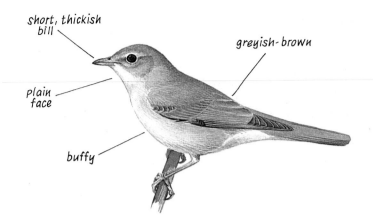

Sylvia borin **Garden Warbler**

short, thickish bill

greyish-brown

plain face

buffy

Compact summer visitor, virtually devoid of field marks. Upperparts greyish brown, underparts buffy white. Short, stubby bill is best identification feature. Frequents open deciduous and mixed woodland with plenty of undergrowth, as well as scrub, overgrown hedgerows and young plantations. Mostly skulks, even when singing.
Status: summer visitor to England, Wales, southern Scotland and central Ireland; double passage migrant.
Similar Species: nondescript appearance could confuse with variety of warblers, including Icterine Warbler (p.227); song similar to Blackcap (p.232), but more subdued and usually longer lasting.

GARDEN WARBLER	
Type	warbler-like
Size	13–15cm (5–6in)
Habitat	gardens, heaths, woods, hedges
Behaviour	flits, takes off and lands on vegetation
Flocking	solitary
Flight	flitting
Voice	fine but quiet warbling
IDENTIFICATION	
Adult	
Crown	grey-brown
Upperparts	grey-brown
Rump	grey-brown
Tail	brown; medium length, notched
Throat	buffy white
Breast	buffy white
Belly	buffy white
Bill	black; short and stubby
Legs	grey; medium length
BREEDING	
Nest	cup in bush
Eggs	4–5; white, blotched brown
Incubation	11–12 days ♂ ♀
Young	helpless; naked
Fledging	9–10 days
Broods	2; May–June
Food	insects, berries
Population	60,000–100,000 pairs

J	0
F	0
M	0
A	3
M	4
J	4
J	4
A	4
S	4
O	2
N	1
D	0

Lesser Whitethroat *Sylvia curruca*

brownish crown, reduced mask

grey upperparts

dark ear coverts

dark legs

juvenile

adult

LESSER WHITETHROAT

Type	warbler-like
Size	13–14cm (5–5½in)
Habitat	heaths, woods, hedges
Behaviour	flits, takes off and lands on vegetation
Flocking	solitary
Flight	flitting
Voice	hard *tac-tac*; also a single-note rattle

IDENTIFICATION

Adult

Crown	grey
Upperparts	grey
Rump	grey
Tail	black, white outer feathers; medium length, square
Throat	white
Breast	white
Belly	white
Bill	black; short and thin
Legs	grey; medium length

BREEDING

Nest	neat cup in low bush
Eggs	4–6; white, blotched olive
Incubation	10–11 days ♂ ♀
Young	helpless; naked
Fledging	10–11 days
Broods	1–2 ?; May–June
Food	insects
Population	25,000–50,000 pairs

Generally a skulking bird of bushy scrub, tall hedgerows and young conifers. Attractive warbler, basically grey above, white below. Male has prominent, dark ear coverts, giving masked appearance. Legs dark; tail has white outer feathers. Song similar to rattle of Yellowhammer but lacking final flourish.
Status: summer visitor mostly to southern England; passage migrant especially to south and east coasts.
Similar Species: Common Whitethroat (p.231) is slightly larger, rusty brown above and pinkish below.

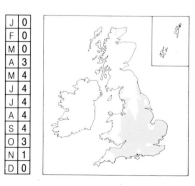

J	0
F	0
M	0
A	3
M	4
J	4
J	4
A	4
S	4
O	3
N	1
D	0

Sylvia communis **Common Whitethroat**

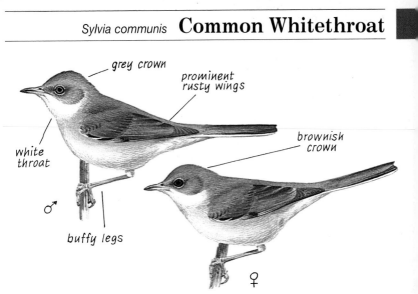

- grey crown
- prominent rusty wings
- brownish crown
- white throat
- buffy legs
- ♂
- ♀

Summer visitor to heaths, commons, scrub and hedgerows. Marked by white throat; particularly obvious in singing male. Upperparts greyish brown; broad rusty margins to wing feathers immediately identify. Head grey in male, buffy brown in female and juvenile. Breast pinkish, belly white, legs pale. Though often skulks in dense cover, in spring will sit atop bushes to sing. Has short, dancing song flight. *Status:* widespread summer visitor to all but Scottish Highlands; decline in 1970s and 1980s associated with extension of Sahara southwards into Sahel wintering grounds. *Similar Species:* Lesser Whitethroat (p.230) differs in colour and size.

COMMON WHITETHROAT	
Type	warbler-like
Size	13–15cm (5–6in)
Habitat	gardens, heaths, woods, hedges
Behaviour	flits, takes off and lands on vegetation
Flocking	solitary
Flight	undulating; flitting
Voice	hard *tac-tac*; song, a brief scratchy warble

IDENTIFICATION

Adult ♂	
Crown	grey
Upperparts	greyish brown, wings brown with rusty margins
Rump	greyish brown
Tail	greyish brown; medium length, square
Throat	white
Breast	pinkish
Belly	white
Bill	buff; short and thin
Legs	buff; medium length
Ad.♀ and juv.	buffy brown head

BREEDING

Nest	cup near ground
Eggs	4–5; pale blue, speckled olive
Incubation	11–13 days ♂ ♀
Young	helpless; naked
Fledging	10–12 days
Broods	2; May–June
Food	insects, berries
Population	500,000–700,000 pairs

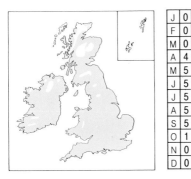

J	0
F	0
M	0
A	4
M	5
J	5
J	5
A	5
S	5
O	1
N	0
D	0

Blackcap *Sylvia atricapilla*

black cap

grey back

rust cap

♂

♀

BLACKCAP

Type	warbler-like
Size	13–15cm (5–6in)
Habitat	gardens, heaths, woods, hedges
Behaviour	flits, takes off and lands on vegetation
Flocking	solitary
Flight	flitting
Voice	a varied warble

IDENTIFICATION

Adult ♂	
Crown	sooty black cap
Upperparts	grey
Rump	grey
Tail	grey; medium length, notched
Throat	greyish white
Breast	greyish white
Belly	white
Bill	black; short and thin
Legs	black; medium length
Adult ♀	rusty cap; browner above, buffy below

BREEDING

Nest	cup in bush or tree
Eggs	5; white, blotched reddish
Incubation	12–13 days ♂ ♀
Young	helpless; naked
Fledging	10–14 days
Broods	2; May–June
Food	insects, berries
Population	c200,000 pairs; 3000 winter

Best known for its delightful song, which some compare to Nightingale; has greater variety of notes and phrases than Garden Warbler. Male has sooty black cap and grey back; greyish white below. Female has rusty cap; browner above and buffy below. Frequents open deciduous or mixed woodland with well-developed undergrowth; generally keeps well hidden among vegetation. Some birds overwinter and visit bird tables.
Status: widespread summer visitor, except to extreme north and west; passage migrant; scarce winter visitor to southern England and south-eastern Ireland.
Similar Species: male could be confused with Marsh Tit (p.242) and Willow Tit (p.243) but is larger and slimmer.

J	1
F	1
M	2
A	5
M	5
J	5
J	5
A	5
S	4
O	3
N	1
D	1

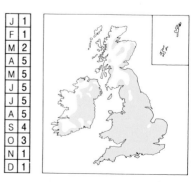

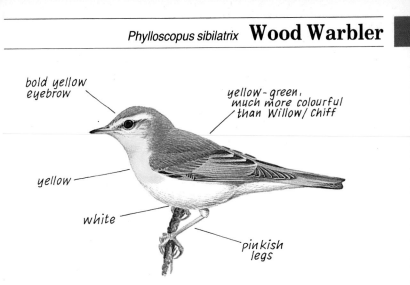

bold yellow eyebrow

yellow-green, much more colourful than Willow/Chiff

yellow

white

pinkish legs

Summer visitor to dense deciduous woods with scant undergrowth. Larger than closely related Willow Warbler, but greener above, with more yellow on wing and head, and pure white below. Pronounced yellowish eyebrow with dark eye stripe. Legs pale. Song flight on fluttering wings below tree canopy quite distinctive.

Status: summer visitor; more numerous in west than east, though almost absent from Ireland; decidedly scarce on migration.

Similar Species: Chiffchaff (p.234) and especially Willow Warbler (p.235) can be quite yellow, particularly in first winter plumage; neither are white on breast and belly, or green above.

WOOD WARBLER

Type	warbler-like
Size	12–13cm (4½–5in)
Habitat	heaths, woods
Behaviour	flits, takes off and lands on vegetation
Flocking	solitary
Flight	flitting
Voice	*peu*; flight song starts *peu-peu*, accelerates into rapid trill

IDENTIFICATION

Adult	
Crown	greeny yellow
Upperparts	greeny yellow
Rump	greeny yellow
Tail	greeny yellow; medium length, notched
Throat	yellow
Breast	yellow
Belly	white
Bill	black; short and thin
Legs	pinkish; medium length

BREEDING

Nest	dome on ground
Eggs	6–7; white, speckled reddish
Incubation	13 days ♀
Young	helpless; downy
Fledging	11–12 days
Broods	1–2; May–June
Food	insects
Population	30,000–60,000 pairs

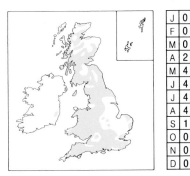

J	0
F	0
M	0
A	2
M	4
J	4
J	4
A	4
S	1
O	0
N	0
D	0

Chiffchaff *Phylloscopus collybita*

short, less marked eyebrow than Willow Warbler

adult spring

buffy white

dark legs

autumn

yellowish

CHIFFCHAFF

Type	warbler-like
Size	10.5–11.5cm (4–4½in)
Habitat	heaths, woods, hedges
Behaviour	flits, takes off and lands on vegetation
Flocking	solitary
Flight	flitting
Voice	distinct *chiff-chaff-chiff-chaff*, repeated; also *hueet*, especially on passage

IDENTIFICATION

Adult	
Crown	olive-brown
Upperparts	olive-brown
Rump	olive-brown
Tail	olive-brown; medium length, notched
Throat	buffy white
Breast	buffy white
Belly	buffy white
Bill	black; short and thin
Legs	black; medium length
Juvenile	yellower below

BREEDING

Nest	dome on ground
Eggs	4–9; white, speckled purple
Incubation	13–14 days ♀
Young	helpless; downy
Fledging	12–15 days
Broods	1–2; Apr–May
Food	insects
Population	300,000 pairs; 300–1000 winter

Widespread summer visitor; named after its characteristic call. Inhabits open woodland but occurs in gardens and scrub on passage. Olive-brown above, dull buffy white below. Eyebrow and eye stripe less distinct than very similar Willow Warbler. Always appears as less well marked and less clean-cut version of Willow Warbler, with shorter eyebrow and (usually) dark legs. Active little bird; flits about foliage in non-stop feeding. Sometimes feeds on ground; continuously flicks wings.

Status: common summer visitor everywhere but highest hills of north; passage migrant; winter visitor to south-west England.

Similar Species: Willow Warbler (p.235) and Wood Warbler (p.233).

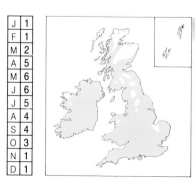

J	1
F	1
M	2
A	5
M	6
J	6
J	5
A	4
S	4
O	3
N	1
D	1

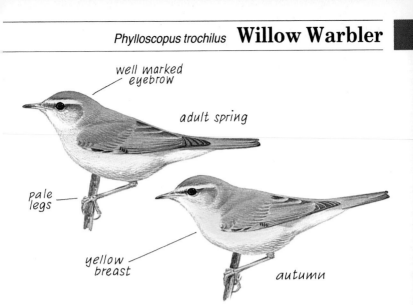

well marked eyebrow

adult spring

pale legs

yellow breast

autumn

Most common and widespread warbler; summer visitor to wide variety of wooded habitats, from forests to bushy commons. Very similar to Chiffchaff – olive-brown above; buffy yellow below. Clear eyebrow extends well beyond eye. Always cleaner-cut than Chiffchaff with pale (not dark) legs. *Status:* abundant and widespread summer visitor.
Similar Species: Chiffchaff (p.234); Wood Warbler (p.233).

WILLOW WARBLER

Type	warbler-like
Size	10.5–11.5cm (4–4½in)
Habitat	heaths, woods, hedges
Behaviour	flits, takes off and lands on vegetation
Flocking	solitary
Flight	flitting
Voice	weak *hoo-eet*; also a descending warbled trill, repeated

IDENTIFICATION

Adult	
Crown	olive-brown
Upperparts	olive-brown
Rump	olive-brown
Tail	olive-brown; medium length, notched
Throat	buffy yellow
Breast	buffy yellow
Belly	buffy white
Bill	black; short and thin
Legs	pale brown; medium length
Juvenile	yellower below

BREEDING

Nest	dome on ground
Eggs	6–7; white, speckled reddish
Incubation	13 days ♀
Young	helpless; downy
Fledging	13–16 days
Broods	1–2; Apr–June
Food	insects
Population	3,000,000 pairs

J	0
F	0
M	1
A	4
M	6
J	6
J	6
A	5
S	4
O	1
N	0
D	0

Goldcrest *Regulus regulus*

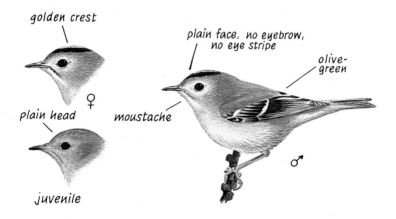

golden crest

♀

plain head

juvenile

plain face, no eyebrow, no eye stripe

olive-green

moustache

♂

GOLDCREST

Type	warbler-like
Size	8.5–9cm (3½in)
Habitat	gardens, heaths, woods, hedges
Behaviour	flits, takes off and lands on vegetation
Flocking	1–10
Flight	hovers; undulating; flitting
Voice	high-pitched *zi-zi-zi-zi*, repeated; song similar but ending in flourish

IDENTIFICATION

Adult

Crown	golden blaze, bordered black; lacks eye stripe and eyebrow
Upperparts	olive-green; wings black with white margins, wingbar
Rump	olive-green
Tail	black; medium length, notched
Throat	white
Breast	buffy white
Belly	buffy white
Bill	black; short and thin
Legs	black; medium length

BREEDING

Nest	cup high in tree
Eggs	7–10; white, speckled brown
Incubation	14–17 days ♀
Young	helpless; downy
Fledging	16–21 days
Broods	2; Apr–May
Food	insects, spiders
Population	1,000,000–1,500,000 pairs; 3,000,000–5,000,000 wint.

Smallest British bird; tiny but decidedly rotund, with shortish tail. Crown has distinctive golden-orange blaze bordered by black. Face remarkably plain with large, dark eye and fine moustachial streak. Back olive-green; wings black with broad white margins and clear, single (sometimes double) wingbar. Underparts buffy white. Ever-active; flicks wings continuously during non-stop search for food among trees. Shows marked preference for conifers. In winter often associates with tit flocks.
Status: common and widespread resident.
Similar Species: closely related Firecrest (p.237) also has orange crown stripe bordered by black, but has distinctive face pattern.

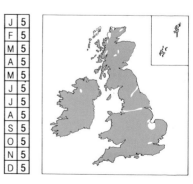

J	5
F	5
M	5
A	5
M	5
J	5
J	5
A	5
S	5
O	5
N	5
D	5

bold white eyebrow
bold eye stripe

yellow-green

golden crest

♀

bold eyebrow

♂

juvenile

Similar to Goldcrest with similar high-pitched call and active, non-stop search for food among conifers. Firecrest is much rarer. Greener on back with distinctive face pattern of bold white eyebrow and prominent black eye stripe. Easily identified if seen clearly. Different call and song; both stronger than Goldcrest, song often ends abruptly.
Status: rare breeding bird in south-east England (often overlooked). Scarce winter visitor to southern England; regular late autumn migrant.
Similar Species: Goldcrest (p.236).

FIRECREST

Type	warbler-like
Size	8.5–9cm (3½in)
Habitat	gardens, heaths, woods, hedges
Behaviour	flits, takes off and lands on vegetation
Flocking	1–2
Flight	hovers; undulating; flitting
Voice	*zit-zit-zit*; song similar, often ending abruptly

IDENTIFICATION

Adult	
Crown	golden blaze, bordered black; prominent eye stripe and eyebrow
Upperparts	yellow-green; wings black with white margins, wingbar
Rump	yellow-green
Tail	black; medium length, notched
Throat	white
Breast	white
Belly	white
Bill	black; short and thin
Legs	black; medium length

BREEDING

Nest	cup high in tree
Eggs	7–11; pale buffy, speckled brown
Incubation	14–15 days ♀
Young	helpless; downy
Fledging	19–20 days
Broods	2; May–June
Food	insects, spiders
Population	10–40 pairs; 200–400 winter

J	1
F	1
M	2
A	2
M	2
J	2
J	2
A	2
S	3
O	3
N	2
D	1

Spotted Flycatcher *Muscicapa striata*

streaked crown

buffy edges

speckled breast

upright stance

SPOTTED FLYCATCHER

Type	chat-like
Size	13.5–14.5cm (5½–6in)
Habitat	gardens, heaths, woods, hedges
Behaviour	perches openly, takes off and lands on vegetation
Flocking	1 or 2
Flight	strong and powerful; flitting
Voice	weak *tzee*

IDENTIFICATION

Adult

Crown	brown and buff
Upperparts	greyish brown; wings pale-edged
Rump	greyish brown
Tail	greyish brown; medium length, notched
Throat	buffy
Breast	white, streaked buff-brown
Belly	white
Bill	black; short and broad
Legs	black; short

BREEDING

Nest	cup against wall or tree trunk, often near ground
Eggs	4–5; pale blue, blotched reddish
Incubation	11–15 days ♀
Young	helpless; downy
Fledging	12–14 days
Broods	1–2; May–June
Food	insects
Population	100,000–200,000 pairs

Most frequently seen perched upright on fence or twig, flying out to catch passing insects and returning to original or nearby perch. Agile flight on large wings; snap of bill audible at close range. Solitary or in pairs. Upperparts greyish brown; narrow, pale edges to inner flight feathers and wing coverts. Crown streaked brown and buff. Underparts white; buff-brown streaking on breast. Short, broad black bill. First winter birds differ only in having broader buff margins to wing feathers.

Status: widespread summer visitor.
Similar Species: female and first winter Pied Flycatcher (p.239) also brownish, but with extensive white in wing; lack streaked breast.

J	0
F	0
M	0
A	1
M	4
J	4
J	4
A	4
S	3
O	0
N	0
D	0

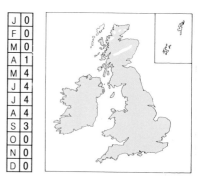

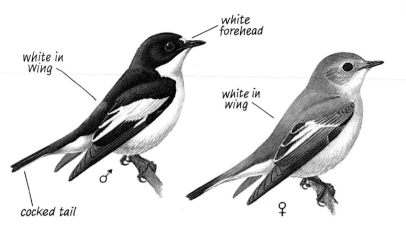

Ficedula hypoleuca **Pied Flycatcher**

white
forehead

white in
wing

white in
wing

cocked tail

♂

♀

Stout little bird with tiny bill. Like
Spotted Flycatcher perches openly
watching for passing insects, but
returns to same perch less frequently.
Summer male black above with white
forehead and bold area of white in
wing; underparts white. Female,
winter male and first winter birds
similar, but brown above with smaller
white area in wing. Takes readily to
nest boxes in open oak and birch woods.
Status: summer visitor to north and
west Britain; passage migrant
elsewhere, including eastern Ireland;
sometimes numerous; usually regarded
as important element of Scandinavian
migration.
Similar Species: Spotted Flycatcher
(p.238) has streaked breast.

PIED FLYCATCHER

Type	chat-like
Size	12–13cm (4½–5in)
Habitat	woods
Behaviour	perches openly, takes off and lands on vegetation
Flocking	solitary
Flight	strong and powerful; flitting
Voice	*whit* or *tic*; also a repeated *zee-chi* ending in flourish

IDENTIFICATION

Ad.♂ summer	
Crown	black and white
Upperparts	black, with white in wing
Rump	black
Tail	black, white outer feathers; medium length, square
Throat	white
Breast	white
Belly	white
Bill	black; tiny
Legs	black; short
Ad.♀, winter♂	brown above; less white in wing

BREEDING

Nest	cup in tree hole or nest box
Eggs	4–7; pale blue
Incubation	12–13 days ♀
Young	helpless; downy
Fledging	13–16 days
Broods	1; May–June
Food	insects
Population	20,000 pairs

J	0
F	0
M	0
A	3
M	4
J	4
J	4
A	4
S	4
O	2
N	0
D	0

Bearded Tit *Panurus biarmicus*

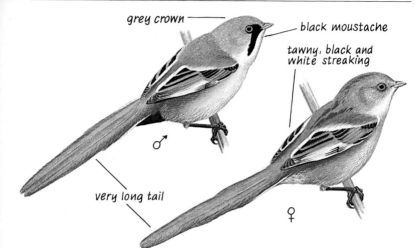

grey crown

black moustache

tawny, black and white streaking

♂

very long tail

♀

BEARDED TIT

Type	tit-like
Size	16–17cm (6–6½in)
Habitat	reed beds
Behaviour	flits, takes off and lands on vegetation
Flocking	1–15
Flight	laboured; direct
Voice	loud *pting*, repeated in flight

IDENTIFICATION

Adult ♂	
Crown	blue-grey
Upperparts	orange-brown; black and white wing margins
Rump	orange-brown
Tail	orange-brown; long and rounded
Throat	white
Breast	orange-buff
Belly	orange-buff
Bill	yellow; short and thin
Legs	black; medium length
Adult ♀	head orange-brown

BREEDING

Nest	cup near ground, over water
Eggs	5–7; white, speckled brown
Incubation	12–13 days ♂ ♀
Young	helpless; naked
Fledging	9–12 days
Broods	2–3; Apr–May
Food	insects, seeds
Population	c 600 pairs

Small buff-brown bird with inordinately long tail. As alternative name Bearded Reedling implies, confined to extensive stands of reeds where most often seen flying low on short whirring wings, long tail streaming out behind. Also perches on reed-tops, especially in early mornings and during autumn. Male rich orange-brown above, with bold black and white margins to wings. Head blue-grey marked by droopy black moustache; both lacking in female. *Status:* highly local; breeders confined to reed beds in East Anglia and south-east England; irrupts across southern England in autumn.
Similar Species: none.

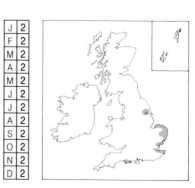

J	2
F	2
M	2
A	2
M	2
J	2
J	2
A	2
S	2
O	2
N	2
D	2

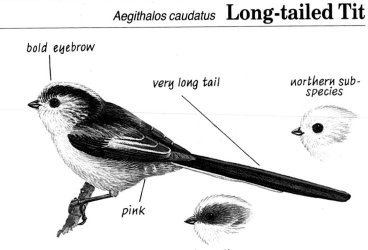

Aegithalos caudatus **Long-tailed Tit**

bold eyebrow

very long tail

northern sub-
species

pink

juvenile

Small, active bird with tail longer than body – no other woodland bird has such a long tail. Crown white with bold black stripe over eye extending to black back; tiny black bill. Wings black and white with broad pink band across upper edge; tail black with white outer feathers. Underparts white with pink undertail coverts. Juveniles lack pink and have sooty black heads. Rare northern sub-species has all-white head. Usually found throughout year in small flocks up to twenty strong. Prefers hedgerows and woods with plentiful secondary growth, as well as bushy heaths and commons. *Status:* widespread resident. *Similar Species:* none.

	LONG-TAILED TIT
Type	tit-like
Size	13.5–14.5cm (5½–6in)
Habitat	heaths, woods, gardens, hedges
Behaviour	flits, takes off and lands on vegetation
Flocking	1–15
Flight	laboured; flitting
Voice	continuous *zee-zee-zee* contact call among flock

	IDENTIFICATION
Adult	
Crown	white, black eye stripe
Upperparts	black and white, wings pink-banded
Rump	black and white
Tail	black, white outer feathers; long and rounded
Throat	white
Breast	white
Belly	white, pink undertail
Bill	black; tiny
Legs	black; medium length
Juvenile	lacks pink; head sooty black

	BREEDING
Nest	dome in bush
Eggs	8–12; white
Incubation	12–14 days, mainly ♀
Young	helpless; naked
Fledging	14–18 days
Broods	1–2; Mar–Apr
Food	insects, seeds
Population	50,000 pairs

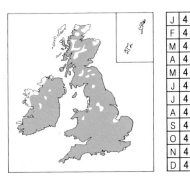

J	4
F	4
M	4
A	4
M	4
J	4
J	4
A	4
S	4
O	4
N	4
D	4

Marsh Tit *Parus palustris*

glossy cap

small bib

MARSH TIT

Type	tit-like
Size	11–12cm (4½–5in)
Habitat	heaths, woods, hedges, gardens
Behaviour	flits, takes off and lands on vegetation
Flocking	1–5
Flight	undulating; flitting
Voice	distinctive repeated *pitchoo-pitchoo-pitchoo*, also repeated *chip-chip*

IDENTIFICATION

Adult	
Crown	shiny black cap
Upperparts	buff-brown
Rump	buff-brown
Tail	buff-brown; medium length, notched
Throat	black bib
Breast	white
Belly	white
Bill	black; short and stubby
Legs	black; medium length

BREEDING

Nest	cup in hole in rotten wood
Eggs	6–9; white, spotted reddish
Incubation	13–17 days ♀
Young	helpless; downy
Fledging	16—21 days
Broods	1–2; Apr–May
Food	insects, seeds
Population	50,000–110,000 pairs

Name misleading as haunts deciduous woods and hedgerows. Typical tit with round head, short bill, black cap and uniform buff-brown upperparts. Behaviour also typical – ever-active forager through tree canopy, often in company of related species. Great care needed to distinguish from very similar Willow Tit; Marsh Tit cap shiny (not dull), bib small (not large and diffuse); lacks pale panel in wing. Marsh Tit is neat and elegant little bird; Willow Tit decidedly scruffy. Calls quite different. *Status:* widespread resident in England, Wales and southern Scotland.
Similar Species: Willow Tit (p.243) as above.

J	4
F	4
M	4
A	4
M	4
J	4
J	4
A	4
S	4
O	4
N	4
D	4

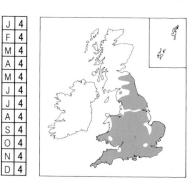

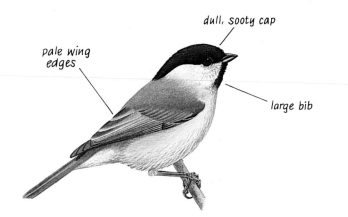

pale wing
edges

dull, sooty cap

large bib

Very like closely related Marsh Tit and found in similar habitats, especially damp alder and birch woods. Somewhat ill-kempt appearance. Distinguished from Marsh Tit by dull black cap, larger white cheeks, larger and more diffuse black bib and (especially in winter) pale wing panel. In summer, must have dead rotting trees in which to excavate nest hole.
Status: widespread resident in England, Wales and southern Scotland.
Similar Species: Marsh Tit (p.242).

WILLOW TIT	
Type	tit-like
Size	11–12cm (4½–5in)
Habitat	heaths, woods, hedges, gardens
Behaviour	flits, takes off and lands on vegetation
Flocking	1–2
Flight	undulating; flitting
Voice	buzzing *erz-erz-erz*; also high-pitched *zi-zi-zi*

IDENTIFICATION

Adult	
Crown	dull black cap
Upperparts	buff-brown, pale wing edges
Rump	buff-brown
Tail	buff-brown; medium length, notched
Throat	black bib
Breast	white
Belly	white
Bill	black; short and stubby
Legs	black; medium length

BREEDING

Nest	self-excavated cavity, thinly lined
Eggs	6–9; white, speckled reddish
Incubation	13–15 days ♀
Young	helpless; downy
Fledging	17–19 days
Broods	1; Apr–May
Food	insects, seeds
Population	50,000–100,000 pairs

J	4
F	4
M	4
A	4
M	4
J	4
J	4
A	4
S	4
O	4
N	4
D	4

Crested Tit *Parus cristatus*

crest streaked

black line surrounds face

Typically active, often associating with other tits but confined to areas of old Scot's Pine with broken tree stumps and scattered birches. Grey-brown upperparts with prominent black and white streaked crest. Face white with clearly marked black eye stripe, black bib and black line extending to enclose ear coverts. Underparts whitish.
Status: scarce, confined to central Scottish Highlands.
Similar Species: only 'crested' tit.

CRESTED TIT

Type	tit-like
Size	11–12cm (4½–5in)
Habitat	forests and woods
Behaviour	flits, takes off and lands on vegetation
Flocking	1–15
Flight	undulating; flitting
Voice	trilled *chirr-chirr-rr*

IDENTIFICATION

Adult	
Crown	black and white, crest
Upperparts	grey-brown
Rump	grey-brown
Tail	grey-brown; medium length, notched
Throat	black bib
Breast	whitish
Belly	whitish
Bill	black; short and stubby
Legs	black; medium length

BREEDING

Nest	cup in excavated hole in old stump
Eggs	4–8; white, speckled purple
Incubation	13–18 days ♀
Young	helpless; downy
Fledging	17–21 days
Broods	1; Apr–May
Food	insects, seeds
Population	*c*900 pairs

J	3
F	3
M	3
A	3
M	3
J	3
J	3
A	3
S	3
O	3
N	3
D	3

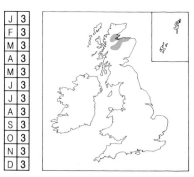

Parus ater Coal Tit

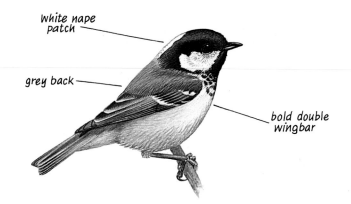

white nape patch

grey back

bold double wingbar

Smallest tit, most often found among conifers, but also visits mature deciduous and mixed woodland, gardens and bird tables. Grey-blue above, with double white wingbar; underparts greyish white. Crown and substantial bib glossy black; white patch on nape distinguishes from other woodland tits. Gregarious, often associating with other tits, particularly outside breeding season.
Status: widespread and common resident except in extreme northern and north-western isles.
Similar Species: white nape patch unique. Call similar to Goldcrest (p.236); song to a similar phrase of Great Tit (p.247).

COAL TIT

Type	tit-like
Size	10.5–11.5cm (4½in)
Habitat	woods, hedges, heaths, gardens
Behaviour	flits, takes off and lands on vegetation
Flocking	1–15
Flight	undulating; flitting
Voice	high-pitched *zee-zee-zee*; also a repeated *weecho-weecho-weecho*

IDENTIFICATION

Adult	
Crown	black, white nape
Upperparts	grey-blue, white wingbars
Rump	grey-blue
Tail	grey-blue; medium length, notched
Throat	black bib
Breast	greyish white
Belly	greyish white
Bill	black; short and stubby
Legs	black; medium length

BREEDING

Nest	cup in tree hole
Eggs	7–9; white, speckled reddish
Incubation	14–18 days ♀
Young	helpless; downy
Fledging	16–19 days
Broods	2; Apr–May
Food	insects, seeds
Population	1,000,000 pairs

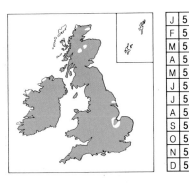

J	5
F	5
M	5
A	5
M	5
J	5
J	5
A	5
S	5
O	5
N	5
D	5

Blue Tit *Parus caeruleus*

greenish crown

blue crown

blue wings

eyebrow and eye stripe

juvenile

adult

Most common and familiar of tits; comes readily to bird tables and other feeders; will also occupy nest boxes and use bird baths. Wings pale blue with single white wingbar; back greenish. Underparts yellow with neat dividing line on centre of breast. White cheeks enclosed by dark line from eye to chin. *Status:* abundant and widespread resident of Britain and Ireland. *Similar Species:* Great Tit (p.247) larger with black cap and face pattern, and bold black line down breast.

BLUE TIT

Type	tit-like
Size	11–12cm (4½–5in)
Habitat	gardens, marshes, heaths, woods, hedges
Behaviour	flits, takes off and lands on vegetation
Flocking	1–30
Flight	undulating; flitting
Voice	*tsee-tsee-tsee*; also harsh *churr*

IDENTIFICATION

Adult	
Crown	pale blue
Upperparts	greenish, wings pale blue
Rump	greenish
Tail	pale blue; medium length, notched
Throat	blue bib
Breast	yellow
Belly	yellow, dark dividing line
Bill	black; short and stubby
Legs	black; medium length
Juvenile	crown greyish

BREEDING

Nest	cup in tree hole or nest box
Eggs	7–12; white, speckled reddish
Incubation	12–16 days ♀
Young	helpless; downy
Fledging	15–23 days
Broods	1; Apr–May
Food	insects, seeds, nuts
Population	4,500,000 pairs

J	6
F	6
M	6
A	6
M	6
J	6
J	6
A	6
S	6
O	6
N	6
D	6

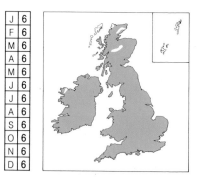

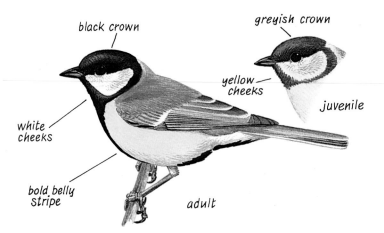

Parus major **Great Tit**

black crown

greyish crown

yellow cheeks

juvenile

white cheeks

bold belly stripe

adult

Largest and most clearly marked of all the tits, with shiny black cap and bib joined by bold black line enclosing white cheeks; black stripe down yellow bib and belly (wider in male than female). Back green, wings and tail pale blue; latter with white outer feathers. Common in all types of woods, including pure conifer stands where often most abundant bird. Comes readily to gardens where aggressive at feeders. Joins mixed tit flocks outside breeding season. Has wide variety of calls and songs – fifty-seven distinct forms described.
Status: common and widespread resident of Britain and Ireland.
Similar Species: Blue Tit (p.246) is much smaller and has fainter belly line and paler cap and head pattern.

GREAT TIT

Type	tit-like
Size	13.5–14.5cm (5½in)
Habitat	gardens, marshes, heaths, woods, hedges
Behaviour	flits, takes off and lands on vegetation
Flocking	1–30
Flight	undulating; flitting
Voice	*see-saw* and *teecha-teecha-teecha* most common

IDENTIFICATION

Adult	
Crown	black
Upperparts	green; wings pale blue, white outer feathers
Rump	pale blue
Tail	pale blue; medium length, notched
Throat	black bib
Breast	yellow, black centre stripe
Belly	yellow, black centre stripe
Bill	black; short and stubby
Legs	black; medium length
Juvenile	crown greyish black

BREEDING

Nest	cup in tree hole or nest box
Eggs	8–13; white, spotted reddish
Incubation	13–14 days ♀
Young	helpless; downy
Fledging	16–22 days
Broods	1; Mar–May
Food	insects, seeds
Population	3,030,000 pairs

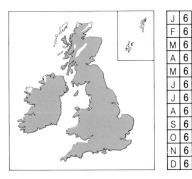

J	6
F	6
M	6
A	6
M	6
J	6
J	6
A	6
S	6
O	6
N	6
D	6

European Nuthatch *Sitta europaea*

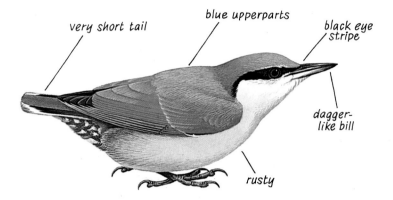

very short tail

blue upperparts

black eye stripe

dagger-like bill

rusty

EUROPEAN NUTHATCH

Type	woodpecker-like
Size	13.5–14.5cm (5½in)
Habitat	woods, hedges, heaths, gardens
Behaviour	climbs, takes off and lands on vegetation
Flocking	1–2
Flight	strong and powerful; direct
Voice	high-pitched *chwit-chwit*; also a repeated *kee-kee-kee*

IDENTIFICATION

Adult	
Crown	pale blue
Upperparts	pale blue, black wingtips
Rump	pale blue
Tail	pale blue; short and square
Throat	white
Breast	warm buff
Belly	warm buff
Bill	black; short and thin
Legs	buff; medium length

BREEDING

Nest	tree hole, plastered mud
Eggs	6–9; white, spotted reddish
Incubation	14–18 days ♀
Young	helpless; downy
Fledging	23–25 days
Broods	1; Apr–May
Food	seeds, nuts, insects
Population	20,000 pairs

Agile tree-climber, similar to woodpeckers but with ability to climb up and down trees. Does not undulate in flight like woodpecker. Upperparts pale blue with bold black eye stripe and black wingtips. Throat white; remaining underparts warm buff, with chestnut on flanks. Tail short and square. Produces sounds by hacking at nuts wedged in tree crevice with sharply pointed bill.
Status: widespread resident of England and Wales.
Similar Species: none.

J	4
F	4
M	4
A	4
M	4
J	4
J	4
A	4
S	4
O	4
N	4
D	4

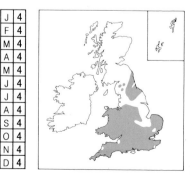

Certhia familiaris Eurasian Treecreeper

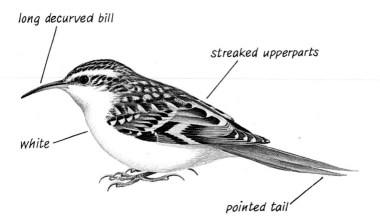

long decurved bill

streaked upperparts

white

pointed tail

Small tree-climber that uses long, decurved bill to search bark for food. Well camouflaged and easily overlooked; streaked brown and buff above with rusty rump. White eyebrow; double wingbar; tail feathers have protruding shafts. Underparts white. Frequently shy, climbing out of view of watcher; call often attracts attention. Joins mixed tit flocks in winter.
Status: widespread resident of Britain and Ireland.
Similar Species: none.

EURASIAN TREECREEPER

Type	woodpecker-like
Size	12–13cm (4½–5in)
Habitat	woods, heaths, hedges, gardens
Behaviour	climbs, takes off and lands on vegetation
Flocking	solitary
Flight	undulating
Voice	Goldcrest-like *tsee-tsee*

IDENTIFICATION

Adult	
Crown	buff and brown, streaked
Upperparts	buff and brown, streaked
Rump	rusty brown
Tail	brown; medium length, pointed
Throat	white
Breast	white
Belly	white
Bill	black; long and thin, decurved
Legs	grey; medium length

BREEDING

Nest	cup behind bark
Eggs	6; white, speckled reddish
Incubation	14–15 days ♀
Young	helpless; downy
Fledging	14–16 days
Broods	1–2; Apr–June
Food	insects
Population	150,000–300,000 pairs

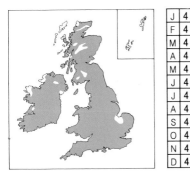

J	4
F	4
M	4
A	4
M	4
J	4
J	4
A	4
S	4
O	4
N	4
D	4

Golden Oriole *Oriolus oriolus*

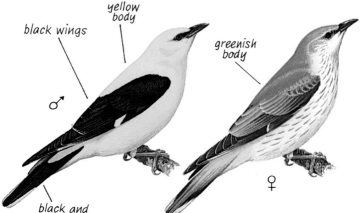

yellow body

black wings

black and yellow tail

♂

greenish body

♀

GOLDEN ORIOLE

Type	pigeon-like
Size	23–25cm (9–10in)
Habitat	heaths, woods, hedges
Behaviour	flits, perches openly, takes off and lands on vegetation
Flocking	1–2
Flight	strong and powerful; undulating
Voice	flute-like whistle *weela-weeo*

IDENTIFICATION

Adult ♂	
Crown	yellow
Upperparts	yellow, black wings
Rump	yellow
Tail	black and yellow; medium length, square
Throat	yellow
Breast	yellow
Belly	yellow
Bill	red; short and thin
Legs	black; medium length
Ad. ♀, Sub-ad. ♂	greenish above, white with streaking below

BREEDING

Nest	cup suspended in tree
Eggs	3–4; white, spotted brown
Incubation	14–15 days, mainly ♀
Young	helpless; downy
Fledging	14–15 days
Broods	1–2 ?; May–June
Food	insects, berries, fruit
Population	30–100 pairs

Boldly coloured but self-effacing woodland bird; more often heard than seen. Male bright yellow with black wings and black base to tail. Females and younger males greenish and black, with varying amounts of white and some streaking on breast. Bill red. Except when flies, easily overlooked among canopy of large deciduous trees.
Status: rare summer visitor, mostly to East Anglia.
Similar Species: none.

J	0
F	0
M	0
A	1
M	1
J	1
J	1
A	1
S	1
O	1
N	0
D	0

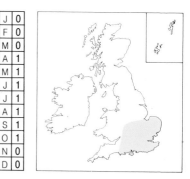

Lanius collurio **Red-backed Shrike**

grey crown

rusty back

grey rump

♂

stubby hooked bill

dark ear coverts

rusty back

♀

Fast-declining summer visitor to open heaths in east England. Spends much time sitting on top or side of low bush waiting for prey – large insects and small birds. Male has grey crown and broad, black eye patch; back rust-red; tail black with partially white outer feathers; underparts white. Female sandy brown above with dark mark through eye and barred underparts; outer tail feathers white. Juvenile similar to female, but barred above as well as below.
Status: scarce summer visitor to eastern England; migrant elsewhere.
Similar Species: Great Grey Shrike (p.252) has grey and black plumage.

RED-BACKED SHRIKE

Type	chat-like
Size	16–18cm (6½–7in)
Habitat	heaths
Behaviour	perches openly, takes off and lands on vegetation
Flocking	solitary
Flight	direct
Voice	harsh *chak-chak*

IDENTIFICATION

Adult ♂	
Crown	grey
Upperparts	rust-red
Rump	grey
Tail	black and white; medium length, square
Throat	white
Breast	white
Belly	white
Bill	black; short and stubby
Legs	black; medium length
Adult ♀	lacks grey head and rump, paler brown above; barred underparts
Juvenile	as ♀ but heavily barred

BREEDING

Nest	cup in dense thicket
Eggs	5–6; highly variable, spotted shades of brown
Incubation	14–16 days ♀
Young	helpless; naked
Fledging	12–16 days
Broods	1; May–June
Food	insects, small birds
Population	1–4 pairs

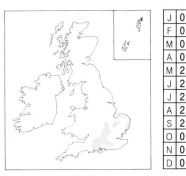

J	0
F	0
M	0
A	0
M	2
J	2
J	2
A	2
S	2
O	0
N	0
D	0

Great Grey Shrike *Lanius excubitor*

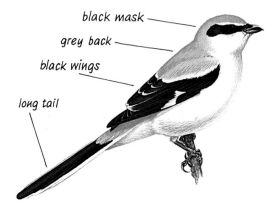

black mask

grey back

black wings

long tail

GREAT GREY SHRIKE

Type	chat-like
Size	23–25cm (9–10in)
Habitat	heaths, hedges
Behaviour	perches openly, takes off and lands on vegetation
Flocking	solitary
Flight	direct
Voice	harsh *chek-chek*

IDENTIFICATION

Adult	
Crown	grey
Upperparts	grey, black wings with white patches
Rump	grey
Tail	black with white patches; long and rounded
Throat	white
Breast	white
Belly	white
Bill	black; short and stubby
Legs	black; medium length

BREEDING

Nest	cup in bush
Eggs	5–7; white, spotted reddish
Incubation	15 days ♂, mainly ♀
Young	helpless; naked
Fledging	19–20 days
Broods	1; Apr–May
Food	birds, voles
Population	150+ winter

Medium-sized, grey and black winter visitor, generally in small numbers. Crown, back and rump grey; wings and long tail black, marked with white patches. Bold black mask through eye. Underparts white. Often sits openly on top of bush or telegraph post, where glistening white breast visible at considerable distances. Like other shrikes, pounces on prey. Invariably solitary.
Status: scarce winter visitor to eastern Scotland and England.
Similar Species: Red-backed Shrike (p.251).

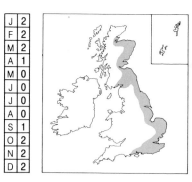

J	2
F	2
M	2
A	1
M	0
J	0
J	0
A	0
S	1
O	2
N	2
D	2

blue- black wings

long, rounded,
green- black
tail

Large black and white crow, with
distinctive long, wedge-shaped, green-
glossed tail. Black head, breast and
back; wings black with glossy blue
wash and bold, white oval patches.
Belly white. Mainly scavenger and
robber, often seen in early morning
picking at corpses along roads. Usually
solitary or in small groups.
Status: widespread resident; has
moved into city-centres in present
century.
Similar Species: only large black and
white bird of the countryside.

	MAGPIE
Type	crow-like
Size	42–50cm (16½–20in)
Habitat	heaths, woods, hedges, gardens
Behaviour	perches openly, hops, takes off from vegetation or ground
Flocking	1–15
Flight	laboured; direct
Voice	harsh *chak-chak-chak*

IDENTIFICATION

Adult	
Crown	black
Upperparts	black, blue-black wings with white patches
Rump	black
Tail	green-black, long and wedge-shaped
Throat	black
Breast	black
Belly	white
Bill	black; short and thin
Legs	black; medium length

BREEDING

Nest	dome of twigs in bush or tree
Eggs	5–8; pale blue, blotched olive
Incubation	17–18 days ♀
Young	helpless, naked
Fledging	22–28 days
Broods	1; Apr–May
Food	nestlings, eggs, carrion, seeds, insects
Population	250,000+ pairs

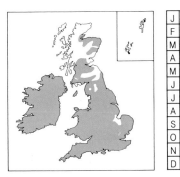

J	6
F	6
M	6
A	6
M	6
J	6
J	6
A	6
S	6
O	6
N	6
D	6

Red-billed Chough *Pyrrhocorax pyrrhocorax*

decurved red bill

square wingtips with fingers

square tail

red legs

RED-BILLED CHOUGH

Type	crow-like
Size	36–41cm (14–16in)
Habitat	moors, sea cliffs
Behaviour	walks, perches openly, takes off and lands on ground
Flocking	1–15
Flight	soars, glides, aerial dive; strong and powerful
Voice	ringing *keear*, repeated

IDENTIFICATION

Adult	
Crown	black
Upperparts	black; wingtips deep-fingered
Rump	black
Tail	black; medium length, square
Throat	black
Breast	black
Belly	black
Bill	red; decurved, long and thin
Legs	red; medium length

BREEDING

Nest	cup on ledge in cave or crevice
Eggs	3–4; pale green, blotched brown
Incubation	17–23 days ♀
Young	helpless; downy
Fledging	38 days
Broods	1; Apr–May
Food	insects, worms, seeds
Population	c1000 pairs

Black, crow-like bird with thin, decurved, red bill and red legs. Wings broad and square, with deep fingering at tips. Found only along cliff-lined shores and in mountain gorges and quarries, where masterful flight involves diving, soaring and aerobatics. Gregarious, forming flocks where numbers sufficient.
Status: scarce and highly localized resident in Islay, Scotland and west Wales and Ireland.
Similar Species: Jackdaw (p.255) is similar size and colour and shares habitat and behaviour, but wings more rounded and lacks red bill and legs.

J	2
F	2
M	2
A	2
M	2
J	2
J	2
A	2
S	2
O	2
N	2
D	2

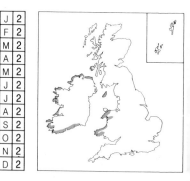

short bill

grey nape

more rounded wings

white eye

longer tail than Chough

Smallest crow; typical black plumage broken by grey nape, not often visible at distance. Short, stubby bill distinguishes from Crow and Rook. Gregarious, forming flocks in wide variety of habitats. Performs aerobatics (like much rarer and more localized Red-billed Chough) along cliff-lined shores, gorges and, in towns, cathedrals, and so on. Feeds mostly on farmland, often in company with Rooks.

Status: widespread and common resident of Britain and Ireland.

Similar Species: Rook (p.256) and Carrion Crow (p.257) are bigger with larger bills; Red-billed Chough (p.254) is rare, with red bill and legs.

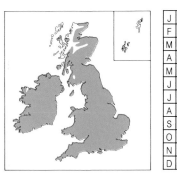

J	6
F	6
M	6
A	6
M	6
J	6
J	6
A	6
S	6
O	6
N	6
D	6

JACKDAW

Type	crow-like
Size	32–34cm (12½–13½in)
Habitat	towns, heaths, sea cliffs, woods, hedges
Behaviour	walks, perches openly, takes off from vegetation or ground
Flocking	1–200
Flight	soars, glides, aerial dive; laboured; direct
Voice	high-pitched *kya*; distinctive *chak*

IDENTIFICATION

Adult	
Crown	black, grey nape
Upperparts	black
Rump	black
Tail	black; medium length, square
Throat	black
Breast	black
Belly	black
Bill	black; short and stubby
Legs	black; medium length

BREEDING

Nest	variable; twigs in tree or cliff hole; also holes in buildings, chimneys
Eggs	4–6; pale blue, spotted brown
Incubation	17–18 days ♀
Young	helpless; downy
Fledging	28–32 days
Broods	1; Apr–May
Food	worms, nestlings, eggs, small mammals, grain
Population	*c* 500,000 pairs

Rook *Corvus frugilegus*

bare face

lacks bare face

thinnish bill

juvenile

slimmer, less bulky than Crow

adult

ROOK

Type	crow-like
Size	44–47cm (17–18½in)
Habitat	hedges, fields, woods, heaths
Behaviour	perches openly, hops, walks, takes off from vegetation or ground
Flocking	1–200
Flight	laboured; direct
Voice	cawing *kaah*

IDENTIFICATION

Adult	
Crown	black
Upperparts	black
Rump	black
Tail	black; medium length, square
Throat	black
Breast	black
Belly	black
Bill	grey; short and thin
Legs	black; medium length
Juvenile	lacks bare face patch

BREEDING

Nest	cup of twigs high in tree; colonial
Eggs	3–5; pale blue-green, blotched brown
Incubation	16–20 days ♀
Young	helpless; downy
Fledging	29–30 days
Broods	1; Mar–Apr
Food	worms, insects, seeds
Population	1,500,000 pairs

Highly gregarious crow, forming large flocks, roosts, and colonial nesting groups, called rookeries, in tall clumps of trees. Crown has distinct peak above eye. Bare skin around base of bill main distinguishing feature; absent in juvenile. Similar to Carrion Crow, but slimmer and more angular, especially in flight. Feeds mostly on arable land, taking more pests than crops.
Status: widespread and common resident, but more numerous in east than west.
Similar Species: Carrion Crow (p.257) as above.

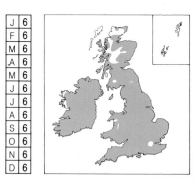

J	6
F	6
M	6
A	6
M	6
J	6
J	6
A	6
S	6
O	6
N	6
D	6

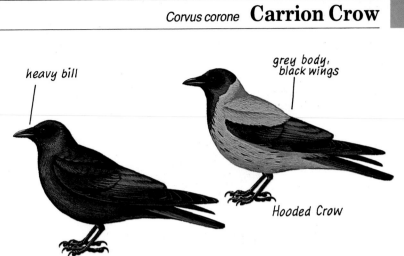

heavy bill

grey body, black wings

Hooded Crow

Carrion Crow

Large, familiar, all-black bird with heavy bill and aggressive habits. More strongly built than Rook and usually found in pairs, though larger numbers may roost together in winter and gather at rich food sources, such as rubbish tips. Generally a scavenger. In northern and western Scotland and in Ireland, replaced by sub-species *C.c.cornix* (Hooded Crow), which has grey back, belly and rump.
Status: widespread in Britain and Ireland.
Similar Species: Rook (p.256) and Common Raven (p.258).

CARRION CROW

Type	crow-like
Size	45–49cm (18–19in)
Habitat	towns, heaths, estuaries, woods, hedges
Behaviour	perches openly, hops, walks, takes off from vegetation or ground
Flocking	1–10
Flight	laboured; direct
Voice	loud *kraa-kraa*

IDENTIFICATION

Ad.*C.c.corone*	
Crown	black
Upperparts	black
Rump	black
Tail	black; medium length, square
Throat	black
Breast	black
Belly	black
Bill	black; short and heavy
Legs	black; medium length
Ad.*C.c.cornix*	grey back, belly and rump

BREEDING

Nest	cup near top of tree
Eggs	4–6; greenish blue, speckled brown
Incubation	18–20 days ♀
Young	helpless; downy
Fledging	4–5 weeks
Broods	1; Mar–May
Food	carrion, birds, eggs, insects, worms, grain
Population	1,000,000 pairs

J	6
F	6
M	6
A	6
M	6
J	6
J	6
A	6
S	6
O	6
N	6
D	6

Common Raven *Corvus corax*

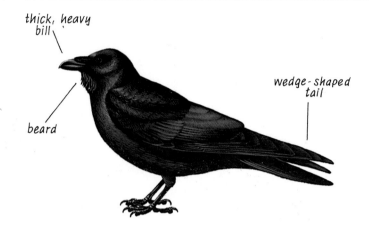

thick, heavy bill

beard

wedge-shaped tail

COMMON RAVEN

Type	crow-like
Size	60–67cm (23½–26½in)
Habitat	moors, heaths, sea cliffs
Behaviour	hops, walks, perches openly, takes off from vegetation or ground
Flocking	1–15
Flight	soars, glides; laboured; direct
Voice	hollow *pruk-pruk*

IDENTIFICATION

Adult	
Crown	black
Upperparts	black
Rump	black
Tail	black; long and wedge-shaped
Throat	black, shaggy beard
Breast	black
Belly	black
Bill	black; short and heavy
Legs	black; medium length

BREEDING

Nest	large cup on ledge or fork in tree
Eggs	4–6; pale greenish blue, spotted brown
Incubation	20–21 days ♀
Young	helpless; downy
Fledging	5–6 weeks
Broods	1; Feb–Mar
Food	carrion, birds, mammals, eggs, snails, grain
Population	5000 pairs

Largest crow, similar to Carrion Crow, but considerably bigger with more powerful head and bill, shaggy beard and large wedge-shaped tail. Found in mountainous and hilly areas, and along cliff-lined coasts; frequently soars like bird of prey. Mainly a scavenger, but also kills small birds and mammals.
Status: widespread in hilly districts of north and west.
Similar Species: Carrion Crow (p.257) smaller with less massive head and bill.

J	5
F	5
M	5
A	5
M	5
J	5
J	5
A	5
S	5
O	5
N	5
D	5

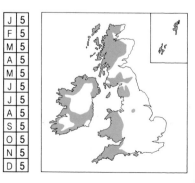

Garrulus glandarius **Eurasian Jay**

streaked crown

brownish-pink

black moustache

Large woodland bird with distinctive plumage, rounded wings and long tail. Crown streaked black and white; black moustachial streak. Back buff-brown; underparts pinkish buff. Wings and tail black; in flight shows bold white rump and white patches on inner wing. Small but distinctive blue and white barred patch on primary coverts. Generally secretive; presence often detected by harsh cries. Gregarious only in early spring.
Status: widespread resident of wooded areas, except northern Scotland.
Similar Species: none.

EURASIAN JAY	
Type	crow-like
Size	33–36cm (13–14in)
Habitat	forests, hedges, heaths, gardens
Behaviour	perches openly, hops, flits, takes off from vegetation or ground
Flocking	1–10
Flight	laboured; direct
Voice	harsh *kaaa*

IDENTIFICATION

Adult	
Crown	black and white, streaked
Upperparts	buff-brown, black wings
Rump	white
Tail	black; medium length, square
Throat	white
Breast	pinkish buff
Belly	pinkish buff
Bill	black; short and thin
Legs	buff; medium length

BREEDING

Nest	cup in tree fork
Eggs	5–7; pale green, speckled buff
Incubation	16–17 days ♂ ♀
Young	helpless; naked
Fledging	19–20 days
Broods	1; Apr–May
Food	nuts, nestlings, worms, insects
Population	100,000 pairs

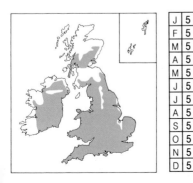

J	5
F	5
M	5
A	5
M	5
J	5
J	5
A	5
S	5
O	5
N	5
D	5

Common Starling *Sturnus vulgaris*

yellow

glossy black

Summer

heavily speckled breast

grey brown

winter

juvenile

COMMON STARLING	
Type	unique
Size	20.5–22.5cm (8–9in)
Habitat	gardens, marshes, moors, sea cliffs, estuaries, woods, hedges
Behaviour	flits, perches openly, walks, takes off from vegetation or ground
Flocking	1–100,000
Flight	glides; strong and powerful; direct
Voice	variety of wheezing calls; much mimicry

IDENTIFICATION

Ad.summer	
Crown	black
Upperparts	black, wings tipped brown
Rump	black
Tail	black; short and square
Throat	black
Breast	black
Belly	black
Bill	yellow; short and thin
Legs	red; medium length
Ad.winter	head and underparts spotted white
Juvenile	grey-buff with white chin

BREEDING

Nest	untidy; in hole in tree, cliff, building, nest box
Eggs	5–7; pale blue
Incubation	12–15 days ♂ ♀
Young	helpless; downy
Fledging	20–22 days
Broods	1–2; Apr–May
Food	insects, seeds, fruit
Population	4,000,000–7,000,000 pairs

Noisy and aggressive bird; walks with a waddling swagger. Highly successful and abundant species; gregarious outside breeding season forming huge flocks, particularly at favoured roosts. Upperparts glossy black with brown margins to wing feathers. Head, back and underparts glossy black in summer; spotted white in winter. Bill yellow, legs red. Juveniles grey-buff with white chin. Pointed wings and short tail give characteristic flight silhouette.
Status: abundant and widespread resident and winter visitor.
Similar Species: none.

J	6
F	6
M	6
A	6
M	6
J	6
J	6
A	6
S	6
O	6
N	6
D	6

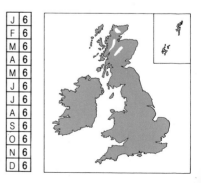

Passer domesticus **House Sparrow**

grey crown

pale eyebrow

large bib

♂

♀

Most familiar of British birds, found everywhere permanently inhabited by people. Male streaked brown and black above, with chocolate nape and grey crown; black bib widens out across breast. Female buffy and brown with streaked back, prominent pale eyebrow and double wingbar; lacks bib. Usually gregarious; forms huge post-harvest flocks in late summer. Nests in holes in houses, but also in bushes when these not available.
Status: widespread resident.
Similar Species: Tree Sparrow (p.262).

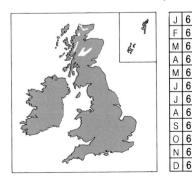

J	6
F	6
M	6
A	6
M	6
J	6
J	6
A	6
S	6
O	6
N	6
D	6

HOUSE SPARROW

Type	sparrow-like
Size	14–15.5cm (5½–6in)
Habitat	gardens, marshes, heaths, sea cliffs, estuaries, woods, hedges
Behaviour	flits, perches openly, hops, takes off from vegetation or ground
Flocking	1–500
Flight	direct
Voice	*chirrup*; various twitters

IDENTIFICATION

Adult ♂	
Crown	grey
Upperparts	brown and black, streaked
Rump	grey
Tail	brown and black; medium length, notched
Throat	black bib
Breast	black and white
Belly	white
Bill	brown; short and stubby
Legs	pinkish; medium length
Ad.♀and juv.	buff and brown above; lack bib

BREEDING

Nest	dome in hole in building, sometimes tree; colonial
Eggs	3–5; grey, blotched dark grey
Incubation	11–14 days, mainly ♀
Young	helpless; naked
Fledging	15 days
Broods	3; Apr–June
Food	seeds, insects, bread
Population	11,000,000–12,000,000 pairs

Tree Sparrow *Passer montanus*

brown crown

white half collar

small neat bib

TREE SPARROW

Type	sparrow-like
Size	13.5–14.5cm (5½–6in)
Habitat	gardens, heaths, woods, fields and hedges
Behaviour	flits, perches openly, hops, takes off from vegetation or ground
Flocking	1–15
Flight	direct
Voice	distinct *chup-chup*; also *tek-tek*

IDENTIFICATION

Adult	
Crown	chocolate-brown
Upperparts	brown and black, streaked
Rump	buff
Tail	brown; medium length, notched
Throat	black bib
Breast	white
Belly	white
Bill	black; short and stubby
Legs	red; medium length

BREEDING

Nest	dome in tree hole, among rocks or against walls
Eggs	4–6; pale grey, spotted brown
Incubation	11–14 days ♂ ♀
Young	helpless; naked
Fledging	12–14 days
Broods	2–3; Apr–June
Food	seeds, insects
Population	250,000 pairs

Both sexes resemble male House Sparrow, but slightly smaller with upperparts more clearly streaked black and brown. Crown chocolate-brown; tiny black bib; black comma on white cheeks. White half-collar visible at considerable distance – best field mark. Underparts white. Prefers parkland and gardens, but often associates with flocks of House Sparrows. Colonial nester, often in boxes erected for tits. *Status:* widespread resident, but curiously absent from some western areas.
Similar Species: House Sparrow (p.261).

J	4
F	4
M	4
A	4
M	4
J	4
J	4
A	4
S	4
O	4
N	4
D	4

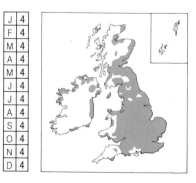

blue-grey crown

buffy crown

creamy breast

pinkish breast

broad wingbar

♂

♀

Most common finch, found in wide variety of habitats. Often seen beside roads, where may fly up showing white outer tail feathers and bold, white, double wingbar (in both sexes). Male has blue-grey crown and pinkish breast. Female duller, in shades of buff. Forms large winter flocks.
Status: numerous and widespread resident; winter visitor.
Similar Species: female similar to female House Sparrow (p.261) but Chaffinch distinguished by bold, white, double wingbar.

CHAFFINCH

Type	finch-like
Size	14.5–16cm (5½–6½in)
Habitat	gardens, heaths, woods, fields and hedges
Behaviour	flits, hops, perches openly, takes off from vegetation or ground
Flocking	1–200
Flight	undulating
Voice	loud *pink-pink*; delicate song ending in flourish

IDENTIFICATION

Adult ♂	
Crown	blue-grey
Upperparts	brown, wings black and white
Rump	buff
Tail	black and white; medium length, notched
Throat	pinkish
Breast	pinkish
Belly	pinkish
Bill	blue-grey; short and stubby
Legs	brown; medium length
Adult ♀	buff-brown above; buffy cream below

BREEDING

Nest	neat cup in low vegetation
Eggs	4–5; pale blue, scrawled red
Incubation	11–13 days ♀
Young	helpless; downy
Fledging	12–15 days
Broods	1–2; Apr–May
Food	seeds, fruit
Population	7,000,000 pairs

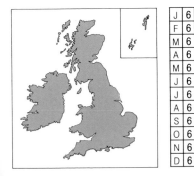

J	6
F	6
M	6
A	6
M	6
J	6
J	6
A	6
S	6
O	6
N	6
D	6

Brambling *Fringilla montifringilla*

black head and back with scaling

black crown and back

scaled black on buff

♂ summer

bright orange breast

♂ winter

♀

	BRAMBLING
Type	finch-like
Size	14–15cm (5½–6in)
Habitat	heaths, woods, fields and hedges
Behaviour	flits, hops, takes off and lands on vegetation or ground
Flocking	1–100
Flight	undulating
Voice	hard *tswick* and *chik*

IDENTIFICATION

Ad.♂winter	
Crown	black and buff
Upperparts	black and buff
Rump	white
Tail	black; medium length, notched
Throat	orange
Breast	orange
Belly	white
Bill	yellow; short and stubby
Legs	red; medium length
Ad.♂summer	cap black; back bordered orange
Adult ♀	paler than winter ♂

BREEDING

Nest	cup in pine tree, near trunk
Eggs	5–7; pale blue, blotched red
Incubation	11–12 days ♀
Young	helpless; downy
Fledging	11–13 days
Broods	1; May–June
Food	seeds, berries
Population	2–10 pairs breed; 50,000–2,000,000 winter

Similar and closely related to Chaffinch, often associating in winter flocks, where may be overlooked. Winter male has blackish upperparts, liberally edged buff on crown and back. Tail black; shows square white rump in flight. Breast bright orange; belly white. Buff margins lost in summer; head and back become pure black with broad orange band below. Female more heavily edged buff at all seasons. *Status:* regular and numerous winter visitor, although more abundant in east; 2–10 pairs breed in north. *Similar Species:* Chaffinch (p.263).

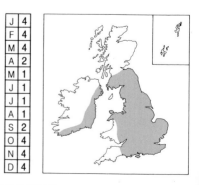

J	4
F	4
M	4
A	2
M	1
J	1
J	1
A	1
S	2
O	4
N	4
D	4

Serinus serinus **European Serin**

yellow
rump

streaked,
often little
yellow

bright
yellow
breast

♂

♀

Tiny yellow finch with bright tinkling song; pure yellow rump a bold field mark. Male has yellow head, back and breast, marked with variable amount of brown streaking. Wings dark with yellowish edges. Less yellow on female, but heavier streaking, particularly on breast. Short stubby bill creates large, round-headed appearance.
Status: rare vagrant, gradually becoming more regular; beginning to breed (1–7 pairs).
Similar Species: Siskin (p.268).

J	1
F	1
M	1
A	1
M	1
J	1
J	1
A	1
S	1
O	1
N	1
D	1

EUROPEAN SERIN

Type	finch-like
Size	11–12cm (4½–5in)
Habitat	gardens, heaths, woods, hedges
Behaviour	flits, perches openly, takes off and lands on vegetation
Flocking	1–2
Flight	undulating
Voice	twittering jangle of notes

IDENTIFICATION

Adult ♂	
Crown	yellow
Upperparts	yellow, streaked brown, wings black
Rump	yellow
Tail	black; medium length, notched
Throat	yellow
Breast	yellow, streaked brown
Belly	white
Bill	buff; short and stubby
Legs	brown; medium length
Adult ♀	less yellow; heavier streaking

BREEDING

Nest	neat cup in bush or tree
Eggs	4; pale blue, spotted brown
Incubation	13 days ♀
Young	helpless; downy
Fledging	14 days
Broods	1–2; Apr–May
Food	seeds
Population	1–7 pairs

Greenfinch *Carduelis chloris*

dark around eye

thick bill

green

yellow at wing edge

yellow underparts

♂

yellow tail sides

♀

	GREENFINCH
Type	finch-like
Size	14–15cm (5½–6in)
Habitat	gardens, marshes, heaths, woods, hedges
Behaviour	flits, perches openly, hops, takes off from vegetation or ground
Flocking	1–100
Flight	undulating
Voice	nasal *skeer*, *chup-chup* flight call

	IDENTIFICATION
Adult ♂	
Crown	green
Upperparts	green; grey wings yellow-edged
Rump	green
Tail	black; medium length, notched
Throat	yellowish
Breast	yellowish
Belly	yellowish
Bill	white; short and stubby
Legs	pink; medium length
Adult ♀	paler and browner

	BREEDING
Nest	cup in bush
Eggs	4–6; pale blue, spotted black
Incubation	12–14 days ♀
Young	helpless; downy
Fledging	13–16 days
Broods	2–3; Apr–June
Food	seeds, berries
Population	1,000,000–1,750,000 pairs

Chunky, thick-set finch with substantial white bill. Male green above, with bold yellow margin to folded grey wing; yellowish below. Female paler and browner. In flight, shows yellow at base of primaries and incomplete yellow edges to tail. Largest and most common of green-yellow finches; found in range of habitats, but most at home in parkland and gardens.
Status: widespread and numerous resident of Britain and Ireland.
Similar Species: female similar to female House Sparrow (p.261) but Greenfinch has narrow yellow edge to folded wing.

J	6
F	6
M	6
A	6
M	6
J	6
J	6
A	6
S	6
O	6
N	6
D	6

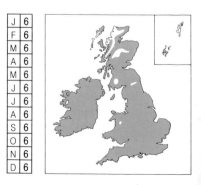

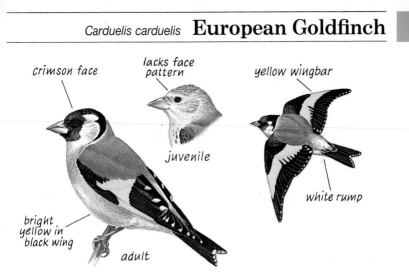

Carduelis carduelis European Goldfinch

crimson face

lacks face pattern

yellow wingbar

juvenile

white rump

bright yellow in black wing

adult

Attractive, easily identified finch with distinctive face pattern of crimson, white and black. Back warm brown; wings black with broad yellow band apparent both at rest and in flight. Shows bold white rump in flight. Feeds on teazles; prefers gardens and overgrown areas. Mostly gregarious. *Status:* widespread resident except in north.
Similar Species: none.

EUROPEAN GOLDFINCH

Type	finch-like
Size	11.5–12.5cm (4¾in)
Habitat	gardens, heaths, woods, fields and hedges
Behaviour	flits, perches openly, hops, takes off from vegetation or ground
Flocking	1–100
Flight	undulating
Voice	sweet tinkling

IDENTIFICATION

Adult	
Crown	crimson, black and white
Upperparts	brown; wings black, yellow bars
Rump	white
Tail	black; medium length, notched
Throat	crimson
Breast	buff
Belly	white
Bill	white; short and stubby
Legs	buff; medium length
Juvenile	lacks head pattern; more buffy

BREEDING

Nest	cup in bush
Eggs	4–7; blue, spotted blackish
Incubation	12–14 days ♀
Young	helpless; downy
Fledging	13–16 days
Broods	2; Apr–May
Food	seeds
Population	300,000 pairs

J	6
F	6
M	6
A	6
M	6
J	6
J	6
A	6
S	6
O	6
N	6
D	6

Siskin *Carduelis spinus*

dark crown

bib

yellow in wing

yellow

streaked flanks

♂

yellow tail patches

♀

SISKIN

Type	finch-like
Size	11.5–12.5cm (4¾in)
Habitat	woods, hedges, heaths, gardens
Behaviour	flits, perches openly, takes off and lands on vegetation
Flocking	1–50
Flight	undulating
Voice	*tsu, tsu-weet*; various twitterings

IDENTIFICATION

Adult ♂

Crown	black cap
Upperparts	green; black wings, yellow wingbars
Rump	yellow
Tail	black and yellow; medium length, notched
Throat	black bib
Breast	yellow
Belly	white
Bill	white; short and stubby
Legs	brown; medium length
Adult ♀	greyish green above; buffy and streaked below

BREEDING

Nest	cup high in conifer
Eggs	3–5; pale blue, speckled reddish
Incubation	11–14 days ♀
Young	helpless; downy
Fledging	13–15 days
Broods	2; Apr–May
Food	seeds
Population	20,000–40,000 pairs; 150,000–500,000 winter

Small woodland finch found mostly near damp areas; has particular liking for alder. Male greenish above, yellowish below with streaked flanks. Crown black, forming distinct cap; small black bib. Wings black with bold yellow wingbars; yellow rump. Female much duller with yellow only in wings and tail; upperparts grey-green, underparts buffy with streaking above and below. Agile feeder, hanging upside down, tit-like, to extract seeds; comes to red-peanut feeding nets in late winter. Gregarious in winter.
Status: winter visitor; breeds in many parts of Britain and Ireland, especially north and west.
Similar Species: European Serin, Greenfinch and Common Redpoll (pp.265, 266, 271).

J	3
F	3
M	3
A	3
M	2
J	2
J	2
A	2
S	3
O	3
N	3
D	3

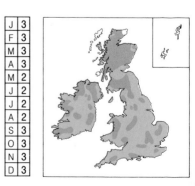

red forehead

white wing flashes

brown back

white in tail

red breast

♂ summer

♀

Small finch abundant in open areas, especially coastal marshes and shingle in winter. Summer male distinguished by red forehead and breast; grey head, brown back. Female lacks red; streaked above and below. Male loses red in winter. Both sexes show white in tail and wings in flight. Gregarious, often forming huge flocks, sometimes with smaller numbers of Twite. *Status:* widespread and numerous resident.
Similar Species: Twite (p.270) very similar to female Linnet but much more heavily streaked.

	LINNET
Type	finch-like
Size	13–14cm (5–5½in)
Habitat	heaths, estuaries, woods, hedges, gardens
Behaviour	flits, perches openly, hops, takes off from vegetation or ground
Flocking	1–500
Flight	undulating
Voice	high-pitched twittering in flight

IDENTIFICATION

Ad.♂summer	
Crown	red
Upperparts	brown
Rump	buff
Tail	black and white; medium length, notched
Throat	buff
Breast	red
Belly	buff
Bill	grey; short and stubby
Legs	grey; medium length
Ad.♂winter	lacks red
Adult ♀	lacks red; streaked above and below

BREEDING

Nest	cup in bush
Eggs	4–6; pale blue, speckled reddish
Incubation	10–14 days ♀
Young	helpless; downy
Fledging	14–17 days
Broods	2–3; Apr–June
Food	seeds
Population	less than 1,000,000 pairs

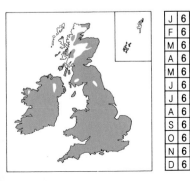

J	6
F	6
M	6
A	6
M	6
J	6
J	6
A	6
S	6
O	6
N	6
D	6

Twite *Carduelis flavirostris*

yellow bill

distinctly streaked

distinctly streaked

buffy throat

pink rump

streaked black on buff

♂ *summer*

♂ *winter*

TWITE

Type	finch-like
Size	13–14cm (5–5½in)
Habitat	moors, estuaries, woods, fields, gardens
Behaviour	hops, perches openly, takes off and lands on ground
Flocking	1–500
Flight	undulating
Voice	similar to Linnet, but harder

IDENTIFICATION

Ad.summer	
Crown	brown, streaked black
Upperparts	brown, streaked black
Rump	pink
Tail	black; medium length, notched
Throat	buff
Breast	buff, streaked black
Belly	white
Bill	grey; short and stubby
Legs	black; medium length
Ad.winter and juvenile	bill yellow

BREEDING

Nest	cup on ground
Eggs	5–6; pale blue, speckled reddish
Incubation	12–13 days ♀
Young	helpless; downy
Fledging	15 days
Broods	1–2; Apr–May
Food	seeds
Population	100,000–150,000 pairs

Northern, upland equivalent of Linnet. Regularly winters along coasts, often in association with large flocks of Linnets; shows similar markings in flight. In all seasons and plumages, Twite warm, buffy brown bird, heavily streaked black above and below. Linnet never as heavily streaked, even in juvenile plumage. Twite has pink rump but difficult to see. Juvenile and winter birds have yellow, not grey, bills.
Status: resident in northern and hilly areas; winter visitor to coast, except in south-west.
Similar Species: Linnet (p.269) as above.

J	3
F	3
M	3
A	3
M	4
J	4
J	4
A	4
S	3
O	3
N	3
D	3

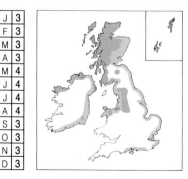

Carduelis flammea **Common Redpoll**

red forehead

streaked back

tiny black bib

pink breast

♂ summer

♀

Small, streaked finch; arboreal, hangs tit-like among trees when feeding. As name suggests, forehead red. Small black bib. Heavily streaked buff and brown above; lighter streaking below, confined to flanks in summer male. Best identified by buzzing flight note. Forms large flocks, particularly among conifers.

Status: widespread resident.

Similar Species: Siskin (p.268) similar size; also forms feeding flocks among tree-tops.

COMMON REDPOLL	
Type	finch-like
Size	11.5–13cm (4½–5in)
Habitat	heaths, woods, hedges, gardens
Behaviour	flits, perches openly, takes off and lands on vegetation
Flocking	1–50
Flight	undulating
Voice	buzzing nasal trill in flight

IDENTIFICATION

Adult	
Crown	red
Upperparts	buff, streaked brown
Rump	buff, streaked brown
Tail	black; medium length, notched
Throat	black bib
Breast	pink, streaked buff
Belly	white
Bill	buff; short and stubby
Legs	black; medium length
Ad.♂summer	loses streaking below, apart from on flanks

BREEDING

Nest	cup in tree
Eggs	4–5; pale blue, speckled reddish
Incubation	10–13 days ♀
Young	helpless; downy
Fledging	11–14 days
Broods	1–2; Apr–June
Food	seeds
Population	300,000+ pairs

J	4
F	4
M	4
A	4
M	4
J	4
J	4
A	4
S	4
O	4
N	4
D	4

Common Crossbill *Loxia curvirostra*

chunky crossed bill

♂   ♀

COMMON CROSSBILL

Type	finch-like
Size	16–17cm (6–6½in)
Habitat	forests
Behaviour	flits, perches openly, takes off and lands on vegetation
Flocking	1–15
Flight	undulating
Voice	distinctive *jip-jip*

IDENTIFICATION

Adult ♂	
Crown	reddish
Upperparts	brown
Rump	reddish
Tail	black; medium length, notched
Throat	reddish
Breast	reddish
Belly	reddish
Bill	grey; short and stubby
Legs	black; medium length
Adult ♀	grey-green, lightly streaked

BREEDING

Nest	twiggy cup high in conifer
Eggs	3–4; pale blue, spotted purple
Incubation	13–16 days ♀
Young	helpless; downy
Fledging	17–22 days
Broods	1; Jan–Apr
Food	pine seeds
Population	1000–2000 pairs

Chunky, thick-set finch with large head and substantial bill. Name derives from distinctive crossed mandibles, visible at close range. Male dirty reddish on crown and underparts; wings dark brown. Female grey-green with light streaking above and below. Large head and shortish tail useful in flight. Mostly gregarious. Regularly irrupts from the Continent; confined to mature conifers and now breeds in various parts of country when new plantations mature to provide food. *Status:* widespread but localized resident; irregular autumn and winter immigrant.
Similar Species: Scottish Crossbill (p.273).

J	2
F	2
M	2
A	2
M	2
J	2
J	2
A	2
S	2
O	3
N	3
D	2

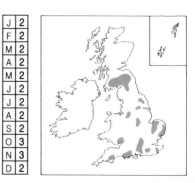

larger crossed bill than
Crossbill

♂   ♀

Almost identical to Common Crossbill; recognized as separate species (and Britain's sole endemic bird) only in 1970s. Differs in larger bill and habitat; restricted to old Caledonian forests of Scottish Highlands.
Status: resident Scottish Highlands.
Similar Species: Common Crossbill (p.272).

SCOTTISH CROSSBILL

Type	finch-like
Size	16–17cm (6–6½in)
Habitat	forests
Behaviour	flits, perches openly, takes off and lands on vegetation
Flocking	1–15
Flight	undulating
Voice	distinctive *jip-jip*, as Crossbill

IDENTIFICATION

Adult ♂	
Crown	reddish
Upperparts	brown
Rump	reddish
Tail	black; medium length, notched
Throat	reddish
Breast	reddish
Belly	reddish
Bill	grey; short and stubby
Legs	black; medium length
Adult ♀	grey-green, lightly streaked

BREEDING

Nest	twiggy cup high in conifer
Eggs	3–4; pale blue, spotted purple
Incubation	13–16 days ♀
Young	helpless; downy
Fledging	17–22 days
Broods	1; Jan–Apr
Food	pine seeds
Population	*c* 750 pairs

J	2
F	2
M	2
A	2
M	2
J	2
J	2
A	2
S	2
O	2
N	2
D	2

Bullfinch *Pyrrhula pyrrhula*

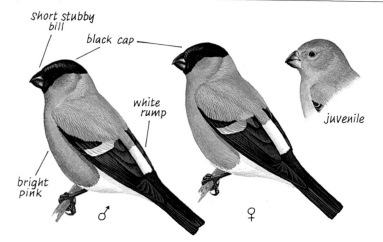

short stubby bill

black cap

white rump

bright pink

♂

♀

juvenile

Portly, bull-necked finch of gardens and hedgerows, most often seen singly or in pairs. Male has black crown with thick, black conical bill and bright pink breast; upperparts blue-grey. Female similar but with pale buffy breast. Both sexes have black wings with broad white wingbar, black tail and square white rump.
Status: widespread resident.
Similar Species: none.

BULLFINCH

Type	finch-like
Size	14–15cm (5½–6in)
Habitat	gardens, heaths, woods, hedges
Behaviour	flits, perches openly, takes off and lands on vegetation
Flocking	1–2
Flight	undulating
Voice	soft *heu*

IDENTIFICATION

Adult ♂	
Crown	black
Upperparts	blue-grey
Rump	white
Tail	black; medium length, notched
Throat	bright pink with black bib
Breast	bright pink
Belly	bright pink
Bill	black; short and stubby
Legs	black; medium length
Adult ♀	buffy below

BREEDING

Nest	twig platform in bush
Eggs	4–5; pale blue, spotted purple
Incubation	12–14 days ♀
Young	helpless; downy
Fledging	12–18 days
Broods	1–2; Apr–May
Food	buds, seeds
Population	600,000 pairs

J	4
F	4
M	4
A	4
M	4
J	4
J	4
A	4
S	4
O	4
N	4
D	4

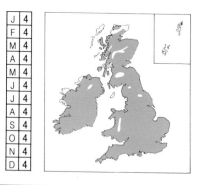

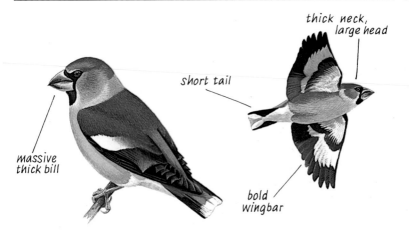

thick neck,
large head

short tail

massive
thick bill

bold
wingbar

Stout finch with huge, thick, grey bill. Large head and bill, thick-set body and short tail obvious in flight; broad wingbars above and below diagnostic. Crown rufous, back brown, wings black, rump and underparts buff. Generally elusive and difficult to find; inhabits old woods and parks, often perching immobile for long periods. Forms communal roosts in winter. *Status:* widespread resident; absent northern Scotland and Ireland. *Similar Species:* none.

HAWFINCH	
Type	finch-like
Size	16–17cm (6–6½in)
Habitat	woods, gardens, parks
Behaviour	flits, perches openly, takes off and lands on vegetation
Flocking	1–15
Flight	strong and powerful; direct
Voice	Robin-like *zik* or *tic*

IDENTIFICATION	
Adult	
Crown	rufous
Upperparts	brown, wings black and white
Rump	buff
Tail	buff with white tip; short and notched
Throat	black bib
Breast	buff
Belly	buff
Bill	grey; short and stubby
Legs	red; medium length

BREEDING	
Nest	twiggy cup in tree
Eggs	5; pale blue, spotted blackish
Incubation	9–14 days ♀, occasionally ♂
Young	helpless; downy
Fledging	10–14 days
Broods	1; Apr–May
Food	seeds, nuts
Population	5000–10,000 pairs

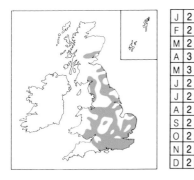

J	2
F	2
M	2
A	3
M	3
J	2
J	2
A	2
S	2
O	2
N	2
D	2

Lapland Bunting *Calcarius lapponicus*

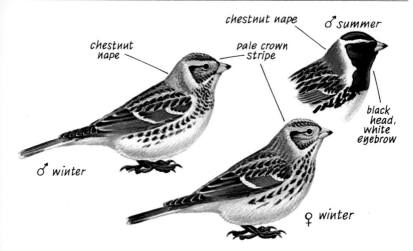

chestnut nape

chestnut nape

pale crown stripe

♂ summer

black head, white eyebrow

♂ winter

♀ winter

LAPLAND BUNTING

Type	bunting-like
Size	14–16cm (5½–6½in)
Habitat	marshes, estuaries, moors
Behaviour	hops, perches openly, takes off and lands on ground
Flocking	1–15
Flight	strong and powerful; direct
Voice	rolling *rrrrp*

IDENTIFICATION

Ad.♀, ♂winter

Crown	black and white with stripe
Upperparts	rusty and black, streaked
Rump	rusty and black, streaked
Tail	black and white; medium length, notched
Throat	white
Breast	streaked buff
Belly	white
Bill	yellow; short and stubby
Legs	black; medium length
Ad.♂summer	black head with bold, creamy eyebrow

BREEDING

Nest	cup on ground
Eggs	5–6; greenish, mottled reddish
Incubation	10–14 days mainly ♀
Young	helpless; downy
Fledging	11–15 days
Broods	1; May–June
Food	seeds
Population	has bred; 200–500 winter

Scarce, ground-dwelling bunting that usually perches on large stone or similar object. Summer male has black head with rich chestnut nape and prominent creamy eyebrow extending behind eye. Back streaked black and white; wings rufous; underparts white. Female, juvenile and winter male similar to female Reed Bunting and often found in same areas; but with pale central stripe on crown, rusty wings and (in male) rusty nape.
Status: scarce winter visitor mainly to low-lying east coast; rare breeder in Scotland.
Similar Species: female, juvenile and winter male similar to female Reed Bunting (p.280).

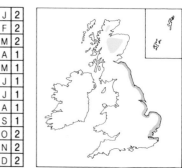

J	2
F	2
M	2
A	1
M	1
J	1
J	1
A	1
S	1
O	2
N	2
D	2

white in wing

buffy marks on head

white head

white in tail

♂ winter

♂ summer

♀ winter

Breeds on high mountain tops; winters along shorelines where forms large flocks. Flies like pieces of white paper blowing in wind. At all times shows much white in wing and tail. Summer male mainly white with black back; wings black and white. Female, juvenile and winter male have mottled upperparts and variable amounts of streaking or buff on head. Feeds on shingle and among dunes, keeping low on ground.

Status: scarce breeder in Scottish mountains; regular but local visitor to east coast.

Similar Species: none.

SNOW BUNTING	
Type	bunting-like
Size	16–17cm (6–6½in)
Habitat	moors, shorelines
Behaviour	hops, perches openly, takes off and lands on ground
Flocking	1–500
Flight	strong and powerful; direct; flitting
Voice	loud *tsweep*

IDENTIFICATION	
Ad.♂summer	
Crown	white
Upperparts	black and white
Rump	white
Tail	black and white; medium length, notched
Throat	white
Breast	white
Belly	white
Bill	black; short and stubby
Legs	black; medium length
Ad.♂winter, Ad.♀and juv.	white below, mottled above; buffy head markings

BREEDING	
Nest	cup on ground in rocks
Eggs	4–6; pale blue, spotted reddish
Incubation	10–15 days ♀
Young	helpless; downy
Fledging	15–20 days
Broods	2; May–July
Food	seeds
Population	6–17 pairs; 10,000–15,000 winter

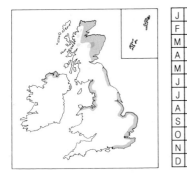

J	3
F	3
M	2
A	1
M	1
J	1
J	1
A	1
S	1
O	3
N	3
D	3

Yellowhammer *Emberiza citrinella*

rusty back

rusty rump

very yellow head

more yellow on head than Cirl ♀

♂

♀

YELLOWHAMMER	
Type	bunting-like
Size	16–17cm (6–6½in)
Habitat	heaths, fields and hedges, gardens
Behaviour	hops, perches openly, takes off and lands on vegetation or ground
Flocking	1–50
Flight	direct
Voice	familiar *'little-bit-of-bread-and-no-cheese'*

IDENTIFICATION

Adult ♂	
Crown	yellow
Upperparts	rust-brown and black
Rump	rusty
Tail	black and white; medium length, notched
Throat	yellow
Breast	yellow
Belly	yellow
Bill	grey; short and stubby
Legs	buff; medium length
Adult ♀	less yellow, darker head markings

BREEDING

Nest	cup in low bush
Eggs	3–5; white, blotched purplish
Incubation	11–14 days ♀
Young	helpless; downy
Fledging	16 days
Broods	2–3; Apr–June
Food	seeds, berries
Population	1,000,000 pairs

Yellow bunting most often seen perched on wire or top of bush. Male has bright yellow head and underparts, brown wings and prominent rusty rump. Female similar but with less yellow; more extensive and darker head markings. Generally solitary, but forms winter flocks. Prefers fields, hedgerows and heaths.
Status: widespread resident.
Similar Species: female could be confused with rarer female Cirl Bunting (p.279).

J	5
F	5
M	5
A	5
M	5
J	5
J	5
A	5
S	5
O	5
N	5
D	5

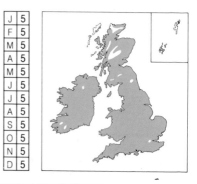

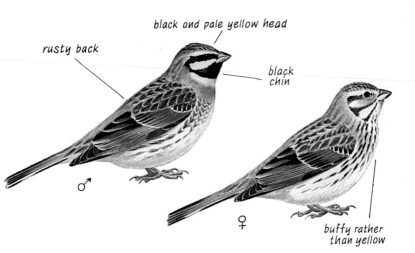

rusty back

black and pale yellow head

black chin

♂

♀

buffy rather than yellow

Male distinguished by bold head pattern of black and pale yellow; greenish breast band, pale yellow underparts and rusty, streaked back. Female rufous buff above, creamy buff below – heavily streaked. Decidedly local and declining resident; inhabits bushy slopes, old hedgerows, parks and gardens – often near sea.
Status: scarce resident in south-west England.
Similar Species: female confusable with female Yellowhammer (p.278), but Cirl never yellow and lacks rusty rump.

CIRL BUNTING

Type	bunting-like
Size	15.5–16.5cm (6–6½in)
Habitat	fields and hedges, heaths, parks, gardens
Behaviour	perches openly, hops, takes off and lands on vegetation or ground
Flocking	1–2
Flight	direct
Voice	*sip*, also a quick rattle

IDENTIFICATION

Adult ♂	
Crown	black
Upperparts	rust and black
Rump	olive
Tail	rust and black; medium length, notched
Throat	black
Breast	pale yellow; greenish band
Belly	pale yellow
Bill	buff; short and stubby
Legs	buff; medium length
Adult ♀	streaked rufous buff above, creamy buff below

BREEDING

Nest	cup low among bushes
Eggs	3–4; white, speckled black
Incubation	11–13 days ♀
Young	helpless; downy
Fledging	11–13 days
Broods	2–3; May–June
Food	seeds, berries
Population	100–250 pairs

J	2
F	2
M	2
A	2
M	2
J	2
J	2
A	2
S	2
O	2
N	2
D	2

Reed Bunting *Emberiza schoeniclus*

black head, white moustache

♂ winter

streaked crown

white collar

♂ summer

♀

black moustache

REED BUNTING

Type	bunting-like
Size	14–16cm (5½–6½in)
Habitat	mårshes, heaths, fields, gardens
Behaviour	flits, perches openly, takes off from vegetation or ground
Flocking	1–10
Flight	direct
Voice	several deliberate notes ending in a hurry

IDENTIFICATION

Adult ♂	
Crown	black
Upperparts	streaked brown and black; white collar
Rump	grey
Tail	black and white; medium length, notched
Throat	black
Breast	white
Belly	white
Bill	black; short and stubby
Legs	black; medium length
Adult ♀	heavily streaked brown and buff above, buffy below; eyebrow and moustache

BREEDING

Nest	cup on or near ground
Eggs	4–5; pale grey and black
Incubation	12–14 days, mainly ♀
Young	helpless; downy
Fledging	10–13 days
Broods	2–3; Apr–June
Food	seeds
Population	c300,000 pairs

Common resident of marshland; has spread to drier habitats, including gardens. Male has black head marked by white moustache and collar; upperparts streaked black and brown. Female similar to other female buntings: heavily streaked buff and brown above, buffy below. Bold eyebrow and smudgy black moustache helpful distinguishing features. Both sexes have white outer tail feathers. Song unappealing and boring.
Status: widespread and numerous resident.
Similar Species: female similar to other female buntings (pp.276–281).

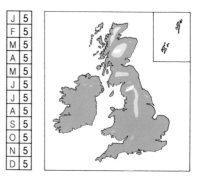

J	5
F	5
M	5
A	5
M	5
J	5
J	5
A	5
S	5
O	5
N	5
D	5

short, thick neck

stubby bill

both sexes streaked

pink legs

Chunky, thick-set bunting that appears almost neckless. Streaked buff and brown above and below; both sexes similar to other female buntings. No white in tail. Perches openly, usually near ground in fields and open bushy areas. Sings with head thrown back; legs trail in fluttering flight. Gregarious in winter.
Status: locally abundant resident; absent from many areas, especially in north and west.
Similar Species: all female buntings (pp.276–280), but Corn Bunting larger and plumper.

CORN BUNTING

Type	bunting-like
Size	17–18.5cm (6½–7½in)
Habitat	heaths, fields and hedges, gardens
Behaviour	perches openly, hops, takes off and lands on vegetation or ground
Flocking	1–2
Flight	direct
Voice	jingling rattle

IDENTIFICATION

Adult	
Crown	streaked buff and brown
Upperparts	streaked buff and brown
Rump	buff
Tail	brown; medium length, notched
Throat	white
Breast	streaked buff and brown
Belly	streaked buff and brown
Bill	buff; short and stubby
Legs	pink; medium length

BREEDING

Nest	cup on ground or in bush
Eggs	4–6; white, spotted grey
Incubation	12–14 days ♀
Young	helpless; downy
Fledging	12+ days
Broods	1–2; Apr–May
Food	seeds, berries
Population	30,000 pairs

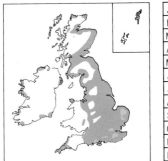

J	4
F	4
M	4
A	4
M	4
J	4
J	4
A	4
S	4
O	4
N	4
D	4

Checklist

- [ ] Red-throated Diver
- [ ] Black-throated Diver
- [ ] Great Northern Diver
- [ ] Little Grebe
- [ ] Great Crested Grebe
- [ ] Red-necked Grebe
- [ ] Slavonian Grebe
- [ ] Black-necked Grebe
- [ ] Fulmar
- [ ] Cory's Shearwater
- [ ] Great Shearwater
- [ ] Sooty Shearwater
- [ ] Manx Shearwater
- [ ] European Storm-petrel
- [ ] Leach's Storm-petrel
- [ ] Northern Gannet
- [ ] Great Cormorant
- [ ] Shag
- [ ] Bittern
- [ ] Grey Heron
- [ ] Purple Heron
- [ ] Spoonbill
- [ ] Mute Swan
- [ ] Bewick's Swan
- [ ] Whooper Swan
- [ ] Bean Goose
- [ ] Pink-footed Goose
- [ ] White-fronted Goose
- [ ] Greylag Goose
- [ ] Canada Goose
- [ ] Barnacle Goose
- [ ] Brent Goose
- [ ] Egyptian Goose
- [ ] Common Shelduck
- [ ] Mandarin Duck
- [ ] Eurasian Wigeon
- [ ] Gadwall
- [ ] Common Teal
- [ ] Mallard
- [ ] Northern Pintail
- [ ] Garganey
- [ ] Northern Shoveler
- [ ] Common Pochard
- [ ] Tufted Duck
- [ ] Greater Scaup
- [ ] Common Eider
- [ ] Long-tailed Duck
- [ ] Common Scoter
- [ ] Velvet Scoter
- [ ] Goldeneye
- [ ] Smew
- [ ] Red-breasted Merganser
- [ ] Goosander
- [ ] Ruddy Duck

- [ ] Honey Buzzard
- [ ] Red Kite
- [ ] White-tailed Eagle
- [ ] Marsh Harrier
- [ ] Hen Harrier
- [ ] Montagu's Harrier
- [ ] Northern Goshawk
- [ ] European Sparrowhawk
- [ ] Common Buzzard
- [ ] Rough-legged Buzzard
- [ ] Golden Eagle
- [ ] Osprey
- [ ] Common Kestrel
- [ ] Merlin
- [ ] Hobby
- [ ] Peregrine Falcon
- [ ] Red Grouse
- [ ] Ptarmigan
- [ ] Black Grouse
- [ ] Capercaillie
- [ ] Red-legged Partridge
- [ ] Grey Partridge
- [ ] Common Quail
- [ ] Common Pheasant
- [ ] Golden Pheasant
- [ ] Lady Amherst's Pheasant
- [ ] Water Rail
- [ ] Spotted Crake
- [ ] Corn Crake
- [ ] Moorhen
- [ ] Common Coot
- [ ] Oystercatcher
- [ ] Avocet
- [ ] Stone-curlew
- [ ] Little Ringed Plover
- [ ] Ringed Plover
- [ ] Kentish Plover
- [ ] Dotterel
- [ ] European Golden Plover
- [ ] Grey Plover
- [ ] Lapwing
- [ ] Knot
- [ ] Sanderling
- [ ] Little Stint
- [ ] Temminck's Stint
- [ ] Curlew Sandpiper
- [ ] Purple Sandpiper
- [ ] Dunlin
- [ ] Ruff
- [ ] Jack Snipe
- [ ] Common Snipe
- [ ] Woodcock
- [ ] Black-tailed Godwit
- [ ] Bar-tailed Godwit

Checklist

- [ ] Whimbrel
- [ ] Eurasian Curlew
- [ ] Spotted Redshank
- [ ] Common Redshank
- [ ] Greenshank
- [ ] Green Sandpiper
- [ ] Wood Sandpiper
- [ ] Common Sandpiper
- [ ] Turnstone
- [ ] Red-necked Phalarope
- [ ] Grey Phalarope
- [ ] Pomarine Skua
- [ ] Arctic Skua
- [ ] Long-tailed Skua
- [ ] Great Skua
- [ ] Mediterranean Gull
- [ ] Little Gull
- [ ] Black-headed Gull
- [ ] Common Gull
- [ ] Lesser Black-backed Gull
- [ ] Herring Gull
- [ ] Iceland Gull
- [ ] Glaucous Gull
- [ ] Great Black-backed Gull
- [ ] Kittiwake
- [ ] Sandwich Tern
- [ ] Roseate Tern
- [ ] Common Tern
- [ ] Arctic Tern
- [ ] Little Tern
- [ ] Black Tern
- [ ] Guillemot
- [ ] Razorbill
- [ ] Black Guillemot
- [ ] Little Auk
- [ ] Puffin
- [ ] Rock Dove
- [ ] Stock Dove
- [ ] Wood Pigeon
- [ ] Collared Dove
- [ ] Turtle Dove
- [ ] Rose-ringed Parakeet
- [ ] Common Cuckoo
- [ ] Barn Owl
- [ ] Little Owl
- [ ] Tawny Owl
- [ ] Long-eared Owl
- [ ] Short-eared Owl
- [ ] European Nightjar
- [ ] Common Swift
- [ ] Common Kingfisher
- [ ] Hoopoe
- [ ] Wryneck
- [ ] Green Woodpecker
- [ ] Great Spotted Woodpecker
- [ ] Lesser Spotted Woodpecker
- [ ] Wood Lark
- [ ] Sky Lark
- [ ] Shore Lark
- [ ] Sand Martin
- [ ] Barn Swallow
- [ ] House Martin
- [ ] Tree Pipit
- [ ] Meadow Pipit
- [ ] Rock Pipit [ ] Water Pipit
- [ ] Yellow Wagtail
- [ ] Grey Wagtail
- [ ] Pied Wagtail
- [ ] Waxwing
- [ ] Dipper
- [ ] Wren
- [ ] Hedge Accentor
- [ ] Robin
- [ ] Nightingale
- [ ] Bluethroat
- [ ] Black Redstart
- [ ] Common Redstart
- [ ] Whinchat
- [ ] Stonechat
- [ ] Northern Wheatear
- [ ] Ring Ouzel
- [ ] Blackbird
- [ ] Fieldfare
- [ ] Song Thrush
- [ ] Redwing
- [ ] Mistle Thrush
- [ ] Cetti's Warbler
- [ ] Grasshopper Warbler
- [ ] Savi's Warbler
- [ ] Sedge Warbler
- [ ] Marsh Warbler
- [ ] Reed Warbler
- [ ] Icterine Warbler
- [ ] Dartford Warbler
- [ ] Lesser Whitethroat
- [ ] Common Whitethroat
- [ ] Garden Warbler
- [ ] Blackcap
- [ ] Wood Warbler
- [ ] Chiffchaff
- [ ] Willow Warbler
- [ ] Goldcrest
- [ ] Firecrest
- [ ] Spotted Flycatcher
- [ ] Pied Flycatcher
- [ ] Bearded Tit
- [ ] Long-tailed Tit
- [ ] Marsh Tit

Checklist

- [ ] Willow Tit
- [ ] Crested Tit
- [ ] Coal Tit
- [ ] Blue Tit
- [ ] Great Tit
- [ ] European Nuthatch
- [ ] Eurasian Treecreeper
- [ ] Golden Oriole
- [ ] Red-backed Shrike
- [ ] Great Grey Shrike
- [ ] Eurasian Jay
- [ ] Magpie
- [ ] Red-billed Chough
- [ ] Jackdaw
- [ ] Rook
- [ ] Carrion Crow
- [ ] Common Raven
- [ ] Common Starling
- [ ] House Sparrow
- [ ] Tree Sparrow

- [ ] Chaffinch
- [ ] Brambling
- [ ] European Serin
- [ ] Greenfinch
- [ ] European Goldfinch
- [ ] Siskin
- [ ] Linnet
- [ ] Twite
- [ ] Common Redpoll
- [ ] Common Crossbill
- [ ] Scottish Crossbill
- [ ] Bullfinch
- [ ] Hawfinch
- [ ] Lapland Bunting
- [ ] Snow Bunting
- [ ] Yellowhammer
- [ ] Cirl Bunting
- [ ] Reed Bunting
- [ ] Corn Bunting

Index

Index

INDEX OF ENGLISH NAMES

Index

Further Reading

Campbell, B. and Ferguson-Lees, J., *A. Field Guide to Bird's Nests*, Constable, London 1972.

Cramp, S. and others, *The Birds of the Western Palearctic*, Oxford, London 1978–1994.

Dymond, J.N. and others, *Rare Birds in Britain and Ireland*, Poyser, Calton 1989.

Gooders, J., *The New Where to Watch Birds*, Deutsch, London 1986.

Gooders, J., *Collins British Birds*, Collins, London 1982.

Gooders, J., *Larousse Field Guide to the Birds of Britain and Europe*, Larousse, London 1995.

Harrison, C., *A Field Guide to the Nests, Eggs and Nestlings of British and European Birds*, Collins, London 1975.

Harrison, C., *An Atlas of the Birds of the Western Palearctic*, Collins, London 1982.

Keith, S. and Gooders, J., *Collins Bird Guide*, Collins, London 1980.

Lack, P., *The Atlas of Wintering Birds in Britain and Ireland*, Poyser, Calton 1986.

Lewington, I. and others, *A Field Guide to the Rare Birds of Britain and Europe*, Harper Collins, London 1991.

Parslow, J.F. (Ed.), *The Status of Birds in Britain and Ireland*, Oxford 1971.

Parslow, J.F. (Ed.), *Breeding Birds of Britain and Ireland*, Tring 1973.

Peterson, R.T. and others, *A Field Guide to the Birds of Britain and Europe*, Collins, London 1974.

Sharrock, J.T.R. (Ed.), *The Atlas of Breeding Birds in Britain and Ireland*, Poyser, Tring 1976.